DON'T

BURN

YOUR

OWN

HOUSE

DOWN

LINDSEY MAESTAS

DON'T
BURN
YOUR
OWN
HOUSE
DOWN

Prioritizing Your Marriage, Your Spouse,
and Yourself for a Deeper Connection

ZONDERVAN
BOOKS

ZONDERVAN BOOKS

Don't Burn Your Own House Down
Copyright © 2026 by Lindsey Maestas

Published by Zondervan, 3950 Sparks Drive SE, Suite 101, Grand Rapids, MI 49546, USA. Zondervan is a registered trademark of The Zondervan Corporation, L.L.C., a wholly owned subsidiary of HarperCollins Christian Publishing, Inc.

Requests for information should be addressed to customercare@harpercollins.com.

Zondervan titles may be purchased in bulk for educational, business, fundraising, or sales promotional use. For information, please email SpecialMarkets@Zondervan.com.

ISBN 978-0-310-36949-3 (audio)

Library of Congress Cataloging-in-Publication Data

Names: Maestas, Lindsey, 1989- author
Title: Don't burn your own house down : prioritizing your marriage, your spouse, and yourself for a deeper
    connection / Lindsey Maestas.
Description: Grand Rapids, Michigan : Zondervan Books, [2026]
Identifiers: LCCN 2025011785 (print) | LCCN 2025011786 (ebook) | ISBN 9780310369479 trade paperback |
    ISBN 9780310369486 ebook
Subjects: LCSH: Marriage—Religious aspects—Christianity | Spouses—Religious life | Married people—
    Religious life
Classification: LCC BV835 .M2243 2025 (print) | LCC BV835 (ebook) | DDC 248.8/44—dc23/eng/20250611
LC record available at https://lccn.loc.gov/2025011785
LC ebook record available at https://lccn.loc.gov/2025011786

Cover design: Lindsey Maestas / Thomas Schwindling
Cover imagery: iStock
Interior design: Denise Froehlich

Printed in the United States of America

25 26 27 28 29 LBC 5 4 3 2 1

For Mom

Thank you for believing in me and my writing since I was just four years old.

We did it! I love you forever.

CONTENTS

CHAPTER 1

MARRIAGE TEMPERATURE CHECK

Imagine standing helplessly as your home, filled with everything you love, is consumed by flames.

Would you wait until every room burned before doing something about it?

It's unlikely.

Most of you would jump into action after seeing the first spark. You'd rush in, ready to save what's precious, to protect the people you love, even if it meant that you got burned.

If your efforts weren't successful, you wouldn't sit back and watch your home turn to ash. You'd call for help, desperate to salvage what you'd built. Because as you watched something you've nurtured with love, commitment, energy, and hope go up in flames, your instinct would be to preserve it at all costs.

We say we'd do anything to save what matters, so why in our relationships do we throw up our hands when the smoke starts rising?

Maybe you have spoken up, prayed harder than ever, given

more of yourself than you thought possible, and still, the flames are smoldering.

You thought love would come more naturally, that it wouldn't feel this lonely, this difficult, this uphill, this one-sided.

Don't Burn Your Own House Down isn't just a title. It's a warning and an invitation.

Disconnection doesn't torch a marriage overnight. It starts small with the words left unsaid, the slow erosion of trust, the lack of partnership, or the quiet grief of being misunderstood.

But the house isn't gone yet. You don't have to abandon what you built. You can still pick up the hose. You can still call for help.

You can still protect your sacred covenant before the fire spreads, or prevent it before it even begins.

It's likely that the disconnect is unintentional at first: You get busy or distracted or assume things will work themselves out until they don't. And other times you know exactly what's happening and still you let it continue. You avoid putting out those small fires: the resentment from unspoken frustrations, the struggle for balance in sex and intimacy, the impact of scrolling and social media distractions, and the emotional distance that creeps in when you stop making time for each other.

And sometimes you don't just ignore the flames, you fuel them with sarcasm or snide remarks, worsening the distance between you, not to hurt your spouse but because it feels like the only way to express what you're feeling when you don't know how else to communicate.

Suddenly, you realize that what might have begun as a minor disagreement, an unforgiven issue, or an unmet need can quickly escalate from one tiny flame of disconnection to engulfing flames that will burn your house down.

Maybe you've stopped feeling like soulmates and eventually become nothing more than roommates.

Or maybe you're one of the lucky ones whose marriage

is thriving; you feel fully alive and deeply connected to your spouse. But I bet that didn't happen overnight, and I guarantee you have some battle wounds to prove it. You know how quickly small sparks can grow if they're ignored. So that's why you keep watch. That's why you fight to stay close. And that's why this book is for you, too, because the best time to protect your home is before the fire ever starts.

The practical steps I'll walk you through in this book aren't only for when things feel tough. They're also for the sweet, happy times. They will help keep your marriage grounded in connection and growth so that you're living in prevention, not damage control.

As you open this book, you might be facing very real challenges in your marriage and feeling disconnected, frustrated, or painfully aware that your relationship is unfolding in a world that often prioritizes lust, pornography, and instant gratification over monogamy and commitment, and where divorce is more accepted than lasting love.

I can relate to that. I've been there.

After my husband, Jesse, and I witnessed the immense strain placed on marriages during COVID-19 isolation in 2020, we felt deeply grateful for all of the effort we'd poured into becoming more than roommates, especially after enduring some very heartbreaking and disconnected seasons of our own.

We kept coming across people in our own lives who felt lost and alone in their relationships, and I thought, *Hold on a second. If the tools we've used have helped our marriage so much, couldn't they also help the hundreds of thousands of people in my audience?*

By then, I had already spent years researching and teaching about marriage and relationships—work that would eventually grow into more than a decade of experience. That foundation gave me the confidence to launch a biblical marriage course: The Wife Project: From Roommates to Soulmates, which has since landed in the hands of thousands of couples in nearly every country around the world.

Shortly after that, my husband, Jesse, and I released another video course called The Sex and Intimacy Project, designed to help couples strengthen their emotional and sexual intimacy. In response to both courses, we received thousands of emails from couples grappling with marital issues—likely issues just like yours.

I hear from couples every day who tell me how tough their marriages are. They feel deeply lonely, incompatible, ignored, consumed by work and parenting, and just . . . kind of *done*.

I share that with you because sometimes the most reassuring words we can hear are simply, "Oh, you too?"

So yes, us too! And if they haven't told you yet, your neighbors, close friends, and family members are likely experiencing similar issues.

Because *marriage can be freaking hard*. Not just for you but for many.

It isn't only the visibly broken marriages carrying the weight of generational wounds that are at risk of burning down. The couples posting smiling Christmas card photos, waving from behind their white picket fences and showing up at church looking perfectly polished, are also feeling like roommates at home.

Many people assume that marriage inherently protects against loneliness because you always have someone by your side. However, the concept of dyadic loneliness, the experience of loneliness shared by both partners within a relationship, is quite common.

Based on his research, Dr. Lars Tornstam revealed that 40 percent of married individuals reported feeling lonelier than those who were unmarried.[1]

Another study on loneliness in intimate relationships found that 20 percent of wives and 24 percent of husbands experience significant loneliness in their marriages.[2]

As this loneliness deepens, the risk of depression also increases, further highlighting the emotional toll that disconnection in marriage can take.

This book is for any couple in any season. You may be recently married and figuring out the bumps of those early years. Or you're in year seven—or year fifty—doing your best to hold it together, searching for something to feel grateful for when gratitude feels out of reach. You've been avoiding the real issues so as not to cause waves because the truth feels too scary to speak out loud.

But just like the loud arguments, the silence can turn into apathy in your heart and home. And apathy becomes a slow death to joy, to passion, and to identity. If neither of you is reaching toward the other anymore, of course you feel like you're drifting.

You no longer feel seen by the person you've committed your life to. Are you even seeing yourself?

There have been many seasons of marriage in which I felt aimless and unsure of what I wanted or who I wanted to be. I didn't feel seen by Jesse. I felt like he simply tolerated me. And if I'm being honest, I rarely did the work to truly see him either. Not with curiosity. Not with tenderness. I wanted to fix him instead.

Countless couples silently sit in these exact trenches where one partner is drowning in sadness or confusion and the other is shutting down because they feel like a failure. And then both walk away feeling misunderstood, unloved, and so far from the intimacy they both desperately want.

During one of these seasons of my marriage, I picked up the phone and called my sister-in-law for what felt like the millionth time. I had learned early on that seeking counsel or wisdom wasn't for the moments when your entire house had already burned down; it was to prevent the fire.

So therapy, resources, sermons, and advice from couples who had gone before me became a lifeline. No, I don't normally recommend going to family about things like this (save your-selves!), but my in-laws are the best kind of unicorns.

During this specific call, I told her I felt weary and lonely. I felt like my needs were being squashed in my marriage, that I would compromise and compromise and apologize, and my husband just got to continue living the way he lived. "It feels unfair," I said. "I want to be selfish. I don't want to do the work anymore."

I knew as I spoke that my heart had been misaligned. I'd been spending a lot of time feeling sorry for myself, wondering when my circumstances would shift. I was actively teaching others how to look at their own shortcomings while rarely looking at my own. I was living in pride and selfishness, and my relationship with God had become distant.

My husband wasn't perfect by any means at the time, and he still isn't, of course, but I was so clouded by what he wasn't doing that I didn't take any time to consider what I wasn't doing, or what I was doing to push him away.

Jesse and I had both been keeping score of pain, of effort, and of who was failing who. But the problem was that we kept waiting for the other person to go first to begin fixing it. Neither of us felt like we could ever be enough for the other.

And somewhere in all of that, the light started to dim.

It didn't happen overnight. It was a million little moments.

But here's the thing: We've never stopped fighting for the good because God never stopped fighting for us.

We serve a God who enters graveyards and calls dead things back to life.

We are called to live in truth, not pretense. And even if your husband or wife doesn't know how to reach for you right now, God still does. Because love isn't dictated by our feelings but by faith and action.

I wrote this book to help you disrupt the patterns you've become so accustomed to, not by begging or blaming but by leveling the emotional playing field and helping you to acknowledge your situation and do the hard, holy heart work. If not for your spouse, if not for yourself, then for your vow to honor the covenant of "till death do us part."

The reality is this: You can implement all of the life hacks you see on the internet, you can brush those comments under the rug as if they didn't bother you, and you can even go on all the dates. But if you're only doing surface-level work, you're just going to be damping down the symptoms. It becomes behavioral modification. And behavioral modification is like taking Sudafed. Sure, it might stop the drippy nose for a while, but it doesn't cure the virus, because the virus isn't on the surface. It's internal. You eventually have to get to the core of the problem if you want real healing. And as you read through, you will have no choice but to face your core issues—not through the lens of defeat but through a lens of hope.

We're human, and we become exhausted when we don't have hope that things can actually get better. Hopelessness can be the very motivation either to do the work or to hit the eject button. Without hope, we start to settle. We check out and coast. We choose fight or flight.

Did you know that around 20 to 25 percent of married couples experience infidelity over the course of their marriages, with some studies showing higher rates (up to 40 to 45 percent)?[3] And that many affairs happen in marriages that most would describe as "good"? The sex is fine. The finances are manageable. The home seems happy and well put together. That's not the issue. The issue is more about someone who wants to feel alive again. The pursuit of something, or someone, that wakes them up and reminds them of the version of themselves they once were before the weight of responsibilities and children took over.

But here's the truth: Instead of choosing to feel alive in their own bodies and minds, in the hard-earned, often uncomfortable space of a relationship that has walked through the trenches of real life, some people choose the easier fantasy. The escape, the divorce, or the affair. The thing or person that hasn't seen them at their worst. The one that doesn't carry the baggage of babies, career loss, in-law drama, or the dull ache of daily responsibility.

And for a while, it might feel like freedom.

But as Dr. Jordan Peterson says, "In all my years as a clinical psychologist, I have never seen anyone ever get away with anything at all. Not even once."[4]

It may feel easier to escape for a season, but reality and destruction will inevitably follow.

Because true connection, the kind that lasts, requires choosing to stay present and awake in the hard stuff. You can't be asleep at the wheel. And honestly, finding someone new doesn't mean you've dodged difficulty. It's still a relationship, just with different crap to deal with, like someone who refuses to make a dentist appointment until their tooth actually falls out, is unable to communicate their feelings, or loads the dishwasher in a way that makes you question their entire upbringing.

Because no matter who you're with, love will still take work, and connection will always require intention. The quirks will just have different names. So before you start packing up and searching for "better," maybe it's time to pause and ask yourself, *Have I done everything I can to build something beautiful right here?*

A couple we love, long-term friends of ours, recently chose to end their marriage. As a child, the husband experienced abuse from every angle at the hands of his father. Disrespect, anger, fear, and heartache became the norm. Those early wounds shaped the way he understood love and commitment.

He was never abusive in his relationship, but it was marked by infidelity, pain, avoidance, and emotional distance. He didn't have a blueprint for healthy love. He grew up surrounded by hurt and did what he could with what he had. Choices were made, mistakes were made, and consequences followed, yes. But sometimes, when we're left without healing or guidance, even our best hopes and efforts still fall short.

Maybe you also come from a home marked by a broken marriage or a disconnected one. Maybe alcohol and work were used by your parents to numb the pain, or you grew up in a home where name-calling and the silent treatment were normal. Maybe you were simply never shown how to do this well.

And now you're desperate to break that cycle, but the struggle is real because you don't even know where to begin. The first step to breaking the cycle is recognizing where the hurt began—and where you're continuing it. If you can own your faults, intentional or not, there's still hope.

Please hear my heart when I say this: This battle isn't a character flaw. You're not broken. You're not struggling in marriage because you're bad at it; you're unequipped. You're fighting not against flesh and blood but against sin, generational patterns, and the evils of this world.

If nobody ever showed you what healthy love, strong communication, respectful disagreements, or playful connection looks like, how would you know how to build it? This is not a character issue. It's a skills issue.

But when you live with a shame-filled, failure-based mindset, you'll either try to avoid the hard stuff or plow through it. And neither of these leads to true healing.

Remember this: There's a big difference between something being *hard* and something being *impossible*.

We've acknowledged that marriage can be hard. Really hard. But the gap from impossible to joyful is wider than the gap from hard to joyful. And the better you become at managing the hard, the less often hard becomes impossible. But when you don't learn how to manage it, hard eventually feels impossible.

You need community. You need honesty. You need educa-tion and support. You need skills.

You are not a failure. You're not broken. You're just human. And you simply need the tools to make your marriage a more peaceful place to be.

I'm here to speak to those of you who need to feel alive again. To the engaged couples and newlyweds who want to start off on the right path. To the person who's on the verge of burning their own house down because they can't handle one more day of feeling invisible. To those who really love their marriage but just need a little boost to their friendship, communication, or sex life. And to those who need to be reminded that the power resides in you and in a God who brings beauty from the ashes.

So I'm pulling back the curtain on my own marriage—the messy parts and the hard-won lessons—to remind you that you are more than your mess. I am sharing the practical tools, research, disciplines, and mindset shifts that have helped me, and now thousands of others, create stronger, more fulfilling relationships. I'll walk you through the changes that will help you reconnect and create the kind of marriage where you both feel desired, heard, and genuinely loved, all while keeping God at the center of it.

I want to come alongside you to help you fireproof your home and become best friends again with your spouse, because who doesn't love a good restoration story?

Let's begin by doing a quick temperature check on your marriage.

What's Your Survival Strategy?

When our marriages struggle, we tend to respond in one of five ways. Which one do you most resonate with in this season of your relationship? Hold on to your answer as you read this book.

1. *Fighting fire with fire.* Do you resort to confrontations, heated arguments, and a sense of control, allowing pride to fuel conflict and intensify the destructive fire within your relationship?
2. *Complaining to others.* Instead of addressing issues, do you vent your frustrations to friends and family, sharing complaints publicly to seek advice but never taking steps to resolve the situation with your spouse?
3. *Throwing a few cups of water on the flames.* Do you sporadically make feeble gestures like giving your spouse flowers or chocolates or throw out an empty "sorry" as an act of penance, hoping these superficial actions will show your remorse without your having to address the deeper issues and change your behavior?
4. *Silently surrendering.* Do you passively watch your relationship deteriorate, avoiding engagement and conversation? Do you stay silent and hope that the flames will extinguish on their own?
5. *Letting it burn.* Convinced that damage is inevitable, do you throw your hands up and let the fire burn? Have you given up so fully that you no longer try to save the structure of your marriage?

It Begins with You

No matter which survival strategy resonates the most, the work begins with you. Walking through this book may feel a bit like working out. I'm no stranger to discipline, but the truth is that most of the time, bingeing a bag—a family-sized one at that—of Salt and Vinegar chips feels like a better, more instantly gratifying choice to me than hitting the gym. And when I don't see the immediate results of sudden weight loss or noticeable muscle tone, it's so easy to feel discouraged and want to quit.

But progress happens over time, and as you know, when you stay consistent, you will notice changes and inevitably feel a sense of great accomplishment.

Here's the truth: The more you lean into the effort of putting out the little fires in your marriage, even when your motivation is low, or even when you don't even have a desire to do the work, the more you'll see the benefits. The fruit of your efforts will come when you choose to steadily and consistently fight for the marriage you've committed to.

Think of it like building strength: The small, daily choices may seem insignificant, but they accumulate. What you put into your marriage today dictates the relationship you'll have tomorrow. The investment is always worth it.

Consider this from the opposite perspective: Jesse and I have two boys, Sutton Rylee (ten) and Saxon Finn (seven), and we are always reminding them to avoid food dyes, such as Red 40, because of their long-term health risks. Imagine eating processed junk food every single day for twenty years. You might not notice any immediate effects, but when health issues surface decades later as a result of those choices, it wouldn't be all that shocking, would it? Poor decisions may not show their consequences right away, but they always catch up to you in the end.

My father-in-law, pastor David Maestas, often shares a lesson from the pulpit that helps to put things into perspective: Imagine you pack a sandwich lunch for yourself and your spouse every day for ten years. You switch up the types of sandwiches, making sure you're both fed and cared for. If someone asked you to recall which sandwiches you had on which days, you probably wouldn't be able to remember. Even if they asked you for a general idea, it would be hard to say. But did you eat? Yes. Did it make you healthier and stronger? Absolutely.

That's what daily investment in your marriage is like. You may not remember every conversation or small effort, but those consistent actions nourish your relationship over time. Like with the lunches, the effort may seem insignificant at the moment, but the results will speak for themselves.

There is a wonderful poem in Cammie Dennis's book *There's Coffee in the Pot* that beautifully captures my hopes for what you'll gain from this book: a deep respect, love, and care for both the spouse you've chosen and the home you're building together:

I'm building a home for myself
where doors don't slam
and people don't yell
and love is scattered across a kitchen table
that was built with kindness and respect,
I'm building a home for myself
where the floors can be painted yellow
and the tables can be painted blue
because there is no right way to do anything
except to do it with you,
I'm building a home for myself
that will echo the feelings
that live deep in my chest,
but you will know that
when you step into the rooms
that were built by people
who love one another
with nothing but respect.[5]

In the upcoming chapters, we'll work together to face the modern challenges of marriage and build, or rebuild, a relationship filled with respect, kindness, playfulness, and joy. We'll get honest about what's getting in the way of deeper connection and focus on creating God-centered homes rooted in gentleness, intimacy, companionship, and lasting love.

CHAPTER 2

HOW I ALMOST BURNED MY OWN HOUSE DOWN

If your house is on fire, the most urgent thing to do is to go back and try to put out the fire, not to run after the person you believe to be the arsonist.

—Thich Nhat Hanh,
Anger: Wisdom for Cooling the Flames

A few years ago, I quietly said to Jesse, "I don't know what else to do. I don't think I can keep living like this. Are we really at the point of divorce?"

It was a sentence I'd sworn I'd never say, but in that moment, I meant every word. I packed my bags and, with my baby and toddler in tow, walked out the front door. I hoped he would stop me. Or say something. But he didn't. So I drove away.

Before that day, it seemed to our friends and family that Jesse and I had a relatively effortless and sweet marriage. From the beginning of our dating relationship, we had a village of people who knew our darkest and brightest moments. They knew that we'd had ups and downs, because it never served us to hide that. But we were also best friends.

Most people saw a strong, respectful partnership. And we were, for the most part. But as you probably know, what happens behind closed doors is often a different story. We still smiled in public and supported each other outwardly, but the inside of our home told a quieter truth. Sleepless nights, babies who needed everything, and conversations that barely scratched the surface. We weren't fighting; we were fading. And that can be just as dangerous.

The beginning of love is exhilarating, isn't it? It's all-consuming, intoxicating, and—whether we realize it or not—a little delusional. Gary Chapman, author of *The Five Love Languages*, describes the "in love" phase as an emotional and obsessive high that tricks us into believing that we've found something rare, something unbreakable. During this time, we convince ourselves that our partners will always make us happy, that our love is different and immune to the common struggles other people face. It feels altruistic; we would do anything for them, and surely they feel the same way. But that belief is an illusion. Not because our feelings aren't real but because they're unrealistic.

By nature, humans are egocentric. We want our world to revolve around us, and eventually individual needs, emotions, and expectations rise to the surface. What once seemed insignificant, like the way our spouses squeeze the toothpaste, their tone of voice, or how they handle stress, begins to matter more than we ever expected it would.

And that's when reality sets in. The laundry never stops. Half-drunk cups of coffee sit on the counter for days. Exhaustion from work, sleepless nights with kids, and the stress of bills and responsibilities replace the effortless connection and deep talks that once came so naturally. Conversations shift from "I love spending time with you" to "Did you pay the water bill?" Suddenly, the way they leave their shoes in the hallway or breathe too loudly when they're tired starts to really get on our nerves. And if we're not careful, those little frustrations turn into resentment. That once-intense infatuation fades, and we start wondering, *What happened to us? Was it ever real?*

Did you know that the "in love" phase has a shelf life? Research indicates that it typically lasts about two years, though its length can vary.[1] This leads to conflicts with the person we once saw as our ideal match, and we feel let down or disappointed instead of enamored with our spouses.

We realize, in time, that being in love isn't enough for a lasting marriage. This is when we throw up our hands and start believing we've picked the wrong person. Or we settle into a life of unhappiness, convinced there's no way out. But did you know that the divorce rate for second marriages is higher than that of first marriages? And that the rate climbs even higher for third marriages?

It seems the idea of a happier marriage the second or third time around isn't as promising as we might think.

Friends, please hear me on this: Being in love rarely sustains a relationship. Real love doesn't live in the rush of newness, it's built in the mundane, in the everyday choices to stay, to show up, and to put in the work. Connection, intimacy, trust, and safety are equally vital. And relationships require a lot more than just the feeling of being "in love." Because sometimes we may love each other, but we don't actually like the other person as much as we used to. But why? What happens to us?

Married couples often allow comfort and familiarity to lull them into complacency. Without effort, even the strongest homes can begin to burn, and ours was no exception.

In one of his teachings on marriage, Pastor Craig Groeschel

wisely notes, "There is no intimacy without intentionality."[2] And it's true. When we let life dictate our schedules, fill our free time, and distract us with endless obligations, we risk missing the moments that matter.

Jesse and I had stopped taking steps to remedy our relationship because everything felt too hard and too exhausting. It seemed like every conversation we attempted went in circles.

We didn't realize, though, that by neglecting to address underlying issues, we inadvertently created a breeding ground for resentment and disconnection.

In their book *You and Me Forever*, authors Francis and Lisa Chan say it this way: "Eternal-mindedness keeps us from silly arguments. There's no time to fight. We have better things to pursue than our interests. Too much is at stake! God created us for a purpose. We can't afford to waste our lives. We can't afford to waste our marriage by merely pursuing our own happiness."[3]

But that's exactly what Jesse and I did: We fixated on ourselves and our own needs, obsessively gazing into the mirror while pointing fingers at each other. We were so wrapped up in our own happiness that we lost sight of our marriage's eternal purpose. Instead of placing God at the center of our lives and prioritizing our relationship, we allowed self-centeredness to take over.

As a result, our home began to burn. We were quick to blame each other for our unhappiness, all while ignoring that our own choices and selfishness were contributing to the disconnection.

And like a fire that had been quietly smoldering, the realization hit that I had been feeling deeply alone for some time, while Jesse silently wrestled with the suffocating pressure I had placed on him within our relationship. That spark of disconnection had grown into a fire that threatened to consume everything if we didn't confront it.

Our lives had become busier and busier as we got caught up in things that stole our attention, energy, and hearts. Mornings were a blur—diaper changes, crying babies, and rushing out the door. Evenings weren't much better, with busy dinner times, work commitments that stretched late into the night, and zero sleep. Weekends had once been a time for family, but they became dictated by errands, business meetings, and work catch-up.

Parenting young kids added its own weight. Sleepless nights, tantrums, severe asthma and other health concerns, along with the demands of daily life left little room for the connection we once loved so much. Slowly, responsibilities and commitments pulled us apart, and the little moments of intimacy and joy we once shared were overshadowed by exhaustion and the pressure to keep up.

By the end of each day, Jesse and I were both worn out. We often found ourselves turning to the ever-present glow of our phone screens to decompress, mindlessly scrolling without even speaking. Even though we were sitting right next to each other, the weight of our individual worlds felt more pressing than the need to connect.

Jesse liked to decompress after work by numbing out. I felt like a second choice to his hobbies. Honestly, I sometimes felt like having to compete against his video games for attention was going to be the end of me, or of us. I wanted to be what helped him to relax. I wanted to be the first thing he ran to when he was overwhelmed or overworked. And so I told him that.

Again and again and again.

I pushed and pushed for him to want me, to choose me, to just freaking pay attention to me.

But the more I pushed, the more he retreated.

Because I wasn't pleasant to be around. I was moody and critical, easily agitated, and perpetually overwhelmed. I could suck the life out of the room with little effort.

We took some time to figure out our attachment styles (I highly recommend doing this as a couple if you haven't already!), and we couldn't have been more different. I have an anxious attachment style, always seeking reassurance and emotional connection, fearing abandonment if I don't get the attention I need.

He, on the other hand, has an avoidant attachment style, pulling back when things get too close or intense, craving space and independence. The more I sought closeness, the more he felt the need to withdraw. This is a common dynamic between anxious and avoidant partners. My emotional neediness triggered his need for distance, and his withdrawal only fueled my anxiety.

We still laughed together, though not as freely as before.

We still talked, but we avoided the messy stuff.

When we did address our issues, emotions erupted and we couldn't resolve anything or find common ground.

We still pursued intimacy, but far less often.

One evening, Jesse and I sat on the couch, scrolling through our phones. Beside him, I felt the familiar weight of silence between us. I took a breath and finally spoke.

"Hey, can we talk for a minute?"

Jesse glanced up and right back down again, distracted. "Yeah?"

Of course he's distracted, I thought.

I wasn't sure where to start, but the words spilled out. "I feel like we've become the thing that we warn so many other people against. We're roommates. I miss the people we used to be. We don't connect the way we did when we were first married. I miss feeling like we're on the same team."

Jesse's face softened, but his eyes still seemed distant. "I know . . . I miss you. I just don't know how to fix it."

The silence between us hung heavily, and the weight of unresolved issues pressed on me.

We had changed. No longer the same kids who got married at twenty-two, Jesse and I had evolved and had grown apart.

Experts estimate that the probability of a first marriage

ending in divorce is between 40 and 50 percent.[4] Half of the people who get married don't make it to the end.

Ouch.

The thought of feeling unwanted or unloved was painful, and I didn't want Jesse to experience that either. Yet if we were honest, there were days when both of us felt that way.

Balancing the emotional burdens of our home had become increasingly difficult. Jesse wrestled with lust and pornography prior to our relationship, and the remnants of that struggle carried over into our marriage and affected the trust between us, while my intense bouts of postpartum anxiety, depression, and emotional overwhelm left Jesse feeling like he no longer knew who I was.

We were both Bible-believing Christians when we got married. But as a pastor's kid, Jesse had openly battled questions and doubts throughout his life. After a few years of marriage and significant church hurt, he questioned whether what he believed was real. He was deconstructing and doubting, which left me to lead our family spiritually and, often, emotionally—even when I had no capacity to do so. Ultimately, this journey of questioning strengthened his faith, but it took years to get to that point.

What a mess we were.

Can you relate?

Does the weight of the world ever make your marriage feel like just another box to check off the list? Another responsibility in the blur of deadlines, dishes, and demands?

My breaking point came one night at 3:00 a.m.

I had just put our son back to bed after a bad dream for what felt like the ten-thousandth time, and then something cracked inside me. My emotions flowed freely, a stark contrast to my usual self. I had always strived to maintain composure, even in front of Jesse. I'd become a master of playing house, meticulously concealing the cracks in our foundation with a facade of normalcy. But that night, the facade crumbled and I could no longer cling to the illusion of "everything's going to be fine."

I resented Jesse for his lack of presence and leadership in our home and often had the thought, *Who did I marry? You were so different when we first met.* In his defense, I had moved far from the bubbly, carefree girl he had known while we were dating.

Neither of us was innocent. In truth, it's rare that anyone in a marriage is. Marriage is two imperfect sinners coming together with high hopes and high expectations, yet often ill-equipped and unprepared for the weight of covenant love.

For me personally, I was exhausted and overwhelmed, trying to navigate new motherhood. And on top of that, I made sure Jesse knew just how unhappy I was. I threw snide remarks his way, fueled by bitterness, every time he came home from work, like, "How nice it must be to just go to lunch or the gym whenever you feel like it." I wanted him to feel the weight of my day, to understand my struggles.

I suffocated Jesse by making him the center of my happiness, relying on him to meet every emotional need. I put an immense amount of pressure on him, expecting him to bring me peace, to make me feel whole, to keep me joyful. In my mind, if he didn't do those things, something was wrong. This left no room for him to be imperfect, no space for him just to be himself. I had made him my source of fulfillment—my god—rather than turning to Jesus for joy and peace.

I came to realize that no human, not even my husband, could provide the peace, joy, and purpose that only God could give me, that I had stopped relying on God for my worth, identity, and emotional stability.

We had a lot to work through. On many days, it felt like we needed to break through a brick wall to feel compatible or we were going to fall apart.

So that night at 3:00 a.m., when our son woke me up again,

I felt entirely out of control of my emotions. *He never wakes his dad,* I thought. *Because his dad won't wake up. It's always on me!* My bitterness was blinding. I was furious. I was exhausted. And I felt completely alone in it.

I tried to wake Jesse, shaking him harder with each attempt, but he didn't budge. The anger surged in my chest. *This is probably how he feels on the mornings when I can't get out of bed and he has to carry the responsibilities of the house alone,* a small voice whispered. But I silenced it. Looking back, I realize I didn't care about fairness or my own failures; I was too consumed by his. To me, his sleeping felt like a choice, a refusal to carry this burden with me. I couldn't see how my anger was making everything worse. Not just for Jesse but for me too.

I had believed him to be the arsonist, but the truth was that we were both holding a match.

Exhausted and frustrated, I took our son back upstairs and stayed with him until he fell asleep. The bitterness lingered, but so did a growing awareness that maybe both of us were running on empty and that neither of us was showing up well for the other.

I walked back toward our master bathroom and found that somehow Jesse had woken up. *Convenient,* I thought. Months of unspoken hurts and unacknowledged pain finally found release the moment the bathroom door clicked shut.

I fell to the floor, tears streaming down my face as I slumped against the cold bathroom tiles, crying the kind of sobs that feel like your chest cavity has fractured. It was the kind of crying that comes only when pent-up emotions have become too much to bear—a desperate release from the burdens that had been weighing me down for far too long. I thought about how insurmountable the whole situation felt. My mind raced through all the ways I could escape this mess.

The sleep issue wasn't huge, it was simply the tipping point.

That's when I realized that I wasn't just angry about the sleep, I was angry about everything. I teach often that when molehills feel like mountains, it's a pretty sure sign that bitterness has taken hold.

I didn't care whether Jesse heard me; part of me wanted him to feel the weight of it all, to finally understand how heavy it was, to carry the burden just once.

But my cries were met with silence. Jesse didn't check on me. He didn't ask if I was okay. Had he ever heard me cry like that before? It didn't seem to matter.

Does he even like me anymore? I wondered.

That night, something settled in me. I knew I couldn't keep doing things the same way. The next morning, I would show Jesse—not out of anger but out of conviction—that something had to change.

We'd promised we'd never let the word *divorce* enter our home, but at that moment, that promise felt irrelevant. We both had checked out. We both had given up. I didn't have a plan, but I knew I couldn't stay in that house for another second. So without giving Jesse a chance to say anything, I packed my bags, grabbed the kids, and left.

Our marriage wasn't horrible. As I look back now, I see that these are real issues that ordinary people face every day. They may wear different costumes, like stress, silence, resentment, or distraction, but they all stem from the same truth: Life is hard, and marriage doesn't protect us from that.

But at the time, I just wanted to be happy. And in my hurt and bitterness in that early morning moment, I was willing to do whatever it took—not to fix our marriage but to feel loved and wanted again. For my own needs and selfishness, I was willing to forsake my family and what I stood for.

Can I share something with you? Love doesn't, and won't, just happen to you. As a society, we often view love as this serendipitous experience that visits us magically and stays without effort, but that's not true.

Love is a discipline. It's a lifestyle. It is an action, a practice, an investment, and a consistent, persistent activity. Love doesn't just visit you one day and take up residence permanently, as nice as that might be. Yet we treat it as if it's exactly that, because in the face of love, we are exceedingly passive.

We try to rely on that sweet spark of the honeymoon phase to keep us going. And because we're so reliant on that, we live without growth, mutual reliance, self-control, structure, and patience in our marriages. We expect our feelings to sustain themselves.

Our feelings at the beginning of a relationship are never the same as those in a lasting one. Though we may say that we know that, we're often still shocked when we first feel uncomfortable or disconnected, and we quickly convince ourselves that we're falling out of love.

But we're not falling out of love, are we? Instead, we're just lifelessly lying on the ground, expecting our relationship to change and work for us instead of our working for *it*.

Jesse and I, along with many married couples, had fallen prey to the ideology that love is a feeling to be received rather than an action to pursue.

Looking back, I see how our expectations of each other were so unreasonably high that we were drowning in them. Our lack of grace seeped into every corner of our relationship. I wanted a husband who never faltered, who met every one of my needs, who was essentially my version of Jesus.

Jesse, on the other hand, wanted me to be happy, but without offering the time and effort our marriage needed. He struggled with feeling inadequate yet still resisted meeting me halfway when I asked for true partnership.

We hadn't done the work to heal our marriage or ourselves; we simply expected those things to heal themselves.

After I walked out, Jesse and I were apart for about seventy-two hours, a brief but transformative time. Many of those hours were spent with both of us in tears, seeking wisdom from trusted friends and mentors.

During that time, we realized that we didn't want to do life with anyone else. We wanted to keep our family together. We chose to stay and wrestle through the trials of our covenant rather than walk away and inherit new problems with someone new.

Because no matter who you're with, there will be work, so we might as well do the work that keeps our family whole.

I want to be clear: Divorce is not the unforgivable sin. At times, it has been treated in the church as if it were the pinnacle of failure, but Scripture doesn't place it above every other sin. There are biblical grounds for divorce, and God himself acknowledges situations where stepping away is necessary. At the same time, everything truly is level at the foot of the cross. Every one of us is in need of grace, no matter what our stories hold. My heart isn't to heap shame on you but to point you back toward the hope, healing, and encouragement that are always available in Christ.

In order to do the work, we spoke with couples who had struggled through the intense early years of parenthood, and we were reminded that we weren't alone in our disconnection.

We revisited the biggest arguments we'd ever had, not only to discuss their effects on our relationship but also to let others speak wisdom into them.

We listened to advice that helped us see beyond the pain and remember the strength of our commitment and God's presence in our difficulty.

Those mentors assured us that it gets easier, that the tough seasons pass, that love can be made stronger than before.

In the end, we sat down together, face to face, and for the first time in a long while, we talked through all of the resentments, hurts, and misunderstandings that had built up. Instead of defending ourselves, we saw each other with compassion. We realized we never wanted to separate like that again.

We wanted to fireproof our house instead of letting it burn down around us. We decided together that we were ready and excited to create a new marriage.

And so we did.

Creating a Second Marriage Together

Esther Perel, renowned psychotherapist and one of today's most insightful voices on modern relationships, says this: "Most of us are going to have two or three significant long-term relationships or marriages. And some of us are going to do it with the same person."[5] Perel is right that marriage isn't a static commitment but an ever-changing experience.

I want to encourage you that you can create a new marriage with your same partner. Each phase of life brings new challenges and opportunities for growth, and navigating them together can be a gift. Imagining ourselves sitting in rocking chairs together in old age symbolizes the hope and joy that can come from evolving side by side as partners.

I know that the idea of undergoing so many changes in a marriage can feel daunting. You chose your partner for specific reasons and have become accustomed to their ways. Whether those patterns are positive or negative, they feel familiar.

But the reality is that who you are in your twenties is vastly different from the person you become in your fifties, and the same is true for your spouse. Changes in personalities and preferences present really sweet opportunities to discover new versions of each other. And if you married at a young age, you will have even more time together to evolve individually and as a couple.

But changes also come with challenges. As you change, your partner is changing too, often in ways that don't align with your own growth. If we want our marriages to remain vibrant, fresh, and alive, we have to be willing to make space for each other to evolve.

A couple of years ago, on my podcast, *Living Easy with Lindsey*, I interviewed David Erdman, an author and highly esteemed divorce lawyer who has consulted on more than five thousand marriages.[6] Tens of thousands of you have listened to that episode, and continue to do so, in which he shares a striking insight: Nearly all of his clients who've been married two or three times wish they had stayed in their first marriages.

When two people marry, they're like two pieces of clay. They begin to blend and reshape, each molding themselves to be a fit for the other. Yet they will each always have contours and textures different from the other person, because complete harmony is not fully possible.

"What people don't always understand in their first marriage," Erdman explains, "is that they've been shaped by that relationship. The next person they meet will have a different shape, and they'll soon realize they brought along the problems they thought they were escaping. I call it baggage; all the baggage they brought into the first marriage will resurface in the second, and they'll also have a new set of problems with that new person."

Erdman says that it often takes people up to three marriages to realize that the issues they face in one relationship follow them into the next, especially if they never did the work to heal what was damaged within themselves. Eventually, they realize that the outside world isn't as perfect as they imagined and that they may never find a fit as comfortable as their first relationship, often recognizing this only after it's too late to save their original marriage.

Jesse and I didn't want to be without each other; we couldn't imagine doing marriage—or life—with anyone else. Yet we also knew we couldn't continue as we were for one more day.

We were ready for a change, and we were prepared to do the hard work—and the heart work—to get there.

CHAPTER 3

MAKE THE DANG COFFEE

Humility is not thinking less of yourself, it's thinking of yourself less.

—**Rick Warren,** *The Purpose Driven Life*

Jesse takes my empty communion cup every Sunday. And every Sunday, I notice.

At our church, each week we eat a small piece of bread and take a sip of wine to remember Jesus' life and teachings. It's an expression of faith and unity among believers. The bread and juice, representing the wine, are wrapped side by side in one little plastic cup. And for as far back as I can remember, Jesse has always reached over to grab my empty cup once I've taken communion.

He has never been any closer to a trash can than I've been. He could easily hand me his cup or choose to keep only his, but he doesn't. It's a small, seemingly insignificant thing, but I notice. I notice that he takes on a teeny, tiny burden that he doesn't have to take just to make my morning a little bit easier. And every Sunday, I look up at him and smile because I feel like he sees me, and I appreciate his thoughtfulness.

For someone unfamiliar with this type of care, or for someone who doesn't typically feel loved by acts of service, it may seem trivial.

But these little acts truly do accumulate in any relationship. It's often the small gestures, the seemingly insignificant actions, that contribute to strengthening the joy and satisfaction of a marriage.

Let's use Disney World and Universal Studios as an example. Orlando is one of our favorite vacation spots as a family. We love eating our way through every country in Epcot. (We work hard to fit in every single spot, even when we're absolutely stuffed. Don't get me started on England's Fish and Chips or Germany's Pretzel Bread Pudding.) We ride all the rides at Universal Studios—twice if we can. We always enjoy taking in the vivid imagery at Animal Kingdom, as well as the fireworks show at Magic Kingdom.

If you've ever visited any of these parks, you've likely felt what people call "the magic." I wouldn't consider myself a Disney adult, by any means, but I have few sweeter memories than the moments when I watched my children's eyes light up as they experienced the lights, the characters, and the thrill themselves. As I think back, I can still hear my little Saxon screaming, "Goof!!!" at the top of his lungs when Goofy walked past him.

As we walked around the parks during our last vacation, I chose to slow down and take in the details. I realized that some of the most enjoyable parts of our experience weren't on the big rides but in the moments that led up to them.

Disney World and Universal Studios are renowned for their meticulous attention to detail. The thrilling rides and grand attractions are undoubtedly the main draws, but it's the subtleties, like the carefully decorated trash cans, the immersive storytelling, the entertainment while standing in line, and the small, thoughtful touches throughout the park that define our experience.

Walking around the park and standing in lines is simply a pathway to our destination. We may not notice all the details, but subconsciously they are what make the experience so sweet and magical.

Just like the exciting rides at a theme park, the big moments and grand gestures in a marriage, a surprise birthday party or a special vacation, do bring joy and are important. They're akin to meeting the in-character Disney princesses or stepping into the magic of Harry Potter Land. But while these grand experiences are meaningful, they're only part of the equation.

The grand gestures won't sustain a relationship. Often when we are going through difficult times with our spouses and are trying to prove our love, we reference these highlights, saying things like:

- "But I took you on that amazing trip!"
- "I bought you an expensive present that one time."
- "I publicly praised you on social media for your birthday!"
- "I let you go out with your friends all weekend and I didn't complain."

If we're honest with ourselves, we often make these big gestures as acts of reparation, penance, or compensation. Not always, but often.

And I want you to ask yourself this: As humans, when do we most often attempt reparative and compensative acts? When do we plan those big dates, give thoughtful gifts, or pour on the affection?

The answer: usually when things aren't going very well.

It's when we want to apologize that we most often give our spouses chocolate and flowers.

We finally plan a date night when we're feeling so disconnected that we don't know what other step to take and realize that we haven't hung out with each other—romantically—in months.

We thrive during our vacations because we are without responsibilities and don't have to bear the weight of the world, but as soon as we get home, we're back in our old patterns and bad habits. (I'm guilty, y'all. I am my absolute best self when lounging by the pool with "girl dinner" in hand—a coconut drink and a giant bowl of chips and guac. Jesse calls me "Vacation Lindsey" for a reason.)

We tend to look forward to the big moments in our relationships because the everyday stuff often feels so exhausting and hard. But what if we stopped waiting for the big to carry us and started placing small moments of joy, romance, and love into our daily lives? What if the connection we're craving is built not in the grand gestures but in the quiet, consistent ones?

If you live out your days with your spouse in numbness and disconnection, gliding through life on autopilot, then of course you are disconnected. You cannot heal that with one occasional grand gesture, an occasional date night, or a short-lived effort to save what is already damaged.

But that's why we're here. I want to help you change that.

Consider it this way: In one day, you ride those big rides only once, or maybe twice if you're lucky. Just like you go on a vacation once a year or have a date night once a week.

But how often do you stand in line for food, for a ride, for the bathroom? How often do you use the trash cans?

Probably once every thirty minutes or every hour.

Disney's themed lines and even the trash cans are micro-attractions designed to make the in-between moments of your entire experience feel just as magical as the big rides. In the same way, the daily interactions in your marriage are the micro-moments that shape the quality of your relationship. They're what you experience most often, and they're what impact the health of your marriage the most.

I want to call you up to begin paying attention to the small things—both what your partner does for you and what you can do for them. It's the morning coffee made just the way they like it, the unexpected compliment, permanently and successfully taking over a chore they hate, or a simple midday "I can't stop thinking about you" text.

These are the minor, but impactful, actions that serve as threads to help reconnect your relationship.

They say, *I see you. I value you. And I prioritize making you feel loved.*

Rebuilding connection in your marriage starts with a heart of daily service.

In a 2020 study, researchers found that everyday experiences of love were linked to higher levels of psychological well-being, feelings of purpose, and optimism. The more expressions of love a person received daily, the better sense of well-being they had in general.[1]

Jesse has always been good at the little things. The way he pays attention to detail and to the things that matter to me has made me want to be better at doing such things for him too. He expresses affection in various ways, such as making me a coffee every morning, bringing me a lemon water while I'm working out, and taking it upon himself to randomly check my water bottle, refilling it when it's empty. He has stepped in when relationships become hurtful or harmful, addressing crossed boundaries with both strength and grace to protect my well-being.

In moments of stress related to friendships or finances, he is the first to comfort me and remind me, "This burden isn't yours to carry alone, Linds. I'm carrying it with you."

When he spends time alone with the boys, he maintains the cleanliness of the kitchen because he knows a clean house helps me feel unburdened when I arrive.

Following his lead, I know that coffee is Jesse's love language, so I make him his espresso drink in the morning before we start our work for the day. He loves Oreos, so when I go to the store, I make sure to grab him a little treat to let him know I've thought of him. He's obsessed with a good breakfast—avocado toast, an over-easy egg cooked in Chili Crunch, and crispy bacon is his jam—so I try to have one ready for him when he comes home from an early morning of pickleball.

When he feels overwhelmed by burdens, I know that he likes to vent and feel heard. I do my best to shut off my phone, look him in the eyes, and listen to his worries.

We fight hard to serve each other in a way that makes the other person feel seen and loved. When something is important to him, I want it to be equally important to me, and vice versa. But these little actions don't come without intentionality.

It's Not Tit for Tat

Here's a hard truth: Even if your spouse doesn't do the little things well, change needs to start with you. You cannot always live within your marriage, expecting your spouse to be the one to take the first step and then feeling resentful that they haven't. This can be extremely difficult to do when you're already hardhearted or hurting, or when you've already poured out so much effort, but I challenge you to try.

Take a small step toward showing love in the way they've told you they need. It may help to remember that you aren't doing this only for your spouse. You're doing this to honor God and his calling for you to live as a servant in your life and in your marriage. As it says in Mark 10:45, "For even the Son of Man did not come to be served, but to serve, and to give His life a ransom for many."

As Christians, we live to mimic the love and life of Jesus, as we see in 1 John 2:6: "Whoever claims to live in him must live as Jesus did" (NIV). I encourage you to submit your heart to Christ, to know that his call to serve applies to your marriage, even when disconnection has taken hold.

I'm always in awe of Jesus' selflessness when, during the Last Supper, he sat at the table with Judas, the one who would betray him. Knowing full well what was coming, Jesus washed Judas's feet. He shared bread with him. Jesus extended dignity and love to a man who had already made up his mind to trade Jesus' life for silver.

And when Jesus said, "Most assuredly, I say to you, one of you will betray Me" (John 13:21), he didn't expose Judas by name to shame him in front of the others. He turned to him and said, "What you do, do quickly" (v. 27). Then, in what I consider to be one of the most remarkable acts of holiness, he turned his attention to the rest of the disciples and gave them the greatest commandment: "A new commandment I give to you, that you love one another; as I have loved you, that you also love one another" (v. 34).

Jesus didn't play the tit-for-tat game. He didn't wait to be treated well in order to act righteously. He served even when he was being sinned against. Yes, he had boundaries, and we will discuss the importance of setting your own in a bit. But he loved without conditions. And that's the example he has set for us. Not just for strangers, not just for friends, but for the people within the four walls of our homes.

My counselor introduced me to the principle of moral proximity, and this is where it comes into play. It's the idea that we carry a greater emotional, physical, and social-moral responsibility toward those closest to us. In other words, the way we treat our spouses and our children holds more weight than how we treat a stranger or a coworker. But too often, it's the people under our own roof who get the leftover version of us. We extend grace to the world and grow cold at home.

Jesus didn't live with divided integrity. He didn't compartmentalize his compassion. And if we're called to love like he did, then our greatest efforts, our clearest honesty, and our deepest kindness must begin with the people who know us best.

Marriage isn't a scoreboard. It is not "If he apologizes, then I'll soften" or "If she respects me, then I'll love her." That's pride. And pride has destroyed far more marriages than even conflict ever has.

Here's the hard truth: The way you love during a disconnected season speaks volumes about the maturity of your faith. Are you choosing to reflect Christ, even when your spouse doesn't? Are you outdoing one another in showing honor, even when it feels one-sided? Are you looking for the good, even when the hard parts are louder?

Even in the seasons when we don't "feel it," our commitment to God, and our covenant promise, is to love one another, without conditions, through it all.

You're not going to nail this perfectly, so go ahead and take a deep breath and release some of that pressure right away. The last thing I want to do is give my anxious friends even more to stress about! You'll definitely have days when you just don't want to serve your spouse or show them small acts of love because you don't feel like they deserve it. It will happen. And as you foresee that, you can prepare to do otherwise. You can choose to remember that faith trumps feelings. Even when you don't feel like doing something for your spouse, you can have faith that doing so will honor God and, likely, soften their heart.

Jesse and I try to do this well. And then we fail. Then we try again. And on some days, we succeed in making the other person feel truly valued. We choose to keep this cycle going, even when we don't want to, to fight for the little things.

Grandma's Lesson

I remember visiting my late Grandma Machac once and perching on the floor next to her as she sat in her favorite chair. Our family last name is Czech and is pronounced "Muh-Hotch," but everyone butchered it as "Ma-Chack." She would smile every time someone got it wrong, and I can still hear her voice correcting them with that mix of pride and playfulness.

I always liked hearing about her life. That day, I asked her what I thought was a simple question: the secret to her happy marriage of more than fifty years. She smiled thoughtfully as she shared her advice with me. "Ever since the beginning of our marriage, your grandpa and I playfully competed when it came to out-serving each other. It started when we were very young. He would wash the dishes before I could get to them, and I would wash his car when he was still asleep. It became a fun competition where we would see who could serve the other more than we were served. It lasted through our entire marriage, and I believe it was one of the main things that kept us happy and soft toward each other. We, quite literally, out-served one another as often as we could."

I have always loved hearing the wisdom of those who have gone before me, so I soaked it in. My own marriage was strained, and I was eager to try anything, so I decided to follow her example.

I began by making Jesse the dang coffee each morning, even when I was angry or hurt and it was the last thing I wanted to do.

I prayed for God to soften my heart and to give me kind words, and I would write those words on a little note that Jesse would find later on in the kitchen. I would flirtatiously tell him how hot he looked or compliment the way he did his hair. I would encourage him in his parenting, in his job, and in the things he held valuable.

And I watched as both of us softened and we both began to out-serve one another. Just as my grandma had said. While our days of frustration tend to be less common now because of the routines and practices we have implemented, we can still find ourselves amid days, or even weeks, when we feel disconnected.

We have come to accept this truth: The faster you can serve each other, while also communicating with gentleness about the hard topics and deep-rooted issues, the more quickly you can get outside of yourselves.

Remember: It's the little actions, the little affections, that make a world of difference when it comes to the peace and joy within your home. These affections enable you to get back to a place of humility, to look up at God to see what he desires for your marriage, and to place him at the center of it all. When he is the foundation of your words, actions, and decisions, the healthier and happier you will be.

A Little Affection Goes a Long Way

Think about those overwhelming days we've all experienced, particularly if you have little ones running around. Imagine that amid the chaos of doing chores at home your partner walks over, gives you a quick kiss on your cheek, and reminds you that they're on your team.

Visualize standing in a room with a group of people, and your spouse finds your eyes, smiles, and comes over to place their hand around your waist or on the small of your back.

Envision that your spouse comes home from a busy day, and rather than handing them a basket of laundry, disappearing into another room, or instantly ranting about your long day, you pause. You look into their eyes, say, "Hi," and give them a long kiss. You choose to connect in a moment when disconnection feels like the easiest option.

How different could your marriage feel with these small adjustments?

These little affections remind you both that your marriage matters. It's not necessarily about opening up the door to anything physical (although that doesn't hurt); it's a subtle reassurance that you're their person—by their side, thinking of them—and that you value their life and their presence.

Take Notes on Each Other

Early on in our marriage, we received a great piece of advice from two people who had experienced a long and healthy marriage. They encouraged Jesse and me to take notes on each other—our likes, our dislikes, our dreams, the little things that make us light up or smile. They meant this figuratively, but we decided to take it a step farther and actually write these things down. We started by writing them in our notebooks and journals, but now we put them in our notes app on our phones.

We write down everything from favorite candies to dreams and aspirations. This requires us to sit together and learn about each other as we change and grow. You aren't doing the work or allowing for that change if you're assuming their favorite things are the same as they were years prior. Keep checking in. Keep updating one another.

I polled my audience about things that make them feel disconnected in their marriages, and you might be surprised to find out that many of them responded, "I feel disconnected when my spouse makes their own coffee but they don't make mine."

If you aren't a coffee drinker, don't fret. This is more about considering your spouse just as you consider your own body.

When you think about what makes you feel cared for, can you take a moment to ask what makes them feel the same? What do you do for yourself that you could also do for them—with just a small amount of effort?

Do that thing. And do it often.

Please, for the Love, Ask for What You Want

Y'all, your spouse cannot read your mind. As much as you desperately wish they could, it will never happen. The reality is that there is usually one spouse who is willing to do the work, and a lot of the time, it's because they're the ones who are vocalizing their desires.

I encourage you to sit down with your spouse, in gentleness and love, and make your requests known. What do you want? Share it with them. And I can already hear some of you saying, "But I don't want to have to ask! I just want them to know." And I understand the hesitation, but you'll have to get over that hurdle. Your spouse was raised differently from you: different upbringing, different parents, different likes and dislikes. They won't ever be able to give you everything, and they aren't meant to, but you must give your spouse the opportunity and the grace to learn and grow. Speak out the things that make you feel loved, because clarity is kindness.

When you work on implementing these little affections, these micro-attractions, you are likely to see a softening in your marriage and the reconnection that comes when a partner feels safe and secure in the relationship. The big moments, the rides, are great and meaningful, but don't lose sight of the day-to-day servanthood that makes your partner feel seen and valued.

Love selflessly. And make the dang coffee.

CHAPTER 4

DEFROSTING YOUR MARRIAGE

Hatred is an affair of the heart; contempt
that of the head.

—Arthur Schopenhauer,

On the Basis of Morality

Do you realize that you can make a home only so cold before
it freezes your spouse out?

I recently heard a powerful sermon by pastor and author
Darren Whitehead in which he shared an insightful analogy
that cuts to the heart of how we view others and ourselves. He
compared people to icebergs: When we look at someone, we see
only what's above the surface—what they allow others to see. But
beneath the surface lies their struggles, fears, secrets, and untold
stories, and what's hidden often shapes them more than what's
visible.[1]

An iceberg will forever remind me of one of my favorite
movies, *Titanic*. Jesse always teases me for my obsession with

that movie, primarily because he has to suffer through the three hours of "Jack!" whenever I make him watch it with me. But I digress.

In the movie, the guests aboard the ship gaze in awe at a massive, glistening iceberg. They marvel at what's visible: the grandeur and beauty of the crown that sits above the surface. But they have no idea how much more lies beneath. The same goes for our marriages. The tip of the iceberg is what we let others see: the curated moments on social media, the laughs at dinner with friends, the hand-holding in public. It's not fake, but it's only a fraction of the whole story.

The portion that is beneath the surface, what eventually destroyed the *Titanic*, are the unspoken tension, the unresolved conflict, the exhaustion, the growth, and the grace. This is what actually determines whether your marriage floats or sinks. And most of the time, that's what we keep hidden.

So who are we within the walls of our homes when nobody's looking?

It has become, or maybe it has always been, the norm in our society to pretend. We pretend that everything is okay all of the time out of fear of burdening others, out of pride, or because of the shame we feel when things aren't going as well as we'd like.

It's similar to those days when you're at church and people ask how you are. The response is usually, "Good! How are you?" when really you and your spouse got into a massive fight on your way to service, or your mom is sick and you feel like you're carrying the weight of the world on your shoulders, or your baby isn't sleeping and it hurts to nurse, or your financial situation is in a scary place.

Your public image is the surface. And surface can't sustain itself.

A relationship often holds a lot of weight and power beneath the surface. What appears to be a calm, collected, and happy partnership may actually be a fractured relationship with a host of issues. Sound familiar? Maybe, for you, it's the tension that arises when you realize how differently you parent. Or the cracks that grief leaves behind in a person when you have to say goodbye to someone you love. Unresolved conflicts, unmet expectations, financial pressures, and betrayals don't just disappear; they pile up and create a divide.

The greatest problems arise when we pretend everything is okay until we can't pretend anymore. Our frustration finally erupts, turning into anger, hardheartedness, indifference, resentment, and contempt.

So many people I speak with feel alone in their pain and disappointment, convinced they're the only ones struggling. It's easy to believe that everyone else has it together, because all we see are the smiles, the highlight reels, and the good moments. And yes, there are couples who are genuinely happy. But the truth is that most relationships carry some level of difficulty. Behind closed doors, many are quietly working through hurt, miscommunication, unmet expectations, or years of disconnect. We have to stop pretending everything is okay without doing the work to ensure that we're actually okay.

Beneath the Surface

I want you to think of your marriage as an iceberg. Consider these questions with your spouse and write out the answers individually:

1. What are you keeping beneath the surface? What are you avoiding or hiding from view?
2. Are you regularly withholding physical touch, compliments, or words of affirmation?
3. How often do you hand over laundry or other

responsibilities without first offering a kiss or eye contact when greeting each other?

4. Are there unspoken resentments or frustrations beneath the surface?
5. Have you avoided tough conversations because you're afraid of the outcome? What are they?
6. Do you find yourself making snide remarks or unkind comments in the heat of the moment? Has that become the norm in your home?
7. Are you using your children as a distraction from your marital issues?
8. Do you find healthy ways to repair and resolve after conflict, or do you have unhealthy patterns that you've permitted for too long?
9. Are there hurts that have been left unforgiven, causing distance between you and your spouse? What are they?

Certain behaviors, such as giving the silent treatment, gaslighting, or prioritizing family and friends over your spouse, are like ice slowly forming around a relationship. When we avoid household responsibilities, show disdain, or communicate with defensiveness or criticism, the emotional coldness can freeze out our spouses, gradually transforming a warm home into a frigid, inhospitable space.

Maybe you've been going through the motions, living a life around your marriage instead of in it. Yet at no point have you talked about yourselves, your dreams, your hopes, your frustrations, and the needs of your relationship. And because of this, underneath the surface much is left unaddressed and unresolved.

Maybe it doesn't feel worth the fight anymore. It feels far easier to quit or to live a life of complacency.

But for anything to change, you have to soften. You need to defrost.

If you take anything away from this chapter, I want you to remember this: You can ice your partner out for only so long before intimacy and connection die. Love cannot grow in a home filled with criticism, contempt, coldness, irritability, or unforgiveness.

The Number-One Predictor of Divorce

Jesse and I sat with our close friends in their living room, the usual laughter and easy banter replaced by a somber stillness. "I miss the peace and partnership," the husband said, his voice heavy with longing as he looked across the table at his wife. "Our happiest days are the days when we have a routine, not when we feel connected. Our marriage feels transactional. We don't have intimacy. I don't even remember what it's like to feel deeply connected to someone. I miss it. I honestly wonder if we'll ever get it back."

Our friends had created a marriage that was a well-oiled machine, efficiently handling the daily tasks of running a household and raising their child. But the coldness they felt toward each other was a chilling reminder that efficiency doesn't equate to happiness.

They weren't angry at each other, exactly. Anger, while destructive, at least acknowledges emotions. Their relationship had become a different kind of cold, an indifference that had settled over their marriage. Bitterness lingered in conversations. There was a resistance to physical touch and basic kindness. They had entered into what I often call the "roommate stage," where they were coexisting peacefully, but without any intimacy.

This situation mirrors the experiences of many couples my husband and I have spoken with over the years. Conversations often devolve into transactional exchanges—packing diaper bags, planning for sports practices, managing illnesses, and running the household: the meals, the dishes, the laundry, the budget, and the weekly groceries. It's all handled with ease, almost on autopilot.

You're simply surviving.

But is survival enough?

Yes, sometimes survival is simply what marriage is. And sometimes that's just fine. Not spectacular or horrible, just fine. And that can also be normal for a season. You'll hear me say time and time again that your spouse is not meant to be your sole source of happiness or a replacement for your relationship with Jesus. When life throws busy or difficult circumstances your way, you may need to tread water until you come out the other side.

But most couples we work with and see in our daily lives aren't content with merely surviving their marriages in the long term. They dream of a lifelong partnership filled with shared experiences, laughter, and a deepening connection that endures through the years. They envision themselves, gray haired and content, sitting side by side on a porch swing or in rocking chairs, smiling over the memories of the life they've built together.

We don't want to live with hearts weighed down by anger, nor do we want to feel like we're stuck in a car with its wheels spinning helplessly in the mud.

These feelings can make our hearts cold. This is what we call contempt—the silent relationship killer that can dig a trench in a marriage. We must refuse to normalize a marriage marked by contempt because contempt poisons the love and intimacy central to a relationship. Rooted in pride and disrespect, it contradicts the biblical call to love and serve others.

Contempt is the eye rolls, the sarcastic remarks, the put-downs disguised as jokes, and the condescending tone that communicate "I'm better than you" or "I deserve better than you."

Ephesians 5:21 instructs, "Submit to one another out of

reverence for Christ" (NIV). Contempt is the antithesis of this reverence. To combat it, we need to focus on deepening humility (Phil. 2:3) and practicing forgiveness (Matt. 6:14–15).

Dr. John Gottman, a renowned psychologist and researcher, has dedicated his career to understanding what makes relationships either tick or crumble. He is known for his groundbreaking work on the four horsemen of the apocalypse in relationships: criticism, defensiveness, stonewalling, and, the most destructive of them all, contempt.[2]

Contempt, according to Gottman, is the number-one predictor of divorce.[3]

Here's why contempt is so damaging:

1. *It breeds defensiveness.* When your partner feels like you're attacking them personally, they're going to shut down. It makes talking things out much more difficult.
2. *It erodes trust.* Disgust, whether expressed verbally or through actions, is a form of contempt that erodes trust and safety. It's a destructive force that can undermine even the strongest bonds.
3. *It escalates conflict.* Contempt is a one-way street, pushing the other person farther away and making conflict resolution nearly impossible.
4. *It predicts divorce.* Studies by Gottman show that couples who frequently express contempt are far more likely to end up in a divorce.

Does any of this feel familiar?

The emotional neglect of contempt, this slow withdrawal from each other, is exactly what our friends were experiencing, and it was taking a heavy toll. Their relationship felt forced and irreparable. For anything to change, they needed to honestly discuss the issues, practice forgiveness, and let humility take root.

Rising Tension

When you share a bed with your children, you're hindered from connecting intimately with your partner.

When your discussions revolve only around the children, work, or responsibilities and don't include time to relearn each other over and over again, you grow farther and farther apart.

When you bring up each other's faults, critiquing and fixing, rarely praising or encouraging, you break each other down day by day.

When you reconcile after hurt and betrayal, yet you keep a record of wrongs that's miles long, you destroy your spouse's will to fight for you.

And underneath the surface, the tension rises.

Our friends sat across from us in their living room, their silence louder than words. The husband's thoughts had landed like a punch, leaving no room for misinterpretation.

The wife finally spoke up. "You tell me you love me all the time, but where is the proof of that? It isn't there. Of course you feel disconnected. Your eyes are always elsewhere, you give bare minimum, and you've fully disengaged from what used to make us 'us.'"

I realized, watching them now, how easy it was to get stuck in that place, coexisting but never truly seeing each other anymore.

Melting the Distance Between You

When our boys were babies, our lives became both sweeter and harder. No one told us how much we'd miss our relationship before parenthood, how much we'd miss being the people we once were before the constant responsibilities and sleepless nights. For a season, we lost each other.

A therapist once told me not to make any big marriage

decisions in the first year of parenthood. Solid advice, because I definitely felt ready to call it quits whenever Jesse strolled in well rested while I looked like a haggard swamp troll after another night of endless nursing. Honestly, I'd add another two years to that advice, just to be safe.

When we're overwhelmed, we're exposed, and it's easy to project our frustrations onto each other.

During that difficult season, Jesse and I were both overwhelmed by the demands of new parenthood.

He felt defeated when I selfishly pulled him into my fog of frustration after we both navigated a sleepless night.

I was so uncomfortable in my own skin that I'd hide from him, even in the bathroom while I showered, and he felt neglected physically.

I became resentful of him when he disconnected emotionally.

I boiled with anger when he stayed up too late playing video games, leaving me to handle mornings alone.

We resented each other when we felt the other wasn't fully taking on their roles.

In addition to that, our oldest son, Sutton, had severe asthma, which led to nights at the hospital, oxygen tanks being wheeled into our home, and three to four nights a week spent monitoring his breathing, with no sleep for either of us. We were constantly worried, constantly overwhelmed.

Health issues, of course, hadn't been part of our plan. We had little time to connect with each other, even though we both desperately longed for the other's comfort. While we knew it wasn't anyone's fault, we still found ourselves carrying the blame—nights spent crying and wishing we could make it all go away. It was heavy. Many days, it still is heavy.

The problem is, many couples get stuck in this phase instead of growing through it, allowing the demands of parenthood to consume their relationship, even after the baby stage has passed.

Sometimes there's no choice but to forge ahead until you can catch your breath. But there are ways to prioritize each other, make time for each other, and keep your marriage the main thing.

The hierarchy in a home should be God, spouse, children, work, ministry. Your life cannot revolve entirely around your children. Your spouse comes before your children for the sake of your children.

I believe with all my heart that one of the greatest gifts a parent can ever give their child is the security of a united marriage. One in which they are united in their love for God and one another, and aligned in discipline, in rhythm, in purpose, and in their values and goals for their family.

I can't tell you how many parents have confided in me that they feel guilty for taking time away from their kids, whether it's for date nights or adults-only vacations. But the truth is, neglecting the time you need to connect does more harm than good.

A healthy marriage creates a happier home—and happier children. Research shows that families where parents prioritize their marriage often enjoy greater emotional stability and overall well-being. Children in these families tend to thrive better educationally, socially, cognitively, and behaviorally. The positive effects of a strong parental relationship can be seen both in the short term and as children grow into adulthood.[4]

One day, your little ones will grow up and leave your home. What will be left between you and your spouse when that time comes? Have you invested in your connection so you'll have plenty to talk about when the house is quieter? Will you still enjoy each other's company when it's just the two of you sitting across from each other at the table?

Remember: It was you and your spouse before them, and it will be you and your spouse after them.

Jesse and I learned the importance of prioritizing our marriage the hard way shortly after having our first baby. Like so many new parents, we found ourselves living in a child-centered home, pouring everything into our boys and leaving almost nothing for each other. We weren't trying to neglect our relationship. It just happened slowly and subtly.

That's when I started building an iceberg between us.

It began with small blocks of ice.

He didn't hold my hand in the car like he usually did. One block.

He came home and was in a bad mood, even though I had been looking forward to seeing him all day. Block of ice.

He brushed off the conversation about our budget when I was feeling overwhelmed. Block of ice.

He shut down emotionally during a disagreement instead of working through it with me. That felt like one hundred blocks of ice.

He didn't seem to notice all the energy I had poured into the boys' birthdays or the little details I was managing at home.

He realized that he didn't actually want to travel as much as he said he did when we first got married.

None of these things were massive on their own. But they went unspoken. And what goes unspoken tends to grow.

Before I knew it, my iceberg was a thousand feet deep. And in my hurt, I let the cold in. I grew distant and irritable. I withheld affection and eye contact. I let sarcasm slip into my tone, saying things that cut just enough to make my disappointment known.

It's so, so easy to silently collect the ways our partner falls short, especially when we're feeling overlooked ourselves. We disregard the many things we could praise and instead focus on the negative. Jesse could very easily write an even longer list about my shortcomings; although, if I'm honest, he is less prone to see the bad in me than I am to see the bad in him. I wish that weren't true of me, but that's the case.

This is how contempt begins. It doesn't show up all at once.

It creeps in slowly, as the warmth starts to fade. One moment you feel a little distant. Then cold. Then, one day, you wake up and realize that every trace of intimacy between you feels frozen.

I started to recognize a pattern in myself: I was internalizing Jesse's actions and emotions, letting them feed my own insecurities. If he didn't reach for my hand, I took it as rejection. If he was quiet, I assumed it was something I had done wrong. And he did the same. If I was having an emotionally heavy day, he often assumed it was because *he* wasn't doing enough—because *he* was the problem.

Can you relate? Over time, many couples build patterns: You react to their withdrawal, they react to your reaction, and the cycle reinforces itself. The only way to disrupt this pattern is to sit in the discomfort long enough to let a new pattern form. That looks like pausing before assuming his quiet is about you, or giving her space without taking it as rejection.

This is where the hard work comes in: You have to let yourself sit in the discomfort instead of rushing to fix it. When you know your spouse's actions aren't meant to wound you, and they've shown through both words and actions that you're loved, you can start questioning the instinct that every silence or mood shift is about you.

Do you find yourself assigning meaning to your spouse's behavior that may not actually be there? Do you jump to conclusions or build silent narratives that stem more from fear than from fact?

Let me offer this truth as a breath of fresh air: Not everything is about you.

And I don't mean that harshly.

For so long, I believed that if Jesse seemed distant or didn't respond how I wanted him to, it was a reflection of something I'd done wrong. I'd spiral. I'd assume. I'd stew. And nearly always, he was just thinking about work or feeling tired from the day.

It's important to do the work not to take everything personally in the context of a relationship where patterns of respect, honesty, and safety have been established. When you know your spouse's actions aren't intentionally hurtful and they've shown you through both words and actions that you're loved, that's when you can start challenging the belief that every shift in mood or silence is about you.

Psychologists call this *self-differentiation*; it's the ability to hold on to your own identity, thoughts, and feelings while staying connected to someone else, even when they're experiencing something different from you.

According to a key concept from The Bowen Center for the Study of the Family, when you're well differentiated, you maintain a clear sense of yourself even when your spouse is upset or distant. You can hold your own thoughts and feelings without being swept into theirs, allowing you to remain calm and clear-headed in emotional moments.[5]

This means that you don't have to internalize every mood they display or interpret their quiet as a personal rejection. Instead, you can choose curiosity by asking, "Hey, are you okay?" rather than jumping to conclusions. That's the wonderful essence of differentiation: You stay emotionally centered and have the power to choose to engage thoughtfully rather than reactively.

Looking back, in nearly every one of these situations, I could have taken a step toward Jesse instead of turning inward and internalizing what I felt. While it always takes two to maintain a healthy relationship, I could have chosen to hold Jesse's hand when I wanted him to hold mine, complimented him first, planned a date for us, or offered a comforting hug after a hard day. Instead, I chose pride and allowed bitterness to take hold when he didn't initiate intimacy or make me feel seen.

So I began to shift.

If I wanted intimacy, I'd send Jesse thoughtful texts

throughout the day, wear some super-short shorts and a shirt with a peekaboo tummy while I cooked dinner, or initiate things in a fun way in the bedroom.

If I needed affirmation, I'd ask if he liked what I was wearing and gently remind him that compliments help me feel more romantically connected to him.

When I felt like he was distracted by his phone, I'd put mine down and engage with him.

Most important, I stopped assuming Jesse could read my mind. If I wanted something from him, I couldn't just hope he'd figure it out. I had to communicate my needs clearly. I realized I needed to take responsibility for my role in making our relationship thrive.

If you allow your relationship to get frigid instead of taking humble, loving steps toward each other, you will often assume that your spouse's actions are driven by malice. You won't believe your spouse is acting with the best intentions if you haven't taken the time to develop a shared language of mutual understanding.

We All Need a Little Emotional Stability

Your spouse is human with their own feelings and stressors. They can't always predict or avoid the things that trigger you. And they're not always prepared with the right response when you project your insecurities, often rooted in childhood or past experiences, onto them.

For example, constantly asking, "Do you love me? Are you sure you love me? Do you promise?" might signal a fear of abandonment or an anxious attachment style. Even if your spouse hasn't given you any reason to feel insecure, you may still find yourself asking these questions. If your spouse doesn't understand what's behind these questions or how to approach them with empathy, or if they have an avoidant attachment style, their response might unintentionally push you farther away. They might feel overwhelmed or suffocated by your neediness, especially if you haven't yet learned how to communicate difficult emotions in a way that brings you closer, not pushes you farther apart.

Think of it this way: When your partner doesn't compliment you in the way you expect them to or doesn't pay you attention as they have in the past, it can throw you off balance, especially if you interpret their actions as a personal slight. This happens because compliments and attention aren't just about the words and actions themselves, they are part of the ongoing pattern of emotional stability in your relationship. The reality is that when someone disrupts your stability, it can feel like a personal attack, even if it's not intended that way.

As I mentioned at the beginning of this book, our inclination as humans is to be self-serving and self-focused. But when we become united in marriage, we are supposed to be spouse-serving and spouse-focused, which calls us to be the one to go first, inviting us to move toward our spouses. Unfortunately, our pride can prevent us from doing this well, or at all. Pride is a deeply destructive drug: The more we give in to it, the more we become trapped by its grip.

If you shove all of your problems, your disagreements, your resentments under the surface, hoping they'll stay hidden or fix themselves, your relationship will eventually slam into that iceberg. And just as with the *Titanic*, the damage may be irreparable.

Have Some Self-Respect (Please)

Have you ever heard the saying "Hurt me once, shame on you. Hurt me twice, shame on me"? What we allow within our marriages can be an act of either self-respect or self-disrespect.

We teach people what we will allow.

Self-respect is so important within a marriage, but it can become muddled when it needs to be balanced with honoring and respecting your partner.

So how do we find that sweet spot? It begins with setting clear boundaries: a limit on what you're willing to accept for yourself and from your partner. Boundaries define what is unacceptable to you, allowing both of you to communicate your needs and protect your emotional well-being.

When we fail to set and enforce boundaries, we signal that certain behaviors are permissible. This can lead to a toxic cycle that normalizes disrespect, emotional pain, or even abuse. As author Lysa TerKeurst says in her book *Good Boundaries and Goodbyes*, "When we allow a boundary to be violated, bad behavior will be validated."[6] Imagine you're sitting on the couch, holding an empty glass in your lap, expecting your spouse to fill it just enough to satisfy your need. Instead, they start pouring water into it. It's fine at first because you think they're filling it for you, but then they don't stop. The glass is overflowing, and water spills onto your lap.

You're surprised, but instead of setting the glass down or stopping them, you just keep holding it, hoping they'll realize they've gone too far. But they keep pouring and you're now soaking wet. Frustration builds and surprise turns to shock at their unwillingness to listen once you protest. You shift your body and try to move the glass, demanding they stop, but they keep pouring.

Allowing your spouse to keep pouring water into your lap is a failure to enforce a boundary. Your tolerance of their behavior by staying in the situation communicates to them what you are willing to accept. You're teaching them that their hurtful action is permissible.

If your partner keeps ignoring your boundaries, that says a lot. It isn't only frustrating, it's revealing. Like the old saying goes, "When someone shows you who they are, believe them." At the same time, it's worth asking yourself: *Have I clearly communicated what I need?* Because sometimes we think we're setting boundaries, but we're actually hinting, hoping, or avoiding conflict. I would encourage you to view boundaries not as walls but as doors that help love flow freely without either person getting lost or run over in the process.

Even Jesus Set Boundaries

It's important to remember that even Jesus set boundaries in his relationships. He made it clear that he needed time to be alone with God, even when his disciples or others sought him out. In Mark 1:35, it says, "Now in the morning, having risen a long while before daylight, He went out and departed to a solitary place; and there He prayed."

Jesus also modeled the importance of setting boundaries when he turned over the tables in the temple. In John 2:15–16, we read, "When He had made a whip of cords, He drove them all out of the temple, with the sheep and the oxen, and poured out the changers' money and overturned the tables. And He said to those who sold doves, 'Take these things away! Do not make My Father's house a house of merchandise!'"

Notice that in this moment, Jesus didn't hurt anyone; his actions were aimed at disrupting the behavior, not the people. He didn't act out of unchecked anger when he turned over the tables in the temple. He wasn't sinning by expressing frustration; he was standing firm against something that was wrong by driving out those who were disrespecting God's house and by overturning the tables of the money changers. His actions were a righteous stand for what was right, not an explosion of sinful anger.

After the miracle of feeding the five thousand, Jesus set boundaries with the crowd. In John 6:15, it says, "When Jesus perceived that they were about to come and take Him by force to make Him king, He departed again to the mountain by Himself alone." Jesus recognized the importance of maintaining his purpose, even when others had different expectations of him.

Boundaries reflect your core values and help you feel safe, respected, and loved. You were not meant to be a doormat, letting others walk all over you, nor are you a bottomless cup, meant to pour yourself out endlessly to your spouse without ever being refilled. You simply cannot give what you don't have. When we follow Jesus' example, healthy boundaries make us stronger in our relationships, both with God and with each other.

The Nonnegotiables

If right now you're saying, "Lindsey, my boundaries have been crossed again and again and again. I feel like I've lost my dignity. I can't do this for another four days, let alone forty years. Something has to give," then please invest time in the following activity.

Sit down with your spouse, write down at least five nonnegotiables, and discuss them: the boundaries, values, and requirements you have to have in your marriage in order for it to succeed and for you to feel safe.

Remember: This isn't about pushing your partner away, it's about creating a space to gain understanding and connect more deeply.

What do you both need—what do you absolutely have to have—for this relationship to thrive and to feel like it's worth the fight or effort?

Here are some examples of nonnegotiables:

- When I share my thoughts and feelings, I need to feel heard and respected.

- To maintain openness and trust, we need full access to each other's phones and accounts.
- To stay connected emotionally, we need weekly date nights or time without distractions.
- To support one another, we will not criticize each other publicly or in front of family or friends.
- To keep our bond strong, we need weekly intimacy at minimum.
- To prevent cycles of arguments, we need couples counseling.

In your marriage, boundaries can cover all sorts of areas—in-law dynamics, phone usage, communication styles, and parenting choices. There will be tough days when the need for boundaries is clearer than ever. It's not normal for a spouse to normalize the practice of demeaning you, belittling you, or behaving in ways that cross the line. The more you tolerate disrespect, the more it can seep into your relationship, leading to a breakdown of trust.

After going through this list together, determine:

- Can I meet my spouse's needs?
- Can my spouse meet mine?
- What must we change for us to meet these needs?

Solid boundaries and a commitment to uphold them prevent harmful behaviors in a marriage while helping each partner understand what matters most to the other.

Just a note: If these nonnegotiables can't be met, or if they're agreed on and the boundary is crossed once again, it is probably time to seek counseling or other outside wisdom to determine what steps to take toward healing yourselves and your marriage.

CHAPTER 5

USE THE ANTIVENOM— AND OTHER WAYS TO BEGIN HEALING

Burying your head in the sand does not make you invisible, it only leads to suffocation.

—Wayne Gerard Trotman,

Veterans of the Psychic Wars

Let's discuss a few ways to prevent contempt.

1. A Spouse Who Pays Attention

We need to take the time to learn and care about what matters to our partners. Just look at the way people react to videos on social media where couples surprise one another with gifts or shower their spouses with kindness—it shows that our society really loves a spouse who pays attention. It doesn't take much, but when someone puts in the effort, we notice, and we're impressed by it.

Partners in a healthy marriage don't worry so much about reacting to crises or brokenness because they are focused on creating a climate where those crises are less likely to happen. The simple act of anticipating another person's needs can be a game changer. It's selfless. It's kind. It's considerate. And it softens the blow of hard moments because they're surrounded by consistent, intentional care.

If you really want to grow closer, take time to figure out what actually lights your partner up. Don't assume. Ask questions. Learn their favorites. A lot of us naturally love in the way we most want to be loved, but that doesn't always land for them. Pay attention to what makes them feel seen, show interest in the things they care about, and meet needs before they have to ask.

2. Look at Yourself First (Yes, You)

You'd be shocked (or maybe not so shocked) to know that very few people who come to me for marriage advice begin by talking about their own faults, shortcomings, and failures. Many of them never bring their junk up at all. Instead, the conversations usually begin with something like:

- "If only he would change this about himself, things would be better."
- "If she just did this more often, our marriage would be so much happier."
- "I've tried everything, but honestly, I don't need the work. They do. It's hopeless."

The reality is that we're all broken sinners in need of grace, restoration, and sanctification. Repentance is a key part of the gospel for a reason: None of us is Jesus, and all of us need forgiveness. The sooner we realize that nothing is hopeless with Christ, and that we are 100 percent responsible for 100 percent of our own behavior and lack of intentionality within our marriages, the sooner we will begin the healing.

Our partners' issues are, of course, much easier to point out, not only because it can be painful to self-evaluate but because we feel and carry the weight of those issues. And yet the greatest growth in any relationship comes when we're willing to do our own internal work first. Jesus was quick to speak the truth about this in Matthew 7:3: "And why do you look at the speck in your brother's eye, but do not consider the plank in your own eye?"

One of the best, though often most difficult, ways to self-evaluate is to ask your spouse to identify the areas in which you need improvement. They see your sin and brokenness more often than anyone else does. They also feel the ways in which they, and your marriage, are affected by your behavior.

The purpose of this process is to engage in open, honest discussion with your spouse—and with others in your life—to discover the areas in which you need to improve in your behavior, patterns, and relationships.

There is a rule to this practice: Your partner will first gently communicate their opinion regarding how you interact with them and with others—both the good and the bad, including the ways in which you create discord in your home and the ways in which they feel unloved or disrespected. You may ask questions, but you have to allow your partner to answer without becoming defensive, no matter what is said. You are not to argue (the last thing I'm trying to do is start fights between the two of you!) but to hear them out and to use that information to begin your improvement journey.

Imagine your partner started a fire in your house and it grew out of control. If you came home and found they were inside that burning house, wouldn't you run in to pull them out, despite the risks?

If your marriage feels like a house on fire, you have to be willing to do the hard work to extinguish the flames and help your spouse, even if it means coming out with burns of your own. Even if they are the one who caused most of the damage, you do what it takes to save what you've built together. That's what fighting for your marriage often looks like: It's realizing that your spouse's mistakes also become yours, then working as a team to fix them. You seek solutions together because their problems become your problems. It's often messy and painful, and it requires both courage and grace.

THE RIGHT QUESTIONS

1. How can I catch myself early on when I begin to display hurtful behaviors toward my partner?
2. When I begin to feel these behaviors coming on, do I need to separate myself? Do I need to pray? Do I need to humble myself and ask for forgiveness quickly?
3. Which Scriptures can I memorize to store in my heart and mind for when the temptation arises to fall into these detrimental patterns?
4. What steps do I need to take to avoid repeating these behaviors?
5. Who can I trust to hold me accountable? How can I create a regular check-in with this person to help me process my brokenness so that I can heal?
6. In what areas do I blame my circumstances or my past for my behavior? How can I stop using those things as an excuse and instead take responsibility for my behavior?
7. Do I need to start therapy or counseling to do the internal work?

3. Use the Antivenom: Gratitude

When contempt strikes a relationship, it injects a venom of negativity. But there is an antidote—an antivenom—to this destructive emotion. It's gratitude.

Gratitude involves choosing to view your spouse not through the lens of frustration but through the lens of appreciation. Expressing gratitude isn't necessarily about creating a high-light reel of your partner's life and romanticizing the good. It's acknowledging the simple, everyday ways your spouse makes your life sweeter. You're choosing to remember the little things: the way they make you laugh, the way they make light of serious situations, the way they always remember to grab your favorite treat on the way home.

Whenever I thank Jesse for something he has done, no matter how small that thing might be, I'm saying, *I see you. I appreciate you. You matter to me.* Those few words help to thaw the icy grip of contempt and reconnect us.

In seasons of conflict, or even in seasons of good, what if you try focusing on what you appreciate about your partner every single day? It will help keep you grounded. Ask yourself, *Is there goodness in our marriage?* Then start naming the good that comes to mind. When you remember what you like about your spouse, you will fight back against the destructive thoughts that serve only to pull you apart. The practice of gratitude requires accountability and taking control of your thoughts.

While you're working on developing a gratitude mindset, it's important to ask, *Do I like my spouse? Do I like myself?* You love them, sure. But do you actually like them? Do you choose to like them even when they're unlikable?

Here's an even bigger question: Do you choose to like *your-self*? Do you live your life as someone who is likable and enjoyable to be around? Would you want to be around you?

If you allow those pent-up frustrations to boil over, you're inevitably going to become someone you aren't proud of. You'll likely do or say things you don't mean, unfairly bring up past arguments, or become embittered and irritable. When you lead with gratitude, you'll be more willing to bend toward grace and kindness. Choose the good.

4. Soften (Even When They Don't Deserve It)

Softening your heart in the face of your spouse's hardheartedness can feel counterintuitive. It may feel like surrendering ground and inviting more hurt when the situation is already unstable. But it is the essence of unconditional love, which imitates the love of God.

And what if your partner isn't willing to soften or even meet you halfway? What if they remain entrenched in their pain and resistance? Sometimes unconditional love is wildly sacrificial, requiring more than we can offer on our own. If that's your situation, then I invite you to lift your burdens to God, who will help you walk in compassion over condemnation. He will give you the ability to extend grace even when it's undeserved. And he has given you the perfect example to follow: Jesus. He did the same for us.

I've learned the hard way that no matter how much I might want to, I can't control another person's choices or reactions. What I can control is my response. When we soften our hearts toward our spouses without any expectations or conditions, we open a door for communication and more understanding. The goal isn't about changing our spouses. It's about becoming better versions of ourselves and learning to love without time limits or conditions.

I cling tightly to the verse that says, "The goodness [or kindness] of God leads you to repentance" (Rom. 2:4).

And just as it's God's kindness that draws us to repentance,

I already mentioned lemon water (and it probably won't be the last time because it's my obsession and fuel), and Jesse shows his love by bringing me a Stanley cup filled with lemon water, extra ice, extra pulp, every morning. Because, priorities.

I once told a friend how much Jesse's gesture makes me feel loved. She responded, "It's not really about the lemon water, is it?" I asked her to explain. She said, "It's more than the fact that he knows you love lemon water. It's a consistent act of love. You're getting it even on days when you might not feel deserving. And he makes sure you have it when you need it, whether you're waking up or working out. It's his thoughtfulness and attention to what matters to you that makes you feel seen and loved."

That insight was spot on. One of the deepest forms of love is consistent consideration. When someone thinks about what will make you feel good, prioritizes their choices based on how they will affect you, and pays attention to the details of your life, it shows just how deeply they care. The depth of your care for your partner can often be measured by how much you consider their needs and feelings.

If consistent, loving care hasn't been a part of your marriage, don't lose hope. It's never too late to start building a home filled with warmth and joy. Begin with small, meaningful gestures. It could be as simple as offering your spouse a glass of lemon water—a small act of kindness that says, "I see you, and I care." Small steps can lead to big changes that don't lead to a walkaway spouse.

CHAPTER 6

FORGIVE EACH OTHER (EVEN FOR THE LITTLE THINGS)

Forgiveness releases our desire for
retaliation, not our need for boundaries.

—Lysa TerKeurst,

Forgiving What You Can't Forget

I've been wronged. I've been betrayed. I've been left speechless
by the words and actions of others. And one of the best lessons
I've ever learned is that harboring unforgiveness rarely harms the
person who wronged you as much as it harms and traps you. I
share this regularly on my podcast and social platforms because
it's a truth that sets me free: "Holding a grudge is like drinking
poison and waiting for the other person to die."

When you refuse to forgive, you end up carrying the burden
of anger and bitterness yourself, while the other person moves on
with their life, largely unaffected.

Every time you dwell on your spouse's wrongdoings, you're consuming a toxic substance, mistakenly believing that it harms them when, in reality, it's slowly destroying you from the inside out.

At this point in your marriage, how many bottles of poison have you swallowed?

Forgiveness is at the heart of Christianity. It's the reason Christ came to us. We all fall short, both by nature and by choice. Without Jesus' sacrifice, we wouldn't experience the grace that forgives and restores us.

Jesus connects our forgiving others with God's forgiveness of us. In Matthew 6:15, he says, "But if you do not forgive [others] their trespasses, neither will your Father forgive your trespasses."

Jesus' illustrates his statement with the parable of the unforgiving servant in Matthew 18:21–35. In the story, a king confronts a servant who owes him a staggering ten thousand bags of gold. Unable to repay, the servant pleads for mercy, and the king, moved by compassion, forgives the entire debt.

But after receiving such incredible forgiveness, the servant turns around and demands repayment from another servant who owes him a much smaller amount. His refusal to show mercy contrasts sharply with the king's compassion.

When the king finds out, he rebukes the servant, saying, "You wicked servant! I forgave you all that debt because you begged me. Should you not also have had compassion on your fellow servant, just as I had pity on you?" (vv. 32–33).

It is the same way with us.

Jesus paid the ultimate price for our forgiveness. Who are we to withhold forgiveness from our spouses or other people in our lives for their wrongs when we have our own debts of sin? Jesus' sacrifice is a powerful reminder that our ability to forgive others is rooted in the overwhelming forgiveness we've received.

Let's do a little heart check.

Think back to your childhood, your high school days, your

friendships, your relationship with your parents, your early marriage, and your current day-to-day. How much forgiveness have you been shown in your life? It's easy to forget how much grace we've received when resentment creeps in. We get so focused on our hurts that we lose sight of our own messes—past sins, current struggles, unintentional offenses, pride, and those hidden idols we don't always want to acknowledge.

But we have to remember Isaiah 1:18: "Though your sins are like scarlet, they shall be as white as snow; though they are red like crimson, they shall be as wool." Our hands and feet may be blood red with sin, but God's grace washes them clean.

It's a radical idea, isn't it? The Bible's view of sin often expands beyond what we might expect. Take adultery, for example: It's not just physical infidelity that qualifies as sin but also lustful desires and intentions.

When we step back and reflect, we realize that sin is much broader than we often care to admit. And that's where Jesus' teachings really challenge us. His radical message upends what society considers good and pushes us to look deeper, examine our hearts, and see how much we, too, need forgiveness. This exercise is humbling, but it also invites us to extend the same grace to others.

It's easy for me to compare myself with someone who is doing a lot worse than me, but when I compare myself with the sinless life of Jesus, I'm quick to see the depth of my depravity. I realize that I deserve nothing without his blood and grace. And yet God has poured out his mercy on my life and washes me white as snow. Even when I feel entitled to cling tightly to bitterness over offenses big or small, his grace abounds.

I understand that discussing forgiveness in the context of relationships can be incredibly complex, especially when dealing with issues of verbal, physical, or spiritual abuse. It's important to me that I emphasize that forgiveness does not mean condoning harmful behavior.

While forgiveness is a powerful tool for personal healing, it should never be used as a justification for abuse. Trust and safety are fundamental to any healthy relationship, and these should not be compromised under any circumstances.

But in the regular, daily struggles of marriage, we have to realize that it's not our place to fix our spouses. We're not the Holy Spirit. Our job is simply to love them.

I first began to understand the importance of forgiving others at the age of nineteen, when I gave my life to Jesus. It has since proven to be a pivotal lesson in my life. I had to let go of everything I believed about forgiveness and my entitlement to what I thought I deserved, ultimately finding freedom from the bitterness I'd held on to for so long.

It is a continual process to know and believe that God sees my brokenness, my mess, and the hurt I've caused others and still loves me. God says, "You are precious and honored in my sight, and . . . I love you" (Isa. 43:4 NIV), and the psalmist writes, "As far as the east is from the west, so far has He removed our transgressions from us" (Ps. 103:12).

Here's a small challenge that you and your spouse can do together:

1. Make a list of the grievances you are holding against your partner. These can range from significant betrayals to minor annoyances such as forgetting to unload the dishwasher. Include anything that has caused you to feel even small amounts of unresolved bitterness toward them.
2. Repent before one another for your lack of forgiveness. You are not justifying the other's behavior by choosing to forgive them, you are simply seeking to be in right standing with God and seeking freedom from bondage.

3. Ask the Holy Spirit to enter your heart and help you forgive your partner the same way God has forgiven you.
4. Pray individually about each struggle, asking God to help you see your spouse with new eyes of mercy and grace. Remember, there's absolutely no shame in seeking professional counseling together if the challenges feel overwhelming.

Forgive and Forget?

I want to repeat that while forgiveness breeds freedom, it is not an acceptance or justification of a person's behavior. It's a decision that says, "I refuse to let that poison rot my heart." But it doesn't mean you don't create new boundaries in the relationship.

We choose to forgive because of who Jesus is, not because of how much the offending person deserves it. Jesus displayed immense forgiveness throughout his own life, and to forgive another is a commandment, not a luxury. This isn't a harsh or unloving command; we know that in all things, God desires good for those who love him and are called according to his purpose (Rom. 8:28).

In Matthew 18:21, Peter asks Jesus, "Lord, how often shall my brother sin against me, and I forgive him? Up to seven times?" He wants to know how many times he has to let go of that sin. But Jesus says to him, "I do not say to you, up to seven times, but up to seventy times seven" (v. 22). By no means do I believe this passage is telling us to keep a tally of how many times someone wrongs us and we forgive them. Jesus wasn't offering a math equation; he was making a heart statement. Our forgiveness, like his, is meant to be complete. When Jesus said, "It is finished!" (John 19:30), he wasn't just declaring the end of his suffering. He was announcing the fullness of his forgiveness. Every sin—past, present, and future—was paid for in that moment. And because of that, we are no longer bound by bitterness or offense. We have been forgiven of far more than we will ever be asked to forgive. His death didn't just save us. It gave us the freedom to live with open hands and soft hearts, even toward those who have deeply wounded us.

Marriage is a sacred covenant that you enter into on the day you say "I do." But what you are also saying to your spouse at the altar is, *I know that you have good in you. I also know you're sinful and that I will need to forgive you again and again and again. I know that you won't fulfill all of my needs or desires, but I'm going to work on it with you for the rest of my life.*

Trials are inevitable. There will be pain in your marriage. Your forgiveness acknowledges the hurt and allows you to move forward free of bitterness, but it doesn't require you to erase the memory or downplay the significance of the things that happened. In all honesty, sometimes the pain remains because the lessons learned from it are vital for our healing.

The Impact of Betrayal

Few things cut deeper in a marriage than the betrayal of an affair. When trust is broken like that, rebuilding it can feel almost impossible. We've walked very closely with friends on both sides of this kind of heartbreak—those who were betrayed and those who made choices they never thought they'd make. Watching the pain, the confusion, and the devastation unfold changes you. And it reminds you just how fragile trust can be and how much work healing really takes.

The impact of an affair is far reaching, causing immense suffering not only for the betrayed partner but also for the offending spouse and for the couple's loved ones. It's a tumultuous, heartbreaking tornado.

To bring hope to those who are walking through it, I want to share that I have personally seen real, miraculous redemption in marriages that were once shattered by infidelity. Couples who seemed irreparably broken have experienced miraculous healing—going from pain and anger to living in a relationship that is stronger and happier than ever before. It is possible.

The reality, though, is that the aftermath of discovering or admitting betrayal can be overwhelming. It's easy to feel like the marriage is beyond repair. Perhaps you're there right now. Or maybe it's not an affair that has pushed you to this point but a series of smaller betrayals, such as pornography use or keeping secrets, that have built up resentment and made you feel the only direction is out.

I believe that restoring a marriage shattered by infidelity requires a miracle of two parts: (1) repeated forgiveness by the betrayed partner, and (2) the continual, sincere repentance, patience, and perseverance of the spouse who committed the betrayal.

Pastor John Piper says this of healing from betrayal: "For the long-suffering that has to happen, he or she recognizes that receiving forgiveness is not the same as receiving trust, nor should it be. The rebuilding of trust requires a patient, humble, long-suffering endurance. Being forgiven is not a right to be demanded but a gift of grace to be received with humility and thankfulness and tears."[1]

Piper goes on to explain that trust is not like a stake you drive into the ground and walk past; it's like an acorn you plant in the ground. And someday, God willing, it may be an unshakable oak tree. But it will grow through tender stages only by patient watering and nurturing and protection through storms that will threaten to kill it.

Many people are reluctant to show mercy because they don't understand the difference between forgiveness and trust.

Forgiveness is letting go of the past. Trust has to do with future behavior.

In his book *The Purpose Driven Life*, Pastor Rick Warren writes, "Forgiveness must be immediate, whether or not a person asks for it. Trust must be rebuilt over time. Trust requires a track record. If someone hurts you repeatedly, you are commanded by God to forgive them instantly, but you are not expected to trust them immediately, and you are not expected to continue allowing them to hurt you."[2]

Love Keeps No Record of Wrongs

If you are struggling with forgiveness in your life or marriage right now, remember that a lack of forgiveness seeps into every single area of a relationship. My boys and I often do a "science project" where we fill a glass container with milk and add a few drops of food coloring. At first the color remains in a concentrated spot, but as time passes, it begins to spread. We then push a soap-covered Q-tip down into the food coloring.

With a little pressure, the colors disperse, creating a rainbow of colors in the dish, completely altering the original color of the milk. Just like the food coloring, certain issues or behaviors in a relationship may start small—almost insignificant—but with some pressure, they gradually seep into every aspect of the relationship.

For example, I recently watched a video where a woman shared her experience after her husband's affair. She described it as a permanent elephant in the room. Every argument, no matter how small, would circle back to that betrayal. "You didn't do the dishes, and you also had an affair." "You're home late, and, oh yeah, you had an affair."

She had chosen to stay, but every little frustration became magnified in light of what had happened. This matters deeply because forgiveness is not forgetting, it's choosing to release someone from the debt they owe you, even when the pain still lingers.

One verse that has always resonated with me is 1 Corinthians 13:5: "[Love] keeps no record of wrongs" (NIV).

How often do we allow "that one time" from two years ago to pop up in our minds and further escalate the fight today?

A friend recently shared something with me over lunch that brought this point to life. She told me her husband often forgets her birthday or gets her something random and impersonal. But this year, he mentioned feeling hurt that she didn't do much for his birthday. She said, "But I heard your words in my head, Linds. I didn't bring up the times he had forgotten mine. I just apologized for not being thoughtful, because I had already addressed my own disappointment with him when it happened last year. We had worked through it, and it felt unfair to drag it back up. I knew if it happened again, we'd talk. But in that moment, I wanted to acknowledge his disappointment, own my part, and respond in love and move forward." This is a great example of sitting through the discomfort in order to eliminate unhealthy patterns.

We all grow up with different traditions, expectations, and definitions of what "thoughtful" looks like—especially around holidays and birthdays. That's why communication matters so much. If you've never talked about how you like to celebrate, what makes you feel seen, or what feels important to you, it's easy to end up hurt or disappointed. Please ask for what you need and be sure to say it clearly!

When it comes to bigger moments, such as choosing to stay after hurt or betrayal, we also have to be willing to do the hard, painful work of rebuilding. Otherwise, bitterness just finds new ways to grow. Restoration can't happen without effort. Forgiveness opens the door, but it's the daily choices like counseling appointments, vulnerable conversations, and the moments we resist bringing up past hurts in unrelated arguments that actually carry us forward.

You can't say you're staying while also holding on to the right to constantly punish your partner.

True healing requires both people to engage: the one who broke trust and the one choosing to rebuild it. And yes, it's slow and it's messy. But it is possible, especially when God is invited into the process.

Standing at the altar is a promise of future grace. It says, *I choose you, even when things are no longer the same as they are right now. I choose you when you fail me and when you make mistakes. I will choose you again and again.*

Proverbs 17:9 reiterates this, saying, "Whoever would foster love covers over an offense" (NIV).

Is there something you need to forgive? Something that lingers in your heart despite apologies and repeated conversations? Have you talked it through, heard the right words, yet still find yourself unable to fully release it?

If so, I want to encourage you to try this activity: Find a quiet space and dedicate an uninterrupted hour to yourself. Identify the source of your unforgiveness. Is it directed toward your spouse or someone else? Write a letter to that person, expressing your hurt, anger, or betrayal without holding back. Be honest about your feelings and the impact their actions have had on your life.

This letter is for your eyes only. It's meant only to release your emotions without judging them. Once it's complete, read the letter aloud, letting yourself fully experience the emotions it expresses. When you're ready, conclude with a statement of forgiveness: "I forgive you. I love you. Jesus loves you. And I'm sorry for any part I may have played in this situation." Offer a brief prayer for the person, releasing your burden.

Finally, destroy the letter. This act symbolizes letting go of the pain and resentment that have been holding you captive.

Then let go.

If you long to have a soulmate relationship and to be best friends with your spouse again, it's time to pour that poison down the sink.

The Enemy comes to steal, kill, and destroy. Unforgiveness in the heart of a believer is one of the quickest ways he can achieve that goal in your life. But Jesus wants to remove the poison and heal your marriage from the inside out. Forgiveness is a beautiful miracle of God.

Remember this truth: Forgiveness doesn't excuse your spouse's behavior. Forgiveness prevents their behavior from destroying your heart.

CHAPTER 7

MORE SCROLLING, MORE PROBLEMS

Do you ever hide from humanity in your home,
only to stare at the worst of it on your phone?

—Joshua Turek,

"In the Land of Wrong Names"

id you know that orgasms release a surge of dopamine?
Exercise, touch, meaningful conversations, sunlight, and feelings of love are natural dopamine boosters as well. These simple, everyday things have a profound effect on our happiness. Our bodies' built-in reward system is a beautiful, God-created gift, designed to bring us joy.

Dopamine is the neurotransmitter that's essential for motivation and learning and that floods your brain when you hug your spouse or kiss your children. Its release is the brain's reward system, designed to encourage behaviors that contribute to survival and well-being.

And yet we have replaced these sweet, life-giving triggers of dopamine with a glowing, plastic, soulless rectangle. Our smartphones' constant stream of notifications and rewards hijack our system, creating an artificial sense of gratification that undermines our capacity for fulfillment. This digital dopamine addiction has numbed our senses and is actively disconnecting us from the world around us.

I've spent quite a bit of time researching the impact of phone addiction, mostly because I started to feel and see its effects not just in my own life but in the lives of so many people around me. It's subtle at first, isn't it? Just a few scrolls to unwind and a quick check during dinner, but over time, I noticed how it was stealing my focus, my presence, my desire for time with real people, and a ton of my peace.

Did you know that excessive screen time disrupts your natural intake of dopamine? This is particularly evident in the phenomenon of doomscrolling—the compulsive consumption of negative news and information—where the brain becomes addicted to the unpredictable hits of dopamine triggered by each new, often distressing, update.

"Why do we do this to ourselves?" I asked my husband one night after a long period of mindless scrolling. We both felt disgusted with ourselves after spending what seemed like hours watching depressing news and social media videos that made us compare our lives with others' lives.

I realized I'd been experiencing this feeling far too often over the past few months. I felt so gross about it that I wanted to throw my phone across the room. Do the hours of endless scrolling ever make you feel that way? Like you're wasting your life away? I was finally waking up to the reality that this constant pull into a digital world gave me nothing in return. It was making me restless, irritable, and, honestly, kind of miserable. I had to be honest with myself and admit that something needed to change.

The impact of our digital addiction as a society is profound; technology is stealing our most intimate moments. Countless couples spend the last five minutes before sleep staring at their smartphones rather than the faces of their partners, and it has become the norm.

We've spent far too much of our lives looking down, distracted and mindless.

Something has to give.

The Distracted Wife

On the day I wrote this chapter, I decided to visit a new coffee shop in Nashville.

After working for a little more than an hour, sipping my iced hazelnut latte, I noticed a man stopping at the table near mine, where a woman sat. He was likely in his mid-sixties and was carefully carrying two cups of steaming coffee—one for himself and one for his wife. I observed him from the corner of my eye as he settled into his seat, his excitement for the day evident. With a gentle sigh and a smile, he absorbed the ambiance of the coffee shop.

I caught glimpses of anticipation flickering in his eyes and heard the joy in his voice as he spoke, his gaze fixed on his wife. *This is a man who genuinely enjoys spending time with his spouse,* I thought. Then I heard him say to her, "It's a beautiful day, isn't it? . . . Did you hear that our new neighbor moved here from Canada? . . . Would you still like to walk the shops today?"

But there was no response. Nothing. Not even an "mmhmm" or a grunt of acknowledgment.

I tried my best to stay focused on my computer, but no matter how hard I tried to ignore it, I couldn't. (Don't judge—I'm a natural eavesdropper. It's unavoidable, so it makes date nights way more fun for Jesse and me. Ever played Guess What

They're Talking About at dinner? Ten out of ten recommend.)
As I waited for her response to him, a wave of emotion swept over me.

The wife had just ignored her husband's very obvious bid for attention. Did she not hear him? Maybe he needed to speak up.

He asked another question.

Silence.

At this point, I was doing my best not to glance over.

Would it be weird if I responded to him on her behalf? I wondered, feeling empathetic. I resisted the urge to speak to the man—*because yes, Lindsey, that would be weird*—but I couldn't resist looking over quickly to see what was happening.

Not to my surprise, the wife was glued to her phone, oblivious to his efforts.

The one-sided dialogue continued for a few more minutes. Then the man's shoulders slumped in defeat as he disengaged. He pulled out his own phone, and only then did the wife attempt to show him something on her screen.

For the next thirty minutes, she scrolled through social media and spoke about people they barely knew. Her chatter, filled with ambiguous mentions of divorces, mistakes, and accomplishments of those on her Facebook friends list did little to bring back the joy that had drained from her husband's face.

The reality is this: The woman was spending more time looking through the lives of people she hardly knew than looking into the eyes of someone who truly mattered, someone who wanted her to see him.

But she didn't see him at all.

My heart was saddened. Not only because I became a little too invested in wanting them to experience more connection during their special day together—which is the goal of my job—but because I saw myself in her.

The Drug That Works Only the First Few Hundred Times

It's so easy for Jesse and me to plop down on the couch together only to immediately gravitate toward our screens instead of each other.

I find myself checking my email countless times per day, texting and scrolling. Jesse is drawn to games and watching video after video of informational content.

While these aren't necessarily bad activities, our lack of moderation in them harms the connection we're trying to build within our relationship.

When faced with certain feelings—like anxiety, fear, regret, or shame—people often want to distract and soothe themselves. We reach for our devices as a way to do that. Are you guilty? This is a pattern of emotional avoidance. It's a coping mechanism, allowing us to escape from negative emotions instead of confronting them. But while it might provide temporary relief, it prevents us from processing our feelings and can lead to reliance on—and addiction to—technology for comfort.

When you choose to stop numbing out by staring at a screen all the time, you'll likely notice things you've stopped paying much attention to. You'll see when your child is struggling with a friendship or when your spouse is having a challenging day. You'll notice how beautiful it is just to sit and listen to the birds chirping in the morning, or how refreshing it is to walk on the dewy grass with bare feet.

Isn't this kind of exciting? You feel real emotions again without shoving them down as far as they can go. You confront the struggles, feelings, and realities of life that rise to the surface. It might not feel great at first, but the more willing you are to work through your issues, the less they will feel like issues. The phone distraction is like a drug that works only the first few hundred times (Hi, Taylor Swift fans!) and eventually causes more destruction than pleasure.

I often reflect on this destruction, specifically how I'm sacrificing the gift of being present, when I bring my phone outside to watch my boys play soccer or do flips on the trampoline. Instead of savoring the moment, I feel a wave of FOMO (fear of missing out), as if I must capture a video of them, especially since keeping people updated on my life is part of my job. But this urge or self-imposed responsibility to document the experience pulls me away from living in it.

I have to remember that I'm the one enslaving myself to the need to document every single moment or to constantly keep my phone in my hand so I don't miss something. I'm tethered to this phone only because I choose to be. It doesn't increase my child's joy when he looks over at me after nailing his very best flip only to see the top of my head because I got distracted by a notification.

The sobering reality is that we may be the very first generation to have more vivid memories of strangers' lives than of our own.

Ugh. Does that idea bother you as much as it bothers me? It's a pretty heavy thought and makes me feel a little sad. But it's not too late to create a different legacy—for our marriages, for our children, and for future generations.

Think of it like bingeing your favorite fast-food meal. You crave it to relieve some emotional stress, but once you finish and feel stuffed, you ask yourself, *Why did I do that? I feel awful*, or you say to yourself, *I've failed again.*

So many of us turn to our phones for that same kind of relief, but instead we end up immersed in regret after an hour of scrolling through videos that offer no real value to our lives. We wonder, *What am I doing with my life?* Yet an hour later we pick our phones right back up again.

Complacency, distraction, and laziness have no place in our

lives. And yet they're a huge part of our modern world right now. By constantly making our phones a priority, we send a message, even if unintentionally, that these distractions are more important than the person sitting next to us. We favor our own comfort, our own decompression, and our own peace of mind over real relationships. Phones are stealing precious moments, not only from ourselves but from our chosen people.

How can we reclaim our families and our marriages from the clutches of our smartphones?

How to Put Down Your Phone (for Good)

Your phone can kill or build emotional and physical intimacy unlike anything else. It's the ultimate tool for immediate disconnection. If you're really serious about getting connected, here's how you can take the first steps:

1. The 2–2–2 Reset. A practical starting point is to establish phone-free zones. Commit to:

- Two hours a day of device-free time
- Two days a month of digital detox
- Two weeks a year unplugged

This approach can help break the grip of constant connectivity and help you create new habits.

2. Ask yourself whether this is a tool or a time trap. Think of "distraction apps" as the apps you click without even realizing you're doing it: your internet browser, YouTube, social media apps, and games. Even email can be a distraction. How many times do you open your email just to close it again? These are the apps to which you lose forty-five minutes of your day without realizing that even five have passed.

Utility apps are for ordering groceries on your phone,

keeping a family calendar, making phone calls, reading a daily devotional, and texting friends.

Set boundaries for your phone use: Delete unnecessary apps, turn off nonessential notifications, and schedule times for checking it. Make your phone a tool, not a source of distraction.

3. Put your phone in another room during meals. A phone-free policy has made such a positive impact on our own family meals. It gives us the opportunity to ask the boys questions, to hear their highs and lows for the day, to share what God is doing in each of our lives, and to discuss the areas in which we need support or encouragement from one another. Our sons can be sure that during this time, Jesse and I will be present, intently listening, and always seeking to learn more about them. When you designate a basket or a place to leave your phones outside of the dining area (not just face down on the table), you show people that you prioritize being fully present with them. Research shows that quality family time is linked to better emotional health and stronger relationships.

4. Use a real alarm clock. It's surprising how normal it is now to wake up in the morning and immediately check our phones for the time or to turn off an alarm. But it doesn't stop there. We see a text notification, so we read it. Then a breaking-news alert catches our eye, and we can't resist clicking on it.

You've barely opened your eyes and said good morning to your spouse or taken a moment to pray. Yet in those opening seconds of your day, you're immediately bombarded with all of life's problems. Yuck. Emails from work, credit card updates. It's all coming at you.

None of us think this is a positive way to start the day, do we? It certainly isn't healthy.

A dedicated alarm clock can eliminate the need for your phone to be right next to you at night. Don't even keep it in your room! The physical separation discourages early-morning or late-night phone use.

Additionally, the blue light emitted by phone screens can suppress melatonin production, a hormone that regulates sleep. When you use a real alarm clock, you minimize exposure to your phone's blue light before bed, giving you better sleep overall.

5. Get a "dumb phone." If you're open to this option, a flip phone could change your life immediately for the better.

6. Use a real paper calendar. The less dependent you are on your phone, the better. Paper calendars eliminate constantly having to check your phone for appointments, deadlines, and to-do lists, thus significantly reducing screen time and the potential for distraction.

7. Set (and stick to) screen-time limits. Start using app timers or screen-time restrictions on your devices. Stick to daily limits for social media or entertainment apps. If you break promises to yourself, you're disrespecting yourself, so keep your commitment.

You can also schedule phone-free times during the day, such as during family meals or the hour before bedtime. Consider creating a weekly plan that includes time for quality, in-person interactions with people for a more balanced lifestyle and stronger sense of community.

8. Remember, breaking the grip of constant phone connectivity starts with you. Guys, please remember that it's a good and healthy thing to embrace boredom, for both you and your children. When you allow yourselves to be bored, you'll be more likely to take adventures that you normally wouldn't, have dance parties, explore, play sports, spend time with friends, compete over board games, and just . . . live. Take the time to appreciate the sounds, scents, and sights around you. This will, without a doubt, lead to deeper, more meaningful connections with your spouse and with your children.

For those of us who are parents, our kids are always watching us. When they see us on our phones, they naturally ask, "Why are they on their phone? What's the purpose?" This is a good opportunity for us, as parents and spouses, to model accountability. If we need to access our phones, it's a good practice to look our kids in the eye and state the reason, like, "Hey, I'm just finishing up this email and then I'll put my phone away and be fully present with you." When we demonstrate disciplined phone use, we help our children understand the difference between engagement and distraction. This, again, says, "I prioritize you."

Phone Fog

You've likely experienced the feeling of "phone fog" once or twice in your life. This is the sluggishness, discomfort, and even discontentment with yourself that you feel when you put your phone down after hours of scrolling or binge-watching a show.

It's neuroscience: As you scroll, your dopamine levels spike quickly and then crash even faster. The high doesn't last, and it drops much more sharply than with normal sources of pleasure.

Long periods of scrolling result in a dopamine deficit—a phenomenon known as the "dopamine cliff." This is your dopamine crash—a physiological response to the stimulation of your screen. The crash after the constant barrage of information and entertainment can often even mimic symptoms of depression.[1]

We weren't built for a 24-7 dopamine drip, a world of instant gratification held comfortably in our palms. In response, our brains adapt, attempting to maintain equilibrium by lowering dopamine production. This creates what is called a "dopamine deficit," a state where the things that once brought us joy are now less appealing.

Do you notice this in your own life? The things that once felt easy and brought you joy—like watching an entire movie uninterrupted, reading a novel, or even having a long conversation with a friend—do they feel more difficult to enjoy now? Like your mind is always halfway somewhere else?

In her book *Dopamine Nation*, Dr. Anna Lembke of Stanford

University says, "We've ended up in this dopamine deficit state where we feel incredibly depressed and nihilistic and unhappy and we don't know why. And so what do we do? We reach for more of those things that give us pleasure in the short term. And yet those are the very things that are creating the despair in the first place."[2]

Did you know that your dopamine won't crash after sex? Or a kiss? Or exercise? It lingers. Dopamine released during real-life connection tends to be more balanced and lasting than the quick spikes triggered by phone notifications or social media. Highs from natural, God-given sources are authentic and enduring.

I recently spoke with a friend who shared about his struggle with phone addiction and desire to break free from it. "The thing is, I know it's addictive. We hear about it all the time. But what I really need to figure out is why I should care enough to stop. I want to be more present with my family, but my whole life seems to exist on my phone."

It's an honest reflection of a common struggle. Our friend went on to encapsulate the mentality of resignation: "It's just a way of life now." But this mindset normalizes the constant pull of our devices, even when we sense its detrimental impact on our lives. It's an acceptance that currently robs us, and will continue to rob us, of our most precious moments and connections.

The reality is that we live in a world with unprecedented technological challenges, unlike anything our parents or grandparents faced. iPad babies? Short attention spans? Cyberbullying? Levels of insecurity unlike ever before? The truth is, the moment you give your child a smartphone, you're fast-tracking their childhood into a world they're not ready for. The accessibility to an uncensored and dark world is unlike anything else. I'm thankful for the resources that are beginning to pop up, but until recently we haven't been given a manual to teach us how to navigate such difficult issues. We're charting a new course, figuring things out as we go, all while attempting to guide our children through it.

I'm here not to villainize phones but to bring attention to the damage they can do to our families and to encourage us to set healthy boundaries before it's too late.

I think when we look back on our lives, we won't regret working too much. We'll regret all the moments we missed—too busy staring at a screen, watching others live instead of truly living ourselves.

Called to Be Outliers

One study conducted by Brigham Young University involving 143 couples found that electronic devices often disrupted shared activities, conversations, and even mealtimes, often heightening conflict within relationships.[3]

This disruption is another new phenomenon in our modern world; it's known as *technoference*—the practice of prioritizing technology over relationships.

It's no shock that our marriages and sex lives are suffering when we rarely touch or look at one another during the day or before bed.

We do need to give ourselves a little bit of grace, though. Honestly, I fantasize often about tossing all of our phones into the trash, unplugging every TV, and retreating to an isolated farm to raise chickens and make sourdough bread—just to salvage my relationships. But I can't get my sourdough past the starter stage for the absolute life of me, and I wouldn't even know where to begin with those cute little chickens.

Moreover, this fantasy just isn't feasible for my life (at least not right now) and likely isn't for yours either.

As Christians, we're called to live above reproach, meaning our lives should reflect integrity, self-discipline, and intentionality in how we engage with the world. In a culture saturated by social media and technology addiction, living above reproach means choosing to step back from unhealthy habits while setting an example of balance and purpose. It's also about being in the world, but not of it (John 17:14–16), resisting the pull of cultural norms that distract us from our higher calling.

We're called to be the outliers—people who prioritize connection with God and others over the fleeting gratification of endless scrolling.

Even when everyone else is glued to their phones.

Even when your child's friend gets a phone.

Even when you're tempted to see what so-and-so posted or who's winning the football game while you're out on a date.

You have the power to make a different choice. It won't be easy. Yet nothing worth having in life ever comes easily.

The reality is this: Relationships need focused attention, open communication, and physical touch to thrive. It starts with taking the first step.

In his book *The Tipping Point*, Malcolm Gladwell affirms the power of a first step: "Tipping points are a reaffirmation of the potential for change and the power of intelligent action. Look at the world around you. It may seem like an immovable, implacable place. It is not. With the slightest push—in just the right place—it can be tipped."[4]

He goes on to say that small actions reach a critical mass and cause a larger change, which is relevant to managing addictive behaviors like excessive phone use.

Do You Need to Make a Change?

Here are some questions to ask yourself regarding your phone use. Consider journaling the answers to get your thoughts flowing.

1. Am I genuinely interested in the constant stream of updates, or do I feel pressure to keep up?

2. Does scrolling make me feel more connected to others, or does it leave me feeling isolated, less than, or sad?
3. Do I feel closer to, or farther from, God when I spend excessive time on my phone?
4. When I reach for my phone, am I trying to avoid an uncomfortable conversation or a difficult emotion?
5. Could the time I spend scrolling be better used to connect with my spouse, children, or friends in a meaningful way?
6. Do I feel anxious or restless if I'm not constantly near or checking my phone?

If you answered yes to a few of these and realize that your phone use is making you feel pressured, insecure, depressed, or anxious, you're not alone. My friends and I were just talking about this during Bible study the other day. We feel far more depleted when we get off our phones than when we first picked them up. Many people struggle with similar feelings because of constant phone use. The good news is that you can break free and reclaim control by setting healthy boundaries.

Remember, breaking any addiction is rarely an all-or-nothing proposition. If you take the time to understand the root of your phone habits and how they make you feel, it gives you the ability to take daily steps toward growth and change. The solution isn't to smash your phone against the wall (unless you want to, of course) but to cultivate a healthier and more mindful relationship with your phone for the sake of your real relationships. Start having conversations with the people closest to you about what needs to change, seek accountability together, and explore where those conversations take you.

You'll create a more intentional, purposeful, and connected life by prioritizing your relationships over your screens.

CHAPTER 8

MARRIAGE DOESN'T SUFFOCATE

You can choose intimacy or you can choose control, but you can't have both.

—Laura Doyle, "How to Stop Being Controlling in a Relationship"

Research shows that marriages with an excessively controlling person in them experience increased stress and dissatisfaction and have a higher likelihood of divorce. Control steals what makes healthy marriages thrive when mutual respect, communication, and shared decision-making are quenched and suffocated.

Trust me. I know from experience. I wish I could say I grew up in a world untouched by the knowledge of infidelity and unhappy marriages, but the reality was quite different. The reality of divorce wasn't hidden from me as a child. I witnessed the complexities and struggles of relationships firsthand, and I watched as commitments were broken and families fell apart, which shaped my understanding of love and commitment from an early age.

Those experiences seeped into my own home and belief system in adulthood, leaving me with an unhealthy view of marriage.

Growing up between two homes left me unsettled, always bracing for the next shift. Since I couldn't control that part of my life, I clung even tighter to control everywhere else. I controlled what I could: my grades, what I ate, and how I looked. When things fell outside of my control, I fell into a spiral. And my future, and the people in it, were very much outside of my control.

More than anything in the world, I longed for the safety of consistency and presence, which were things I never fully experienced as a little girl. I wanted someone who genuinely enjoyed my company. I didn't want to be left. I clung to the idea of steady love and did whatever it took to avoid abandonment.

Even now, I carry an anxious attachment style. Letting go of someone who matters to me feels almost impossible. I battle a deep fear of being abandoned. I overexplain, overapologize, and hold on, even when I know something is unhealthy, because the ache of being unwanted or not chosen feels heavier than the ache of staying.

In the past, I often internalized rejection as proof that I wasn't enough and wrestled with the belief that if I could just do better, try harder, be less, or be more, maybe then I'd finally be chosen. That kind of desperation and fear led me to ignore red flags and accept breadcrumbs of affection in many relationships. I jumped from relationship to relationship, simply because I didn't know how to be alone. People ended up getting the worst version of me when conflict or tension arose, and in turn, I got the worst version of them. I hadn't yet done the work to heal.

I realize now that having this insight into unhealthy marriages affected me far more deeply than I knew at the time. It shaped my perception of marriage (I was convinced my future marriage would never last) and made me exceptionally cautious of the individuals I allowed into my heart.

I vividly remember my calls to my family after Jesse's proposal.

What should have been celebratory news became instantly choked by fear. My heart guarded itself before the phone even rang. The conversations were strained, filled with my anxious, bumbling disclaimers: "Hey! Guess what? Jesse proposed. We know we're young, marriage is hard, but we won't get divorced, he won't cheat, we'll be different than everyone else. We'll make it work."

Wow, Linds. Way to celebrate!

I don't know if I was desperately trying to convince them or clinging to those words for myself. Their loss for words was understandable.

Though I had witnessed many marriages succeed and couples navigate difficult challenges as a team and, by God's grace, emerge even stronger than before, I was afraid that my story would end in divorce like so many others had.

Even now, as I write this book, I'm fully aware that I'm not immune to divorce. None of us are.

Back when I got engaged, I understood and believed that God could redeem both sin and trials and use them to deepen relationships and draw a couple back to him. But I didn't want to endure that kind of pain. I wasn't ready or willing to face the hardship. I just wanted to experience the lighthearted, easy parts of marriage.

The verse on my car dashboard at the time—"Be strong and courageous. Do not be afraid or terrified . . . for the LORD your God goes with you; he will never leave you nor forsake you" (Deut. 31:6 NIV)—didn't hold the same weight in my life then as it does now.

Jesse and I, fresh-faced twenty-two-year-olds, dove headfirst into our tiny fixer-upper right after the wedding. We were best friends—we had been inseparable for two years before we started dating—and enjoyed spending every waking moment with each other. Life with Jesse was effortless. We never would have said it out loud, but we didn't understand why all the new couples around us thought marriage was so hard.

We spent our evenings creating makeshift indoor picnics: blankets sprawled across the floor, a symphony of dipping strawberries, popcorn, and pretzels in melted chocolate. Chilly fall afternoons found us bundled in oversize coats, driving to the mountains for whispered conversations while overlooking the city lights. Communication was our safe haven; nothing was left off the table.

Jesse's commitment to open honesty and communication was a pillar of our relationship, beginning on our honeymoon, and it taught me how to live the same way.

Everything was good. We were good.

Until we weren't.

I remember sitting on our living room couch one warm summer night about a year after our wedding. The back door was open, and a gentle breeze wove its way through our home, carrying the soft scent of the New Mexico desert air. The smell of smoke from our neighbor's bonfire wafted in through the door. In that moment, I felt an overwhelming sense of peace and calm as I soaked in the summer night.

In a fleeting moment of excitement, I felt a strong urge to share with Jesse the childhood memories that the smell evoked. It was a nostalgic feeling, and I wanted him to be a part of those recollections. But as I searched for him, I realized he was in his office with the door closed.

Just as quickly as I felt that sense of calm, it disappeared and shifted into deep, desperate mistrust and fear that my husband was being unfaithful. There was absolutely no evidence to support the idea that anything was wrong; my feeling was based solely on my fear that he was doing something he shouldn't be.

Looking back, I realize that the emotional shift stemmed

from a fear of losing control of my life, and of our marriage, but I didn't know it then. I do recall thinking, *Jesse's been alone in his office for a long time. What if he's talking to someone else? What if he's looking at something that makes him stop loving me or wanting me?*

Jesse had been open with me during our engagement about his struggle with pornography, and I was deeply thankful for his honesty. He had sought out and committed to having accountability partners and installing software blockers, all in a dedicated effort to honor God and hold himself accountable. He has since spoken about it openly on my podcast in the hope of helping other couples through that same struggle.

Jesse and I had walked through numerous conversations about how his temptation made me feel—primarily how insecurity infiltrated my every thought and action after I learned of it. We made our phones and computers fully available to each other, communicated through the difficulties of intimacy, and navigated the complexity of addiction. I knew he had been working toward growth and had overcome so much already.

Jesse was a good man, a very good man, but he was also a sinful man. An imperfect man. One who had the power to hurt me deeply. I wanted him to be just like Jesus, at least in this area. I needed him to be sinless when it came to lust and attraction to other women. I didn't want him to fail or fall. I demanded perfection. It was a heavy, and nearly impossible, burden for him to carry. I knew that a spouse shouldn't ever have to carry such weight or be so responsible for their partner's joy, but I had handed my heart to him on a silver platter, rather than entrusting it to Jesus. You'll notice a pattern throughout this book: I had a habit of placing far too much responsibility on Jesse for my peace and happiness.

But in that moment in my home, I found myself convinced that Jesse was being unfaithful to me. It was sudden and confusing. The Enemy had established a foothold in my thoughts, and rather than taking them captive, I sank into them. I couldn't muster up sympathy for Jesse's struggles. I hated that he desired to look at someone other than his wife. I was convinced that his history of watching porn would inevitably progress into sinful actions, leading to betrayal and the ruin of our marriage.

My mind consumed by fear, I marched into Jesse's office, accusation etched on my face, overwhelmed by the notion that the man I had married was not the person I once believed him to be. Whew—those spirals sure can come on quickly.

Jesse looked up when I burst in, a welcoming smile crinkling the corners of his eyes. He was studying for the sermon he would be sharing with our church's youth group that week. He'd had his head buried in his Bible and was typing out notes.

I breathed more easily when I realized everything was okay, but my fear of abandonment that summer night marked a turning point in me. The Enemy got a foothold in my heart, and it spiraled into immense distrust. It created a deep disconnection between us. It took years for those anxious thoughts and beliefs to loosen their grip on me.

I would wake up in the dead of the night, gripped by panic, and go through his phone.

I would control his actions, ask accusatory questions, and pick apart his answers.

I would repeatedly scrutinize his social media pages. He had made poor decisions in the past; what would stop him from pursuing things further?

I didn't want him looking at girls on TV or going to the gym where pretty girls were.

The thought constantly consumed me that something would eventually happen. It had to. How could he not betray me? The lies kept filtering in, and my responses were anything but gracious.

Jesse was patient, but he was being suffocated.

And I was drowning in fear.

To make matters more difficult, numerous couples close to us had experienced divorce, brokenness, or emotional or physical affairs during the first few years of their marriages. We walked through the devastation alongside them to the best of our ability, but their experiences, often unexpected, left us feeling blindsided and confused.

I was waiting for it to be my turn.

But it never happened. He didn't betray me.

To this day, my flesh wants to add "yet," as in "it hasn't happened yet," but God's sanctifying work and my growth won't let me go there.

Thirteen years into our marriage and fifteen years into our relationship, I am thankful to say that my husband has been a faithful man. He hasn't been perfect—just as I haven't. There have been times when his struggles have reawakened old fears, and we've had to face them together, again and again.

And yet even if he hadn't been faithful, I know now that no matter what I did, no matter how much I tried to control his every move, I never could have prevented temptation from surrounding him.

And neither could he.

You may have experienced unfaithfulness or struggles with lust in your marriage, and your mind likely has at some point reeled at the idea that you could have prevented it:

- "If only I had checked their phone more."
- "If only I hadn't let them be alone that one time."
- "If only I were a better cook or a more physical person."

Can I give you a sense of freedom? If your partner betrayed you, that betrayal was their decision and it's their responsibility.

It was not your fault. Yes, your actions or mistakes may have contributed to tension or feelings of disconnection in the relationship, but their choice to betray you was theirs alone. You are not accountable for it; they are. Each person is responsible for their own actions, no matter the circumstances.

The truth is that Jesse can't stop men from coming up to me at the gym.

I can't control the algorithms that bombard him with sexual content.

He can't stop me from seeing attractive men out in the wild.

I can't stop women from complimenting his smile or wearing low-cut shirts.

As much as I wanted to be always just around the corner, peeking in on him (call me crazy, because I felt crazy), there was no freedom in that. I lived consumed, bound by worry and skepticism, always waiting for the other shoe to drop and our happiness to shatter. But what I didn't realize then was that this need for control, this constant fear, was the true thief of our joy.

It wasn't the external temptations but my internal struggle that poisoned our relationship.

The truth is this:

A healthy marriage does not suffocate.

A holy marriage does not seek to exert control.

A spouse who is drowning in their fears cannot breathe life into their family.

And a marriage built on God's love and grace does not dominate or constrain.

It breathes and grows freely.

The Illusion of Control

Healthy relationships thrive on a foundation of mutual respect, trust, and open communication. Partners in these types of relationships feel safe expressing themselves, contributing equally to decisions, and maintaining a sense of autonomy; although they are "one," they also have a strong sense of self.

But when one person exerts excessive control, it breeds resentment and frustration, and it silences communication. This, I now realize, was the unhealthy dynamic I unknowingly created in my marriage.

The need for control goes beyond just worrying about lust or infidelity; it can affect every aspect of your marriage. It can also show up when you attempt to take over your partner's emotional, financial, or logistical responsibilities.

Take a second to reflect: In what areas do you try to exert control in your marriage?

Maybe you've believed that if you could just get your spouse to be cleaner, more thoughtful, or more romantic, everything would be fine. You repeat that desire to them over and over and find that it creates tension and hostility in your home rather than amity. In moments like these, ask yourself, *Do I want to feel connected right now, or am I more focused on trying to control the situation?*

People with controlling tendencies may justify their actions as helpful or generous, but they often have the opposite effect. When we treat our spouses as if they can't handle things on their own, we unintentionally undermine their ability and make them feel inadequate. This includes both taking over responsibilities and imposing our expectations on what they should do. In doing so, we risk damaging their sense of autonomy and weakening our partnership.

This type of control can take the form of statements like:

- "They won't do it themselves, so I need to take over for them."
- "They won't do it how I do it or as well as I do it, so I'm going to take care of it."

- "If I don't check on it regularly, they will take advantage and abuse their freedom."
- "They didn't remember the argument just right. They didn't say they'd be home at 6:15. It was 6:00. So now I have to fact-check them, in the name of honesty, and make sure they know they're wrong."

Does your spouse tell you how to organize the pantry? How to handle your work tasks? What to say in a social setting? It's exhausting to live with someone who is constantly giving orders, treating you as if you can't manage on your own.

Here are a few patterns of controlling behavior:

- *Micromanagement.* Constantly critiquing everything you do.
- *Dishonesty.* Lying or hiding information, especially about finances.
- *Manipulation.* Pressuring you to comply, often downplaying your feelings.
- *Overprotectiveness.* Extending controlling behavior to your kids.
- *Emotional bullying.* Using criticism, taunting, or gaslighting to make you doubt yourself.
- *Interrupting.* Frequently cutting you off in conversations.
- *Making decisions alone.* Choosing for you without consultation, such as when dining out or during activities.
- *Nagging.* Repeatedly criticizing your health habits, such as eating poorly or smoking.
- *Jealousy.* Projecting insecurities onto you, revealing their low self-esteem.
- *Defensive attacks.* Lashing out when you set boundaries, often flipping the accusation back on you.

For a man, this can feel deeply emasculating, and for a

woman, it often comes across as wildly condescending. Control steals from your connectedness and turns your partner into a competitor instead of a teammate. When taken too far, these behaviors can cross the line into emotional abuse.

Spouses who crave control often fall prey to an illusion. You're fearful to surrender because you don't want to lose your sense of control. But you didn't actually have control; all you had was anxiety.

Have you succumbed to it? You believe you can dictate your partner's behavior by taking over their emotional, financial, or logistical tasks and then attempt to "fix" them by doing so. This dominance only creates distance and stifles individuality.

You can check your spouse's phone only so many times before it makes your partner feel like they're being parented.

You can rearrange the dishwasher only so many times before they feel they're incapable and give up.

You can criticize their parenting only so many times before they withdraw and let you take the reins.

My pride often convinces me that I can handle things better than Jesse can. You might hear a similar whisper from your own pride, saying, *If only my spouse did things exactly the way I do, our lives would be so much easier.*

But honestly, two of you in one marriage could result in a disaster, couldn't it? There's a reason why opposites tend to attract. What if, instead, you embraced the power of being complemented by someone different from you? The healthier you become as an individual by leaning into trust and recognizing that a healthy partnership thrives on mutual respect, the sooner you can shed the illusion of control and embrace a connected dynamic within your relationship.

Take a second to think about your greatest strengths and your spouse's greatest obstacles. What if you took on the roles that they despise, and they did the same for you? Your strengths would balance out their limitations and vice versa. For example, Jesse does the dishes because I despise them. I do the taxes because Jesse wants nothing to do with them. We've worked to cooperate as a team, knowing that we're fighting toward the same goals: unity and eternity.

The heart-level changes you and your spouse need will never come from pressure, manipulation, or control. Those things are likely coming from a place of fear, but fear is a terrible architect for intimacy, because real change can't be forced. It's genuinely impossible for true connection to thrive in an environment of control. One of the most important things you can do is release your grip and ask God to work in the places you can't reach. Focus instead on what you can control: your tone, your reactions, your healing, and your surrender.

Surrender isn't weakness, it's wisdom. And the sooner we release the notion of control and trust that God is guiding our lives and our spouses' lives, the more at peace we will be.

It took time and a good amount of heartache in our marriage, but God took hold of my heart and shook me awake.

Fear Not

Did you know that the most common command in Scripture is "Fear not"? It isn't a suggestion or a subtle nudge, it's a command given by God not to be afraid.

When I'm struggling with this, I often lean into some of my favorite verses, including:

> Have I not commanded you? Be strong and of good courage;
> do not be afraid, nor be dismayed, for the LORD your God is
> with you wherever you go.
>
> —Joshua 1:9

For God gave us a spirit not of fear but of power and love and self-control.

—2 Timothy 1:7 ESV

And, of course, the reminder about how well we are cared for:

Therefore I tell you, do not worry about your life, what you will eat or drink; or about your body, what you will wear. Is not life more than food, and the body more than clothes? Look at the birds of the air; they do not sow or reap or store away in barns, and yet your heavenly Father feeds them. Are you not much more valuable than they? Can any one of you by worrying add a single hour to your life?

And why do you worry about clothes? See how the flowers of the field grow. They do not labor or spin. Yet I tell you that not even Solomon in all his splendor was dressed like one of these.

If that is how God clothes the grass of the field, which is here today and tomorrow is thrown into the fire, will he not much more clothe you—you of little faith?

—Matthew 6:25–30 NIV

If God takes the time and care to nurture these things—things that aren't created in his image like we are—how much more will he care for our hearts and our marriages?

Jesse told me long before we got married that he had chosen to entrust my heart to Jesus, recognizing that he could never love me more than God does. He regularly reminded me that he could never force me into a version of a person that God didn't create me to be. It was a powerful lesson, and I needed to apply the same principle in my life: to entrust my husband's heart to Jesus. This meant acknowledging that Jesus alone has the power to convict Jesse when necessary, to lead him to repentance, and to guide the sanctification of his heart.

It had never been my role to control Jesse's decisions, his life, or the way that he loved me. I was not the Holy Spirit. I wasn't ever meant to be his savior or the molder of his heart, and honestly, thank God for that. I finally accepted that I really didn't want to be in control of it.

Four Ways to Manage Fear and Control in Your Marriage

1. The Worst-Case Scenario

If you have ever grappled with a strong desire for control or the fear of losing control in your life, this small but weighty question can help you navigate your fears: *What is the absolute worst outcome if my worst-case scenario actually occurs?*

When you ask yourself this question, whether it pertains to your marriage, your job, your finances, your fear of abandonment, or the challenges of never having been married at all, give yourself the freedom to provide a sincere answer.

I've often heard people respond along the lines of "My life would crumble into pieces" or "Everything I've ever wanted for my family would disappear in the blink of an eye."

If the worst-case scenario happens, yes, it will be devastating. But we will not crumble if our lives are built on the solid foundation of Christ and his promises. He is our sustainer. For he himself has said, "I will never leave you nor forsake you." So we may boldly say: "The LORD is my helper; I will not fear. What can man do to me?" (Heb. 13:5–6). Our jobs, marriages, and savings accounts do not define our stability.

Our spouses are gifts to us, but they were never intended to be God in our lives. We have to give them space for failure and growth. We must also acknowledge that their imperfection is backed by an infallible God who is completely and entirely trustworthy.

This doesn't mean that life wouldn't be incredibly difficult if your spouse betrayed you, walked out on you, or deeply failed you. For those who have endured these things, my heart aches for you. I'm so sorry. Some of the most cherished people in my life have faced this kind of pain, and it's never okay. You didn't deserve it. But know this: Even in the darkest moments, there is still hope. You are not defined by someone else's choices.

I've seen these decisions cause destruction. But do you want to know what else I've seen?

I've seen these hurt individuals draw on their faith in Jesus in ways they never had before.

I've seen them, even while single, choose to live faithfully for the kingdom, serving the church and the people around them. Gradually, their joy returned.

I've seen their marriages restored and renewed, often ending up better than they were before.

God's promise to us isn't that we will be exempt from difficulties in our lives or marriages. His promise is that he will be with us through it all.

2. Stop Carrying Receipts

Love does not suffocate.

It does not control.

Love is patient; it is kind.

It surely doesn't walk around carrying receipts.

Have you ever been mid argument, about to unleash on your spouse a laundry list of their past mistakes? We've all been there.

But a powerful verse in 1 Corinthians 13 says love "keeps no record of wrongs" (v. 5 NIV).

Craving understanding, especially when fear or control clouds our judgment, can cause us to piece together past experiences, bringing up "that one time" and trying to fit old mistakes into the current puzzle.

Here's the key: Treat each situation as if it were new. Issues need to be addressed and resolved, and once that happens, you have a clean slate. When a new concern arises, resist dragging in old baggage.

Imagine this: You're in your work performance review, excited to discuss your accomplishments. But your boss launches into a tirade about every minor slipup you've made all year. Despite your best efforts, your hard work, and your improvements, your boss dwells on the past mistakes.

That would be a great discouragement. It would hinder your potential for growth and improvement because you wouldn't feel like you'd ever be able to do anything right, so why try?

The same happens in marriage. Constantly bringing up past mistakes creates a toxic atmosphere. It hinders growth and disconnects you from your partner.

New disagreements are new disagreements—treat them as such. Keeping a mental checklist of your partner's mistakes isn't innocent recordkeeping, it's fear of vulnerability, fear of being hurt again, fear of losing control.

So pray, journal, repent, and destroy that record of wrongs.

3. Pray Together

Research conducted by the National Marriage Project at the University of Virginia suggests that couples who pray together report higher levels of emotional intimacy and satisfaction with their communication.[1]

A few months ago, Jesse and I started something new. One of our friends recommended it, and it has been a really sweet addition to our nightly routine. Every night before bed, we read a few verses from the book of the Bible we're in, talk through what stood out to each of us, and then pray over each other. Jesse always goes first. He prays over my business, my ministry, my motherhood, and whatever life circumstances or heart issues I'm facing at the time. Then I pray for him: the heavy burdens he's carrying, for his role as a godly father to our boys, his closeness with them, his real estate work, and the friendships that keep him grounded and growing. It's a simple addition and doesn't take long, but it's been really encouraging, vulnerable, and surprisingly powerful. I feel like I'm seeing more of his heart, and he's seeing more of mine. We've shared things we might not have otherwise said out loud. It's helped us feel more connected not just to each other but to God too.

If weaving prayer into the fabric of your relationship is new to you, or if you or your spouse feel uncomfortable praying together, start small. You don't need to craft elaborate prayers; the purpose of praying together is to be genuine and honest together. It isn't meant to be a pristine or lofty experience.

Begin by getting on your knees in prayer, which is a physical position that humbles you and shows reverence for God. Praise and thank him, and share some of the worries, fears, joys, and hopes you've been experiencing as a couple.

I completely understand that it isn't always easy to communicate vulnerabilities like this with your spouse, or in front of your spouse, but I truly believe that the more you do it, the more natural it will become.

4. Speak Out Your Fears to Other Wise Couples

Community is the backbone of marriage. You were never intended to experience your marriage alone. When you let people in—to your arguments, your frustrations, your fears, and your successes—you allow yourself to learn from people who have gone before you in marriage.

Jesse and I have relied heavily on marriage counselors, church leaders, and even friends to help us navigate the difficulties in our relationship. More often than not, after vocalizing all of our hesitations and worries, we hear them say, "Oh! You too?"

If nothing else, allowing people to see into your marriage lets you realize that you're not the only couple who faces your struggles. They have likely been faced by many of the couples who surround you.

During some of the biggest disagreements in our marriage, when we are struggling and talking in circles, our first response is always to call a couple close to us and ask them to help walk us through it. We have chosen not to hide or sugarcoat our issues. We let the other couple in fully and let them help determine the root of our fear and control. We are open and honest while still maintaining respect for each other.

I recognize that many men have a difficult time sharing their struggles with people in their lives. I often hear these kinds of things from women:

- "My husband refuses to talk to anyone, but we're falling apart."
- "He says it isn't their business to know what we have going on in our lives."
- "He doesn't want to air our dirty laundry."
- "He doesn't think it's bad enough to seek help."

Let's be honest: These excuses are often rooted in pride. It's a dangerous thing to prioritize your pride over your marriage. If you do, you may want to evaluate if your motives are self-serving and if they are worth sacrificing the most important relationship in your life.

But I also understand that there are times when individuals

feel the need to seek God first, reflecting on their own struggles before involving others. Sometimes we need to wrestle with our thoughts and prayers privately before reaching out.

Ultimately, the choice is between facing some momentary discomfort to seek help for your marriage or waiting until the pain becomes too heavy to carry. One path leads to healing—the other to regret. The choice is yours.

The Deposit More Love Challenge

Start a Thank-You Economy

Imagine your marriage is a household budget. When you only track every expense (their forgotten chore, your raised voice), resentment builds like an ever-increasing credit card bill. You aren't depositing anything, but you're taking a lot out. This creates a stressful environment and fosters feelings of obligation rather than love.

Instead of keeping score by bringing up every misstep with each opportunity, try to "invest" by appreciating the positive contributions your partner makes.

Here's how it works:

The Spouse-Fulfilling Prophecy

A spouse-fulfilling prophecy happens when one partner's beliefs or expectations about the other shape how they act, often leading to the very outcome they feared.

For instance, if I frequently voice doubts about Jesse's reliability, he might start feeling insecure or pressured. Over time, those feelings could lead him to act in ways that make my worries come true. It creates a cycle where my negative expectations become the reality of our relationship, fueling distrust and tension.

On the flip side, when I tell Jesse what a reliable man he is and express my confidence in him, it enhances his reliability and helps both of us to grow together.

It's a win-win.

Control will suffocate the sweet things that make a marriage thrive. You can choose intimacy or you can choose control, but you can't have both.

CHAPTER 9

YOUR MIND AND BODY GLOW-UP

> Only the disciplined ones in life are free. If
> you are undisciplined, you are a slave to
> your moods and your passions.
>
> —Eliud Kipchoge, marathon runner

Picture this: You wake up tomorrow morning, no longer married. You're freshly single. Whether or not you plan to date again, how would your life change? Take a second to think about it and be honest. What would you do differently?

Would you start taking better care of your body and your appearance?

Would you invest more in the relationships you've allowed to fall to the wayside?

Would weekend trips and moments of adventure become a priority?

Maybe you'd pursue that dream you've always wanted to

achieve, start budgeting more responsibly, or even choose an earlier wakeup time so you can be more productive.

Would your discipline change?

Most people I've asked this question answer with a resounding yes, or at least a probably.

The real question is, Why would single life open the door for you to become the best version of yourself? Shouldn't the person who's committed to you for a lifetime—your spouse—get that best version?

If you've been letting things slide for a while, why are you not working toward becoming the best version of yourself right now in this season of life? All things considered, coasting is not exceptional, and wouldn't you agree that someone who has committed their entire life to you deserves you at your most exceptional?

Discipline is one of the greatest gifts Jesse and I have given each other the past few years. Not only have we lost about forty pounds combined after navigating a tumultuous season of life but also we have experienced a profound shift in our mental and physical health.

I had wrestled with depression for more than a year and felt stuck. Honestly, *stuck* doesn't even feel like a strong enough word. There were days when getting out of bed was a monumental task; it felt like ten thousand pounds were pressing down on my chest from the second I opened my eyes. I felt emotionally overwhelmed by nothing in particular and constantly felt like I could hardly move. I would wrap myself in a blanket and slowly trudge from my bed to the couch, feeling as though concrete had hardened around my ankles.

The heaviness I felt was both physical and emotional, consuming my entire day without a clear cause. I was trapped in a cycle of sadness, worry, anxiety, and emotional fog, and my family felt the weight of it. Irritability poured out of me like a slow leak I couldn't seal. I snapped over the smallest things. I withdrew from my family and friends because I had no energy and didn't even know how to explain what I was feeling. I came up for air for a day or two, but then I'd slip right back under the cloud. And I hated it. I hated that my boys were seeing me like that and that Jesse never knew what version of me he'd come home to. I felt like a nightmare to be around. But I didn't know how to fix it.

To be honest, it felt like I was failing at everything that I was called to do, and I couldn't name a single reason why. That's the hard part about emotional overwhelm, isn't it? It doesn't always come with a label or a cause. Sometimes it's just a fog you learn to navigate with your hands out in front of you, hoping to bump into some kind of clarity.

I needed a change, so I started with an antidepressant. It was a lifeline during that season and helped me to feel human again. But over time, I started to feel numb, like the edges of my emotions, both good and bad, had been dulled. I had lost joy in the things that once made me feel alive. My sex drive had decreased. I didn't feel heightened emotions. My creativity had all but disappeared (and as someone who's required to use my creative brain every day for a living, this didn't sit well with me).

I was forced to acknowledge that medication was just one piece of the puzzle. I couldn't rely on it alone. I needed to make real, tangible changes in my everyday life in order to live well again. I needed to do hard things that actually stuck.

I needed discipline.

Stop Breaking Promises to Yourself

I saw a video recently that impacted me in a way I wasn't expecting. It said something along the lines of "If you want to grow in confidence in a way you never have before, then stop breaking promises to yourself."

I realized then that I'd been letting myself down for a long time. Skipping workouts. Ignoring the goals I'd set. Eating my kids' leftover chicken nugget scraps for lunch instead of preparing a meal for myself. Saying I'd make a consistent effort toward my new work goal, only to quit after the first month. Eventually, it all added up. I started to feel like I couldn't trust myself.

Did I even believe in my own growth?

My discipline, or lack thereof, impacted my family. When I felt behind, I was stressed. When I was disappointed in myself, I got defensive. When I gained weight, I felt insecure in the bedroom and uncomfortable in social settings. And when I procrastinated on a deadline, I took my overwhelm out on the people who love me most: my husband and my boys.

I had to begin asking those necessary questions that I'm still asking today: If I can't keep a small promise to myself, how am I supposed to believe I'll show up when it really matters? If I can't be faithful with little, how will I be faithful with much? This wasn't just an issue of discipline for me. I genuinely had to learn how to rebuild my self-respect and master the art of following through. I needed to love myself enough to finish what I started.

As I often tell my boys, "Let your yes be yes." This biblical principle from Matthew 5:37 is a call to integrity—to be someone whose words can be trusted. Trust is built when others know that we'll do what we say, but even more important, when we know that about ourselves. Not for perfection but for peace. For the future we want. For the people we love. For the one life we've been given.

Do you feel like you're stuck in a cycle of unfulfilled promises or missed goals for yourself? One thing I had to learn is that we don't have to wait until Monday or the New Year to start fresh. In fact, the more we wait for the "perfect time," the more we delay the healing and change we're craving. So even if you've skipped three days, three months, or you're just starting now, it isn't too late. You can start over on a random Thursday afternoon in June, if you wish, simply because that's what you've chosen. The most powerful changes don't depend on a certain day or time; they depend on you finally deciding to no longer break promises to yourself.

I started fulfilling my own promises by making shifts. My mindset tends to lean toward all-or-nothing thinking, so I've learned to avoid diving into big, overwhelming goals or trying to change too many things at once. Oftentimes when a person sets too many goals, or they jump from zero to one hundred, they eventually stumble and end up stopping altogether.

So instead, I began making small, manageable changes and implemented little habits that would eventually make a big difference. Each little win of the day sparked another win, creating a cascade of fulfilled promises and small victories. I started the day by following through with a nonnegotiable like taking a walk, and those nonnegotiables became my anchors on the days when I struggled to accomplish anything else.

Can you relate? Do you feel like you're stuck in a cycle of unfulfilled promises or missed goals? I have a litany of them. But the reality is that no one is coming to rescue us from ourselves.

Addicted to Your Own Suffering

Do you realize that you can be addicted to your own complacency or suffering? You wake up and replay the same emotions, the same fears, the same patterns, and start to accept that that's just the way things are. You're accepting your reality without giving any energy to change it. But the truth is that what you're calling "reality" is often just your past circumstances and decisions showing up on repeat, projecting themselves onto your present. And because it's familiar, you stay still. You're numb. Asleep. You want change, but you're not willing to give up the habits and identity you've built around your comfort or fear.

Hear me out: The life you're living now isn't happening *to* you, it's happening *because of* you.

I feel so strongly about this chapter because I truly believe that so much of our relationship contentment starts with how we view ourselves. The way we speak about ourselves, the thoughts we let linger, the shame we carry, or the confidence we lack—it all spills over. It shapes how we show up in our marriages.

When you're constantly criticizing yourself, you tend to project that same criticism onto your spouse. When you're battling insecurity, it can show up as defensiveness, jealousy, or control. If you don't believe you're worth celebrating, it's hard to fully celebrate your partner. The way we talk to ourselves, the way we talk to others, and the way we respond to our spouses' successes or failures are all connected to how we see ourselves and what we believe about our identity in Jesus.

Whether we realize it or not, it impacts everything.

And maybe you're thinking, *But I'm comfortable, Linds. Maybe we've given up on ourselves a bit, but this is just who we are.*

Comfort is a nice thing, but it makes an awful god. It always leaves us wanting more. It becomes an idol when we seek it more than we desire God's presence and will, when we shift from enjoying his gifts to worshiping the gift itself. What gift are you worshiping? Sleep? Wealth? Happiness? Distractions?

The best, most grounded, most God-reflecting version of you is on the other side of the things that have been holding you back.

The 1 Percent Shift

"Old habits die hard" is a phrase that resonates with many of us because, despite our ambitions and goals, it is challenging to replace long-standing habits with better ones. We implement something new in our lives but then struggle to remain consistent with it.

The key to real, lasting change is to make just a 1 percent shift in behavior every single day.

In one of my favorite books, *Atomic Habits*,[1] James Clear emphasizes that significant change stems from small, consistent improvements. The tiny 1 percent adjustments, while they may seem insignificant in the moment, accumulate into remarkable results over time. Statistically, an all-or-nothing or cold-turkey approach to change backfires because:

1. *It's more likely to fail.* Extreme goals and rigid plans are difficult to maintain, especially in the face of unforeseen circumstances and inevitable setbacks. With an all-or-nothing mindset, a single slipup is a complete failure, leading to discouragement and abandonment of the entire effort.

2. *It discourages progress.* The all-or-nothing mentality focuses solely on the result, ignoring the value of incremental progress. But small wins provide positive reinforcement and keep us motivated on the long road to change.

3. *It's inflexible.* Life throws curveballs. An all-or-nothing plan crumbles when faced with unforeseen circumstances. Small, daily adjustments allow for course correction and adaptation, ensuring consistency even during disruptions.

A disciplined and fulfilling life isn't necessarily about seeking peace, and it isn't about being comfortable—though comfort and peace will come from the healthy patterns you establish. It's more about creating rhythm and consistency in your life in a world that's anything but predictable. The more we say yes to hard things, the more we can experience certainty in a world of uncertainty.

What would your discipline look like if you gave just thirty minutes each day to doing the hard things?

It feels a lot less daunting to me when I consider going for a walk for thirty minutes each day for the next week instead of telling myself that I need to run a marathon in three months. We can run the marathons, but let's start with the daily walks to eventually achieve the bigger goal.

But how does this commitment to small changes help your marriage? Acts of care toward yourself—the ones that make you a better, happier, and healthier version of you—are bound to flow out onto your partner. When you stop breaking promises to yourself, you bring a new energy to everything else you do within your home, in your life, and in your marriage.

How often do you catch yourself saying things like, "I'll do that tomorrow," or, "I'll start on Monday," or even, "I promised myself I'd work out [or finish that project], but I'll just skip it today"? It's so easy to put things off, isn't it?

Time is relentless, friends. And as I watch my boys grow far too quickly before my eyes, I am realizing it now more than ever. Whether we act now or put things off, a month or a year will pass us by regardless. So why not use that time to accomplish something meaningful? You have a choice: to let time drift by without making progress or to invest time in pursuing a healthier home, your goals, and your dreams. I wish I could scream this from the rooftops. It really, really matters.

A close friend of mine said it this way: "Think about a workplace team. If you're a high performer but the rest of your team isn't pulling their weight, how long will you stick around? High performers tend to leave low-performing teams when there's no accountability, because they want to be surrounded by people who challenge them, push them, and grow alongside them. Poor performers who are allowed to stay on the team without any improvement drag everyone down."

Marriage is no different. You and your spouse are a team. When one person consistently ignores the other's needs, resists growth, or repeats harmful behaviors, it can feel like being stuck on a team with someone who isn't pulling their weight. And when someone expresses their needs clearly and asks for change, only to be ignored, it chips away at the relationship.

It's especially hard for someone who is driven by goals and a desire for self-betterment to stay in a stagnant relationship. You're wired to move forward, to improve, to level up together. But if one partner refuses to engage in that process, the other will eventually tire of settling for less.

It's likely that you and your spouse won't always hit the mark at the same time. God's Word reminds us that we are one in marriage. There will likely be seasons when you are running full speed ahead while your spouse is struggling to walk and vice versa. You're teammates, so live well, but be cautious not to race so far ahead of them that they can't ever catch up, abandoning them along the way. Instead, you should use your strength to support and encourage your partner, to the best of your ability, and bring them along with you.

This is why personal discipline and growth within marriage matter so much. Yes, discipline is about avoiding bad habits and keeping yourself accountable, but it's also about creating an environment where both partners thrive and support one another.

The Best Version of Yourself

If it's hard to think of areas in which you need more discipline, here's a little activity that might help. Grab a piece of paper and a pen or open your notes app, and dream big about who you want to be and how you want to live. Step outside your current reality and explore the possibilities of your future. What kind of person do you want to be?

Answer these ten questions about your dream version of yourself:

1. How would they start their day?
2. What food do they fuel their body with?
3. What does their daily time with Jesus look like?
4. What are their core values, and how do they live them out?
5. How do they present themselves to others?
6. How do they interact with their loved ones?
7. What does their body look like and how did they achieve it?
8. How do they spend their free time?
9. What type of friends are they surrounded by? In what areas do those friends make them better?
10. What are their greatest accomplishments, and how do they maintain their momentum?

Remember, this is an ideal version of yourself. Couples with children often make sacrifices that prevent them from realizing every aspect of this dream, and that's okay, because perfection isn't the goal. For instance, if you're pursuing a dream body, you might want to go to the gym five times a week, but if you have a family, it might be impractical and detrimental to your marriage to leave them that often.

It can be challenging to balance the priorities of your first ministry—your spouse and family—while practicing self-discipline. But people around us do this every day. It's difficult, but it's possible. Sometimes it's important to accept that good enough is sufficient when life doesn't allow for perfection.

A quote floating around online says, "You would die for your children, but will you actually live well for them?" Our discipline affects our little ones and their future.

We always have a choice.

We can choose to eat greasy food in front of the TV, or we can talk about life together over a healthy meal at the family dinner table.

We can choose to isolate ourselves in our rooms with video games, or we can throw around a ball together as a family.

We can choose to wake up and silently sit in front of our iPads, or we can read a book together.

Self-discipline is saying yes when it's easier to say no. It's when the desire to become the best version of yourself and the choice to honor God with your life outweigh temporary satisfactions.

C. S. Lewis insightfully remarked, "It would seem that our Lord finds our desires not too strong, but too weak. We are half-hearted creatures, fooling about with drink and sex and ambition when infinite joy is offered us, like an ignorant child who wants to go on making mud pies in a slum because he cannot imagine what is meant by the offer of a holiday at the sea. We are far too easily pleased."[2]

Contrary to what we might tell ourselves, self-discipline doesn't trap us, it liberates us from the narrow confines we've created for ourselves.

What is a nonnegotiable you can hold yourself to today?

The Positive Domino Effect of Routines

I've noticed that good self-discipline has a domino effect. When I do one thing I don't want to do, I feel better, and then it encourages me to do the next thing that follows.

For example, there are still some days when depression seeps in and I struggle to get out of bed. I tell myself, *Lindsey, all you need to do is put your feet on the floor.*

On the hard days when I feel powerless or hopeless, I do

only that. It's my first and only step. Sometimes, when I'm really exhausted, I will crawl like an animal from my bed to my exercise mat. (It's definitely a sight for my boys to see, and it makes them laugh, but it does the trick!) Feet—or knees—on the floor is the first step. I don't force myself to do anything else, but almost always it leads to step two, which is getting my butt on that Pilates mat. I turn on a YouTube Pilates or weight-lifting video and start the process. Most of the time, I don't want to do it at all, but I've learned that exercising gives me energy, even when I don't have any to begin with.

This act of discipline then leads to chugging down some water, hydrating my body. And that small discipline leads to the next, which is getting out in the sunshine for fifteen minutes. And because I'm now energized from my workout and the vitamin D, I have more energy to come inside and start breakfast for the family. I'm a happier, better, kinder version of myself.

But on mornings when I lie in bed, scrolling through a dopamine high until the crash leaves me moody and frustrated, and then I mindlessly start my day, the mood in the house is different.

I regularly remind myself of this concept:

- Laziness kills ambition, but ambition kills laziness.
- Anger kills wisdom, but wisdom kills anger.
- Jealousy kills peace, but peace kills jealousy.
- Fear of failure kills dreams, but accomplished dreams kill fear.

The Pursuit of Discipline Together

The truth, friends, is that the more disciplined and independent you are, the more effective you'll be in your life and in your marriage. Isn't it a huge testament to how well someone is living when they're insanely fit in their thirties, forties, or fifties? We often envy such discipline because it's a rarity. But for couples who desire oneness, it's a blessing and a joy to pursue discipline together.

I'm so thankful that Jesse has walked alongside me through my anxiety and depression. Most days, he leads me in it well. He boosts me and picks me up out of bed when I'm having a hard day. He asks the questions I already know the answers to but need to remember. He talks me through my emotions with selflessness and consideration.

On the hard days, he invites me to the gym or on a walk, leads me in going to church, asks hard questions, and occasionally takes me on mini adventures to get me out of my head. I've learned that having a partner who is willing to do the heavy lifting when I'm hurting is invaluable. (Reminder: Be that person to your spouse when they struggle; we're all going through some kind of battle, aren't we?)

But there are times when it can be very difficult for Jesse to show up for me, especially when I'm not showing up for myself. He can say or do only so much if I'm unwilling or simply unable to care for myself. Eventually, it all boils down to my personal responsibility and work to maintain my health.

If you take anything away from this book, hear me on this: Your partner is on their own journey, and that journey will not always align with yours, and that's okay. You were never meant to fix or control your partner; the only thing you can control is yourself. But life spent together is better and it's sweeter. You can improve your lives better as a team, and that time spent together is irreplaceable.

Ask yourself this: *If I were to look in on my life and my marriage one year from now, and I were in the exact same place I'm now in, would I feel pride or disappointment?*

If the answer is disappointment, I want to remind you that you're not alone. It's normal for your relationship to go through peaks and troughs, but there are many easy ways to make the peaks more common than they have been for you in the past.

Your Schedule Never Lies

"What you're doing speaks so loudly I can't hear what you're saying." Another way to say this is, "Show me your schedule and I'll show you the truth about what matters to you." I repeat this phrase often, both to myself and to individuals I work with, because a schedule never lies.

When you declare that family is your top priority, but your schedule doesn't have time for them, the reality is that family time isn't as important to you as you claim it is.

You might say being in top physical shape is one of your key values, but if your weekly routine doesn't include workouts, your health isn't as high on your priority list as you profess.

You can talk all day about wanting to fix your marriage, but if you haven't scheduled with your spouse counseling sessions, daily prayer, or weekly conversations about your relationship, you're giving your marriage only your leftovers.

You can say that your sex life needs to improve, but if it isn't on your mental or physical calendar, I'd say that fixing that issue doesn't matter to you as much as you might believe.

We make time for what we care about. Plain and simple.

It is unlikely that you and your spouse will grow together in success and lasting happiness if your daily schedule doesn't reflect your deepest values. You have to consistently make time for one another. Doing so requires both desire and discipline. And yes, of course, discipline can be tough. But prioritizing what matters creates a ripple effect, improving not just your relationship but every area of your life.

What if you don't have your priorities straight, though? How can you make the shift?

The Habit Loop

Have you ever heard of a habit loop?[3] It's a simple pattern I learned from the book *The Power of Habit* that has helped me to create new, healthy habits:

1. *Cue:* Something triggers your brain to start a habit.
2. *Routine:* You perform the habitual behavior in response to the cue.
3. *Reward:* You experience a positive outcome or satisfaction, reinforcing the habit.

In the context of marriage, let's consider a common scenario:

1. *Cue:* Your partner frequently works late, and you feel lonely or unimportant.
2. *Routine:* In response to these feelings, you turn to a distraction, such as binge eating or spending excessive time on your phone.
3. *Reward:* This distraction provides a temporary escape from loneliness or negative emotions.

Try this alternative:

1. *Cue:* Your partner frequently works late, and you feel lonely or unimportant.
2. *Routine:* Instead of turning to a distraction, you use this time to work on a project or goal, like learning a new skill, starting a creative endeavor, or organizing a part of your home that needs attention.
3. *Reward:* This activity provides a sense of fulfillment and growth, which helps you manage feelings of loneliness in a constructive way.

When you take time to recognize the habit loops in your marriage, you will be able to address their root (in this case loneliness).

What are some habit loops you've created in your marriage? Take a few minutes to identify them, either by yourself or with your spouse.

Habits for Connection

Now consider the following patterns and habits that can significantly enhance your discipline and connection as you level up together as a couple.

1. Wake Up Together

Are you an early riser, or a night owl? Do you choose to wake up with your partner?

A study published in *The Journal of Marriage and Family* looked at sleep patterns and relationships and found that couples who sync up their sleep schedules—going to bed and waking up at the same time—report higher relationship satisfaction, more emotional intimacy, better communication, less stress, and a stronger overall connection.[4]

This finding has certainly proven true for Jesse and me, and even more so now that we have kids. When Jesse and I manage to wake up before our kids get up, it gives us a precious window of time to focus on each other. We have our coffee, laugh and pray together, and talk about the day ahead. Sometimes we even manage to work out together before the day begins, which boosts our mood immensely. The time we set aside for each other and for our mental health sets a positive tone for the entire day. We know that we'll be needed and touched over and over and over once the kids wake up, so this time together gives us space to be just us for a little while.

It's also really good for our kids, because instead of feeling groggy and rushed, we're fully awake and engaged with them. We're able to be playful and lighthearted with them, which invites these little people to start their day with joy.

Think about it: If the house feels warm and inviting when your kids get up, how different does the experience of waking up become for them? They won't feel like a burden or an inconvenience, as if Mom and Dad are forced to wake up for them. They feel welcome and wanted.

2. Clarity Is Kindness

I speak with so many couples who think and feel many things about their marriages but only drop hints or make passive-aggressive comments about their desires, not clearly asking for what they want. Do you wish your partner would wake up with you in the morning or join you on morning walks? What specific ways do you want to level up together?

Clarifying your wants and desires is an act of kindness toward your husband or wife because they can't read your mind. When you communicate your needs clearly, you prevent any confusion that can lead to resentment or frustration.

Marriage counselors often recommend using "I" statements (rather than "you" statements, which often create defensiveness) to communicate your needs without shifting blame onto your spouse. It's also more effective to address only one of your needs at a time and to kindly and clearly make realistic requests. Making one request at a time ensures that your partner understands and hears you without feeling overwhelmed by multiple requests.

For example: "I feel energized and more connected to you when we're active together, and I would really appreciate it if we could make time a few days a week for a walk or a workout at home."

Or: "I feel closer with you when we go to bed at the same time, and I would love it if we could make an effort to do that more consistently."

While verbalizing your needs doesn't guarantee immediate change, at least you can feel good about having clearly communicated to your spouse instead of assuming they can read your mind. Their response is now their responsibility.

3. The Sunday Meeting

Jesse and I can be very transactional in our marriage. We can talk about business day in and day out. Something that we both love is accomplishing new, difficult things in our careers and finding new financial investment opportunities. We happily discuss business, finances, kids, sports, and schedules. But it's too easy for these to become the only things we talk about.

Once we recognized this pattern, we decided to create the Sunday Meeting—a dedicated time to address all the things that piled up during the week, while also making space simply to be together. Every Sunday, we set aside one or two hours to discuss everything happening in our lives. We grab some snacks, maybe a glass of wine, get cozy under blankets, and reflect on our week. It's the key ritual that keeps us connected, and I believe it can do the same for you.

Following are the questions Jesse and I regularly ask each other, broken up into four categories.

1. The Budget

1. What are the largest expenses we have coming up this week, and have we budgeted for those?
2. Are there any areas in which you're feeling stressed about our finances? What can we do to alleviate that stress?
3. Did we stick to our budget last week? What steps do we need to take to stick to our budget this week?

4. What are our financial goals? What can we work toward paying off or investing in this month?
5. How are you feeling about our finances and the pressures of work and home life? How can I help or pray for you?

2. THE MEAL PLAN

The meal plan includes the grocery list and meal prep for the coming week. Putting a meal plan together prevents the pressure of planning and preparing daily meals from falling on one person. One thing we're never warned about as children is the fact that we will have to decide what to make for dinner every single night for the rest of our lives. Honestly, who has the energy for that? Ha. So you might as well make it a team effort.

Simply discuss what sounds good to eat, what the kids have been enjoying lately, and (bonus points) add a new recipe to the menu that you can cook together. Cooking in the kitchen together can be a really romantic and fun way to connect.

3. SCHEDULING

What's on the calendar? Is Jesse playing pickleball? Am I going to brunch with friends? Whatever we have going on, we put it on the calendar. If one spouse forgets what the other has planned, it's on them to make other arrangements or figure out childcare.

1. Let's sync our calendars. What do you have going on this week?
2. Are there any important dates I need to be aware of this month?
3. Which days have you set aside for alone time? How can I support you to ensure you feel refreshed and have the time and space to pursue what brings you joy?
4. How did we do last week with dividing household responsibilities and living as partners in our home? Was

there a fair balance, or do we need to adjust our schedules for next week?

5. What night this week or month are we going on a date? Have we scheduled a babysitter and made a plan for that date?

4. MARITAL CONNECTION

We discuss our ups and downs for the week and ask each other relationship questions that help pinpoint goals and our trajectory.

1. Name something that I said or did this week that made you feel loved.
2. Name something (if anything) that I said or did that made you feel unloved.
3. How can I best support you this week?
4. Name one activity or adventure you'd like to do together to keep our friendship alive and bring more excitement into our relationship. (Extra points if you add it to the calendar right away!)
5. How do you feel about our sex life right now? What is one thing I can do to make our intimacy more desirable or enjoyable?
6. How was your time with God this week? How can I encourage you and support you in that?

4. Daydream Together

Do you and your partner regularly discuss your goals and dreams? Do you make it a point to follow up and check on each other's progress? One of the things I cherish most about my marriage is how Jesse and I frequently talk about our future. We imagine the dream destinations we want to explore as a family, envision the future we hope for our boys, and think up adventures we can pursue together.

The concept of building a future together is often undervalued in relationships, but it's powerful. When you and your partner work toward collaborative goals, it increases your chances of success, and it also builds a strong connection between you.

5. Work Out Together

The saying "The couple that works out together stays together" holds more truth than you might think. A 2021 study published in the *Journal of Social and Personal Relationships* found that couples who exercised together reported higher levels of positive mood during exercise, increased daily positive mood, and greater relationship satisfaction.[5]

6. Bad Friends Corrupt Good Marriages

Are your friends *for* your marriage?

The people you spend time with can have a big impact on your marriage relationship. Friends who mock your commitment or encourage negativity can slowly chip away at the bond you've built. Even if you're not engaging in toxic behavior, their influence can make you question your spouse, grow critical, or feel disconnected.

To evaluate a friendship's impact, ask yourself, *Are they for my marriage? Do they root for me, or do they feed negativity and gossip?*

How does your friend talk about their own spouse? Constant complaints about their person is likely to drag you into a critical mindset, which may eventually lead to you joining the conversation in a way you aren't proud of.

Does your friend always take your side? True friends don't pander to you. They challenge you to grow and are willing to share the truth in love. Proverbs 27:6 reminds us, "Faithful are the wounds of a friend, but the kisses of an enemy are deceitful." First Corinthians 15:33 says, "Do not be deceived: 'Evil company corrupts good habits.'" You, of course, don't think your friends are evil, but do they and their advice align with the Word of God?

Does your friend respect your spouse? They don't have to love them, but they should honor your choice and your marriage.

Jesse and I realized early on how important it is to surround ourselves with supportive friends and mentors.

We've joined community groups through our church that have connected us with people who share similar values. We seek out relationships with friends and neighbors who are growth-minded—people who challenge us, inspire us, and hold us accountable to becoming better versions of ourselves.

These friendships have allowed us to glean wisdom from more experienced mentors and also to invest in individuals who are younger than us. We gain insight from couples who have been married for more than twenty-five years so that we can learn the should-nots and must-dos. We also spend time with friends who acknowledge their wrongdoings, live out repentance, and work to improve their own lives.

People tend to reflect the characteristics of the five people they spend the most time with, so choose your circle of friends wisely.

7. Read Educational Books

In a world where fifteen-second videos and snippets of unverified advice flood our social media feeds, there is nothing like stimulating your intellectual growth through educational books.

Social media can overwhelm you with a constant stream of information, much of it conflicting or superficial. Books offer a more focused and manageable way to consume information together as a couple. They can be a catalyst for personal development for you and your spouse. Nearly always, I will read to Jesse in the car on road trips, and he reads to me as we lie in bed.

One of my favorite parts of reading together is that it prompts conversation about topics we might not have discussed before.

As you consider leveling up together as a couple in your discipline and habits, think about this: If you never commit to making changes, you won't know what you're missing out on. It could be the exact shift you've been waiting for.

What if working out together is the key to relieving the pent-up stress in your home? What if praying together reveals a level of vulnerability in your partner that you've never seen before? How might Sunday Meetings change the tone of your marriage and balance out responsibilities? How could increased confidence in your body and health improve your sex life?

You won't know until you try.

It takes about twenty-one to thirty days to establish a new habit. Every day you let go by without making a change is another day you allow your quality of life to decline. But daily small, 1 percent shifts—even if it's as little as thirty minutes a day—will shift you toward a more fulfilling and healthier life and marriage.

CHAPTER 10

BECOMING BEST FRIENDS AGAIN

Happy is the man who finds a true friend, and far happier is he who finds that true friend in his wife.

—Unknown

I often reflect on the powerful moment in the movie *The Notebook* when Allie responds to her parents' assertion that she doesn't know anything about love. She retorts, "Oh, and you do? You don't look at Daddy the way I look at Noah. You don't touch or laugh. You don't play. You don't know anything about love."

There's a special sweetness to a first crush, to a teenage romance, to the engagement and honeymoon stages of life. There's playfulness. Genuine fun. Laughter that makes your stomach hurt. I'm sure you have a lot of very sweet memories from that season of your life.

I'll never forget one moment when our boys came out of their rooms to find Jesse and me in the middle of a Nerf-gun fight. We had the black stripes under our eyes and were hiding behind corners, laughing so hard that tears filled our eyes. Our boys lit up and they grinned from ear to ear. They instantly wanted to join in and be part of the fun.

That same glow appears on their faces during mine and Jesse's hugs, kisses, tickling, wrestling matches, and other playful interactions. These moments aren't always convenient or easy for us, and they can honestly be a little bit vulnerable, but the more we make time for them, the more they become a natural part of our home.

But life is finicky. And circumstances can steal our friendship right out from under us if we aren't careful.

Jesse and I have been there. As I've shared with you, we dealt with many late-night asthma scares with our oldest son, Sutton. After one specific grueling stretch filled with relentless coughing, sleep deprivation, and my heavy heart, I found myself retreating to Jesse's office in search of solace.

Sutt was so patient and faithful through it all—relying on prayer and reminding us it was going to be okay, even when he was the one suffering. His big heart, steady calm, and deep empathy make me want to be a better person. But even with his composure, the worry and fear were unrelenting, pressing in no matter how much we prayed or how carefully we tried to manage his medicine.

On top of this, our lives had been consumed by to-do lists, heavy responsibilities, and an endless stream of serious, exhausting challenges for months on end. Playfulness had faded between us; everything felt rigid and transactional, void of emotion or romance.

In that quiet space, I faced a choice: I could spiral into self-pity and doubt, or communicate my concerns to my husband. I, hesitantly, chose communication and vulnerability.

The prideful part of me wanted to wallow in negativity. I

could have believed that Jesse simply didn't love me like he used to, or that being a parent damages the fun of marriage. The lies were loud. But the verse I had stored in my heart, "We take captive every thought to make it obedient to Christ" (2 Cor. 10:5 NIV), reminded me to take captive those destructive thoughts that threatened to consume me.

So I walked in, sat on Jesse's lap and said, "I really miss laughing with you. Adulthood and marriage are so freaking hard, and I feel like, more often than not lately, we allow it to pull us under. I miss sitting on the couch together, making jokes, looking into each other's eyes, flirting, and laughing at stupid things. Can we work toward that again?"

Instead of letting resentment build, I opened up to Jesse about my feelings. To my relief, he responded with understanding and a shared desire for change.

We promised to bring more laughter into our home. We started with little things: sharing jokes, scrolling through funny videos, spending time with people who make us laugh, random dance parties with the kids, and watching comedies together after a long day. We realized how much we needed to choose laughter, especially during heavy seasons of life.

Are You Looking in the Same Direction?

C. S. Lewis said of friendship, "It is when we are doing things together that friendship springs up—painting, sailing ships, praying, philosophising, and fighting shoulder to shoulder. Friends look in the same direction."[1]

Are you looking in the same direction as your spouse? Or are you both looking to the side, away from each other, at your busy lives, and filling your calendars with lists of to-dos? Are you looking back and wishing you had made a different decision to keep life easier or to have more freedoms?

So many couples I speak with believe that their sex life has grown stale solely because too many years have passed. But I want to push back on that thought. The real issue typically is not the bedroom but the life you're building outside of it.

Sex is usually the byproduct of connection that's already happening in a hundred little ways before you even touch each other. If we haven't laughed together, if we haven't looked up from our phones, if we haven't flirted, kissed, or shared anything meaningful all week, why do we expect the sex to suddenly be passionate and alive? In what world does that add up?

Few of us get married with the goal of having a mediocre marriage or sex life. We often begin our relationships with a healthy friendship. But as time goes on, we stop looking in the same direction.

Jesse and I were best friends for a few years before we were married. We were practically the same person: We were obsessed with Marvel movies and fiction books; we loved to gather people together; we shared a deep faith in Jesus; and we were addicted to board games and good food. We could talk for hours without running out of things to say. Fifteen years later, we still share a lot of the same loves, though our passions and hobbies have shifted and evolved.

Many people just accept this slowing down as a normal part of marriage: "Well, that's what happens after a decade or two with kids around." But countless studies show that strong friendships are the backbone of lasting relationships. They matter.

Do you enjoy spending time with your spouse? Do you laugh together? Can you playfully tease each other without hurting feelings?

When you think of true friendship and the friends who have stuck by you, who comes to mind?

Would you say that your strongest friendships are with people who bear with you in love?

Are they the ones who are understanding when you're the worst version of yourself?

Do they help you walk through your brokenness, your emotions, your struggles, and your sin without judgment or condemnation?

The friends you're envisioning are likely the people who have walked through life with you—*in spite of you.*

I have been fortunate enough to have some of the most incredible friends a person could ever ask for. Many of them I've been friends with for more than twenty-five years. I know how lucky I am, because let's be real, they have had plenty (plenty!) of reasons to give up on me. But they never have. They show up, they pursue, they love, and they invest—because of who they are, not necessarily because of who I am.

They've displayed to me what unconditional love really looks like.

Our marriages can have that same depth of friendship.

I vividly remember a family I spent countless hours with during high school. At that age, I desperately longed to feel chosen, but they did far more than that. They fully embraced me. My guy friend, his siblings, and their parents became a living example of the kind of home I dreamed of building one day. There was something steady and sacred about the way they did life together.

I observed them with quiet attentiveness, studying the architecture of their family, mentally collecting the patterns of love and stability they lived out each day. I filed away the details, hoping to one day have something similar of my own. They laughed loudly, loved fiercely, and navigated life's challenges with a grace that captivated me. Fridays were spent with all of us on the floor playing video games, and Sundays were filled with football, food, laughter, and a sense of belonging that seeped into my soul.

Nearly every time I stepped through their front door, I was

met with the smell of something sweet baking in the oven, like warm cinnamon rolls or gooey chocolate chip cookies. Shoes were kicked off in every direction, the sound of laughter and overlapping conversation filled the space, and someone was almost always yelling a loving "Come in!" from the living room, even if they weren't part of the family. Nothing was staged. If the house was messy, it was messy—and no one cared. That was part of what made it feel so safe. The kids opened the pantry every few minutes, the parents didn't flinch, and every guest was treated like family the second they walked in.

I remember countless weekends when I'd walk through their door, exchange warm hugs, and immediately sink into their cozy couch, the soft weight of a blanket draped over me as someone handed me the remote for the next video game. I felt fully at ease. Their home was a refuge, a place where friends were welcomed with open arms.

It felt so much like home that I never wanted to leave.

But what I noticed most was how the parents set the tone. They weren't only managing a home; they were doing their best to shape a legacy. They were always looking in the same direction when it came to their values, what they wanted for their children's lives, and how present and intentional they wanted to be. They were united in how they showed up, in joy and kindness, even when life battered them.

Their playful banter, inside jokes, and sweet flirtation created this easy, welcoming vibe that everyone felt the moment they walked in. They were confident and comfortable with themselves as individuals, which allowed them to be confident and comfortable with one another. They joined in on the games and the inside jokes with the kids. I always noticed that they were never afraid or dismissive of the fun.

Their friendship was the heartbeat of the house.

As I look back now, I realize that I witnessed the reality that a thriving marriage and a happy home are often rooted in a solid friendship. It's easy to get caught up in the day-to-day, letting the demands of life overshadow the importance of companionship. But it's in the moments of spontaneity, fun, playfulness, and laughter that we connect within our marriages.

Ever since Jesse and I married, we've tried to create the same warm, open-door atmosphere I experienced with that family, where laughter, shared meals around the dinner table, and connection are the norm. We're not perfect at it, especially when work and life feel overwhelming, but opening our home is very important to us.

Because it's often in those moments, when our home is filled with the people we love, that Jesse and I feel closest to one another. We are lighter, freer. And our children are also able to see the value of relationships and community.

If we want a life like that, it begins with us.

So how do we build, or rebuild, a friendship well?

Face to Face Versus Side by Side

Friendship is often understood as a bond built on affection, trust, intimacy, and mutual respect between two people. But do you ever feel like you and your spouse are losing that bond? You both long for understanding and peace, yet the paths you're taking to connect seem to be leading you farther apart.

Conversations, like the genuine, face-to-face connections, are invaluable. In a world constantly vying for our attention, choosing to be vulnerable, to look into each other's eyes, and to openly share our hearts is, frankly, a radical act of love. Whether you realize it or not, when you and your spouse sit down with coffee instead of zoning out in front of a movie, or go for a walk without your phones instead of bingeing another show, you're saying something really important. You're saying, *I want to be here with you. I care about what's on your mind. You matter to me.* For many women, especially, this kind of attentive presence speaks the sweetest love language.

But even a good connection or conversation can start to feel heavy when things aren't clicking. If you're stuck in the same frustrating conversation over and over again, it can feel more draining than helpful. Instead of rejuvenating each other, you end up draining each other.

The truth is, we're all wired differently when it comes to connection.

Men often find strength in shared experiences. Much of the time they spend together is side by side, shoulder to shoulder, doing projects, sports, playing games, or building something new. This often fulfills a deep-rooted desire for teamwork and partnership, tapping into the protective, masculine role often expected of them.

When we look at relationships between women—risking overgeneralization here—they often enjoy activities like brunching, walking together, shopping, or sitting on the couch with a glass of wine, chatting about every detail of everything. They're face to face, sharing moments and conversations.

While conversations are important, it's likely (I hope) that you've had a lot of them. So maybe instead of facing each other across a table, dissecting your issues and repeating that same battle for the thousandth time, you might consider choosing to experience life side by side.

The bonus? You get a front-row seat to your partner's growth. You get to watch them step into their calling, pursue their goals, or simply become more of who God created them to be, and it's all very attractive. Jesse has always told me that I'm never more attractive to him than when I'm confident, happy, and chasing my goals, and I feel the same way about him. When you grow together, desire follows.

In my marriage, I've found that when things feel serious, hard, or stressful, spending time shoulder to shoulder with Jesse reminds us that we're on the same team. It reassures us that we don't have to be at odds, even when life feels chaotic. More than anything, it rebuilds and strengthens our friendship.

This is why I'm such a big fan of day dates. With two wild boys and a million things going on, Jesse and I are often wiped out by the time evening rolls around. Honestly, half the time we finally get out, we're just counting down until we can crawl into bed.

But there's something about a midday date that feels lighter. Day dates feel refreshing because we're rested, energized, and excited for the day.

Whether it's a hike, a super competitive (but fun) game of pickleball—Jesse's current obsession—a board game night, spontaneously going to a waterpark, or learning something new together, these little moments help wake our relationship back up. They pull us out of the routine, remind us we're more than just tired parents or busy people, we're thirtysomethings living our lives for the first time, too, and we're friends. And friends need to laugh and play and make space for joy.

In the earlier stages of a marriage, most of us often have time-filling tasks, like raising kids or building a business. This can strengthen bonds, but if all of your energy is going toward the "doing," it's easy to forget how to just be together. What happens when your business changes or your kids go off to college? What will be left to bind you together then?

The reality is that both men and women crave (and need) experiences beyond the confines of their relationship. Jesse and I have always enjoyed hosting barbecues or parties and going out to do fun things with the people we love. Opening our doors to neighbors, friends, and family strengthens and energizes our marriage because it isn't just about us and our issues. We're able to get outside of ourselves, to care about other people, and to take the focus off of our marriage. We hear their stories and share in their joys, and one of the greatest parts is that we have something fresh to talk about together when the night is over.

It's a win-win-win.

Research supports the idea that shared experiences can enhance relationships. A 2021 study published in the *Journal of Social and Personal Relationships* explored how engaging in new and challenging activities with a romantic partner can increase happiness and relationship satisfaction. The researchers identified feelings of growth and security as key mechanisms through which these shared experiences improve relationship quality.[2]

What Are You Building Together?

Psalm 127:1 says, "Unless the LORD builds the house, the builders labor in vain" (NIV).

Many couples waste their lives chasing empty pursuits, and then they wonder why their marriage feels lifeless, dull, or empty.

Do you and your spouse regularly step outside of yourselves? What I mean is, do you spend time with people beyond your immediate circle? Do you help the homeless? Do you invest in the lives of orphans? Do you share the gospel together and show love to the less fortunate? Are you ministering to your children and preparing them to go out into the world? The primary question is this: Do you have a shared kingdom purpose that you both work toward?

In my conversations with others, I often find that when couples lack a purposeful vision, their efforts toward worldly success, personal ambition, and fulfillment fail to provide a life of meaning. They spend their years together squandering the little time they have, figuratively staring at themselves in the mirror, gazing over the fence at others, and seeking their own comfort, while simultaneously asking, "Is this really all there is to life?"

In his book *Don't Waste Your Life*, John Piper says, "I am wired by nature to love the same toys that the world loves. I start to fit in. I start to love what others love. I start to call earth 'home.' Before you know it, I am calling luxuries 'needs' and using my money just the way unbelievers do. I begin to forget the war. I don't think much about people perishing. Missions and unreached people drop out of my mind. I stop dreaming about the triumphs of grace. I sink into a secular mindset that looks first to what man can do, not what God can do. It is a terrible sickness."

Building on John Piper's warning, when a marriage is rooted in the pursuit of worldly desires—whether it's wealth, status, or image—it becomes dangerously disconnected from its true purpose. A marriage that isn't focused on making an eternal impact is a marriage on shaky ground. We eventually lose sight of one another.

And in response to that, instead of fighting for the marriage we have, we:

- Daydream about the what-ifs of having a "better" partner
- Chase temporarily satisfying achievements
- Pour the little time we have into building noteworthy careers
- Seek worldly affirmation, beauty, and success

Here's the harsh truth: Without a shared purpose, something bigger than yourselves, you will likely drift into emptiness and frustration. And you may turn that frustration toward each other, blaming the other for your dissatisfaction when, in reality, the cause is a lack of alignment with God's kingdom.

The goal here isn't to measure success by the world's standards or even by works of faith. You don't have to do anything for God to love you; he already loves you. Having a shared purpose isn't an obligation that you check off your list but a way of life.

It's a display of the fruit of your faith. Think of it as a response to the fact that you love Jesus so much that you are excited to serve and love others. You *get* to do it. You may not always align in your vision for service, and that's okay. It may look different for each of you. But when you choose to get outside of yourselves and commit to building a life outside of you, you will begin to feel your contentment change.

Do the Fun Things

As Jesse and I have grown together, we've come to realize that some of the things we used to enjoy no longer resonate with both of us. Our tastes and interests have shifted over time, and that's okay. Fun isn't one size fits all, and we may be doing a disservice to each other if we always feel like we need to impose our idea of fun on our partners. If your spouse doesn't find certain things as much fun as you do, it may be helpful to do the following:

1. Compromise on Fun

Fun takes compromise. What exhilarates one person might bore another. This fundamental difference can create a rift if we insist on imposing our preferred activities on our partners. It's like expecting a cat to enjoy a dog park.

Remember, compromise isn't about surrender, it's about enrichment. It's a choice to celebrate our partners' passions and personalities, rather than feeling threatened or deprived by them. Again, what matters to them matters to us because we care for them.

Do you (secretly) despise video games, but your spouse loves them? Dive headfirst into their world. Grab a controller, put on some headphones to drown out the noise, and give it a shot. You might discover a hidden passion for puzzle solving or competitive gaming. Even if you don't, your willingness to participate shows support for and interest in their hobby.

Does your partner love thrifting and shopping, but you can't think of a worse way to spend your day? Shift your perspective. Try to view it as an adventure in finding hidden treasures together. Do something you *do* love that day along with the shopping, like treating yourself to a coffee or one of your favorite lunch spots. Remember, it's about spending quality time with your person, not necessarily about the activity itself.

2. Avoid Being a Hobby Hater and Have Boundaries with Your Own

It's easy to fall into the trap of resenting your partner's hobbies. Trust me, I've been there. I spent a lot of time absolutely despising Jesse's video games. Because when someone's passion consumes their time and energy, it can feel like a personal slight or even neglect. But your constant complaints about their hobbies will probably do the opposite of your intended goal by creating a rift and turning what should be a source of joy into a battle. It's important to remind yourself that everyone deserves outlets and interests beyond the relationship.

But (and this is a big but) a hobby should enrich your life, not dominate it. A common complaint, particularly among women, is the disproportionate emphasis placed on hobbies like golf or gaming. When these activities consistently take precedence over shared experiences, it leads to feelings of isolation and loneliness.

This imbalance of priorities will inevitably create some fires in a home. Jesse and I have seen this in our own marriage in many ways, and so as not to burn our own houses down, we have to regularly check ourselves and one another—lovingly—to ensure that we're maintaining a proper balance of our hobbies and our time together. For example, our rhythm right now is three nights of alone time and four nights together. Because when it's imbalanced, a spouse will typically feel like an afterthought, as if their needs have been subordinated to the pursuit of external gratification.

Have you felt this in your own marriage? Has bitterness started brewing over hobbies, too much time with friends, work commitments, or screen time? Both partners deserve outlets for personal growth, but as a couple, our marriage is our first ministry and priority.

3. Establish Daily Habits

Luke 16:10 reminds us that "whoever can be trusted with very little can also be trusted with much" (NIV). Isn't that incredible? The smallest, most seemingly insignificant actions in our marriages can ripple into waves of change.

Imagine if we could fill our days with tiny gestures that scream, *You are my absolute favorite person!* Take a minute to write down five small habits that you can implement daily in your marriage. Hold on to them for safekeeping. For the next thirty days, take turns practicing one habit each day. Serving without expecting anything in return can be life-changing.

Maybe every day you choose to serve your spouse with a foot rub before bed. This is a display of kindness and also selflessly pours into your spouse's soul. It's a tangible expression of *I see you, I value you, and I'm here for you.*

I also encourage you to try quantifying your capacity to contribute to the relationship each day on a scale of one to one hundred. For example, you can come home and say, "Hey, I'm at a fifteen today—low on energy, patience, and kindness." Your partner might reply, "I've got you; I'm at a seventy-five. Let me take over so you can recharge." You're not keeping score but rather recognizing where each person is and adjusting to support the other. Practicing this displays a commitment to fight against circumstances, not against one another.

Some of you might feel far removed from this kind of connection. But Romans 12:10 reminds us to "be devoted to one another in love. Honor one another above yourselves" (NIV).

Submission and respect aren't about power dynamics, they're about honoring each other. Respect means valuing your spouse's worth and opinions. Submission means yielding to their leadership while trusting God to guide you both.

4. You're on the Same Team

When you said "I do," your partner became your teammate for life. When it comes to your marriage versus the rest of the world, your partner should always be your top priority, even over your children, parents, in-laws, and friends. The first book of the Bible makes it clear that we are meant to cleave to our spouses, prioritizing them above all other relationships, including our parents and extended family. Genesis 2:24 says, "Therefore a man shall leave his father and mother and be joined to his wife, and they shall become one flesh."

Being on the same team is not only about accepting differences but about fighting for each other, not against each other.

When disagreements arise, whether between yourselves, with in-laws, or even regarding your children, you have to remember that you're on the same side, working toward a solution that honors Christ, not yourselves. This shifts your perspective, allowing you to see the best in each other and cheer each other on.

Depletion Is Contagious: Take Care of Your Joy

Have you ever spent hours with someone who is perpetually shrouded in negativity? Or with a person who has to find something to complain about, no matter how good the situation might be? It's exhausting, isn't it? It's a recipe for emotional depletion, not just for the complainer but also for those around them.

Chances are, you wouldn't look at that person and think, *Them! I want to be just like them.* Or, *I want to spend all of my time with someone like that!* So if we act this way as partners, it's likely that our spouses are feeling just as exhausted or even longing for escape.

A while back, I took my sons to the theater to watch a much-anticipated cartoon. It was cute and funny but left me unexpectedly emotional and teary-eyed. One of the characters shared a poignant observation: "Maybe this is what happens when you grow up. You feel less . . . joy." I felt something jolt in my stomach when I first heard that, and then I replayed that thought over and over in my mind throughout the week.

I've shared that I have had seasons, even years, when I felt like I completely lost my joy. I couldn't find fun in the things I used to love. And as much as I believe that that's just life sometimes, I equally believe that we can refuse to accept that as our norm. I hope you choose to do that with me. Life is as fun as you choose to make it! But you have to fight for it. Your spouse and your friendship are directly impacted by your happiness, or lack thereof.

I frequently speak to my community via my podcast and Instagram about my passion for actively finding joy:

When I'm driving, I almost always choose the longer, prettier route to soak in the scenery.

I'm constantly on the hunt for new and exciting restaurants to keep life interesting. If I've been to the same place twice, it has to be really, really fantastic. A creature of habit? Never met her.

And instead of the usual dinner-and-a-movie date night, I always seek out something more out of the box, like a waterfall hike, a sushi-making class, a throwback concert from one of our high school favorites, or a cozy morning wandering an apple orchard. These things bring me joy. And joy matters.

I want to encourage you to prioritize filling up your cup. This doesn't just mean bubble baths and Oreos (though I'm all about that kind of self-care); it's also about filling your soul with purpose and connection. I'm talking about digging into the truths of the Bible, exercising regularly, choosing discipline over ease, finding fun, taking days off where you aren't wanted or needed by anyone, soaking up the sun's warmth and vitamin D, and surrounding yourself with life-giving friendships.

You can't dig from the bottom of the well and then expect to give the best to your family.

I tell my boys all the time, "We're each responsible for the tone of our home." I've learned the hard way that someone who is constantly depleted will deplete those around them. It's contagious and bound to damage a friendship.

When someone walks in frustrated or starts snapping, it spreads. And when someone else walks in with laughter, joy, and positivity, it's just as impactful. Science backs this up. It's called *emotional contagion*, and it refers to our tendency as humans to absorb the emotions of the people around us. It occurs when we unconsciously mimic the emotions of others, activating similar neural and physiological responses in ourselves, which creates shared emotional experiences.[3] If one person is extremely joyful, their joy lifts the entire room. If someone is noticeably irritable, they weigh everyone else down.

Our brains are wired for this through something called *mirror neurons*, specialized cells in our brains that activate both when we perform an action and when we observe someone else performing the same action. These cells help us read and reflect other people's emotions. That's why we yawn when someone else yawns, or feel tense when someone walks into the room angry.[4]

In the context of family life, this means that the emotional tone set by one member can significantly influence the entire household. There were seasons when my negativity, overwhelm, and anxiety grew from a flame to a fire and consumed my home. I was burning my own house down by trading joy and peace for productivity, filling my days with tasks instead of joy. This realization has made me hyper-aware of the fact that if Jesse or I walk into the room and seem tense, our kids pick up on it immediately. It shifts their sweet, pure joy into feelings of confusion, concern, or sadness. I don't want to be the person who sucks the energy out of the people I love, so I need to remember that self-control and emotional awareness aren't just about me individually, they shape the peace, connection, and safety in our entire home, so I need to ensure that rest is a part of my pattern.

Rest gives us the ability to increase in emotional awareness. Sabbath rest isn't a simple suggestion in the Bible. It's a command, and it's for our good. Our humanity requires us to rest, and the Sabbath is our way of surrendering to God's will in all things. It's our weekly act of worship that says, *God, I trust you to hold everything together while I pause. I believe you are powerful enough to care for my life, my needs, and my responsibilities even when I'm not hustling to keep them all afloat.*

Rest truly is a discipline that humbles you. Sabbath rest is a reminder that you are not the glue holding your family, home, finances, or life together. He is. And when you ignore that rhythm of rest, you often forget who you are and who he is because you're placing yourself on a pedestal you were never meant to stand on.

There is no guilt in prioritizing alone time and self-care. It is an essential. Jesse and I have become better friends to each other, more successful in our businesses, and more loving parents because we choose to do the things that fill our souls.

It's wild how much better things are when we're not a total wreck, isn't it? The foundation of our space doesn't crumble, the flames subside, peace fills our home, and friendship thrives.

Pressing Reset

Let's get honest. As the saying goes, "The definition of insanity is doing the same thing over and over and expecting different results." It's time to press reset.

Frustration, anger, and resentment are the toxic by-products of unhealthy patterns, patterns you've likely been repeating for years. These negative emotions don't come out of nowhere; the repeated actions solidify them in your heart. But if you're dedicated to healing, strengthening, or saving your marriage, you must remember the wisdom of 1 Corinthians 13:5: Love "keeps no record of wrongs" (NIV).

What an immense calling it is to create a renewed marriage. So how do we put this into practice?

We look to the heart of God.

Imagine if God held every one of your failures against you, or if he constantly reminded you of your shortcomings. You'd be lost in despair. Yet we often deny our spouses the same grace we desperately crave from God.

Isn't it ironic that the Enemy thrives on resentment, bitterness, and the stubborn refusal to change? These toxic things are his playground; we have to fight against them if we expect to see any shift within our marriages.

One easy (and actually fun) way to bring a little spontaneity back into your relationship is with a date jar. We have used a date jar for more than ten years and love it just as much as we did in the beginning. Fill a mason jar with a mix of simple ideas and draw one whenever you're feeling stuck in the same old routine. Whether it's having a living-room picnic or trying a new hike, the jar takes the pressure off planning and brings the excitement back to date night.

The Date Jar Instructions

1. Start by writing ideas for dates on popsicle sticks. (See the suggestions in the following list for ideas.)
2. Drop the sticks into a mason jar.
3. When you're ready for a spontaneous adventure, simply reach into the jar and pick a stick.

4. Pro tip: Create themed jars for more control over the type of date you choose, such as Adventurous Dates, Cozy Nights In, or Free Fun.
5. Replenish the jar regularly to keep the excitement alive.

20+ Date Jar Ideas

1. Enjoy a scenic hike together.
2. Challenge yourselves with an escape room.
3. Build a campfire (or simply use your stove) and roast s'mores.
4. Go on a spontaneous road trip without a destination in mind.
5. Pack a picnic and enjoy the outdoors.
6. Get active at a trampoline park.
7. Indulge in relaxation with massages or a DIY spa experience.
8. Test your batting skills at the batting cages.
9. Unleash your inner chef by baking a delicious dessert together.
10. Have a friendly competition with video games.
11. Explore your thrifting skills with a $15 shopping challenge.
12. Discover new shops and window displays together.
13. Enjoy a fun-filled night of bowling.
14. Venture to a place neither of you has explored before.
15. Recommit to your love by rewriting your vows and enjoying takeout.
16. Have a playful and competitive Nerf-gun battle.
17. Spend a day watching each other's favorite movies.
18. Dress up and enjoy a fancy dinner out.

19. Get some exercise with a bike ride.
20. Have a game night playing your favorite board games.
21. Clear out space for a dance floor at home and dance together.
22. Give back to the community with a surprise gift for a family in need.
23. Spend quality time together with intimate moments and movie marathons.

As people who are created to set an example of unconditional love to the world, let us pray tirelessly to keep that spirit alive in our marriages, even when it tries to slip away as easily as it came. It's a fight worth fighting, because our love is a reflection of something far greater than us.

CHAPTER 11

ARE WE ACTUALLY IN THIS TOGETHER?

Two are better than one,
Because they have a good reward for their labor.
For if they fall, one will lift up his companion.

—Ecclesiastes 4:9–10

Companionship

> **Companionship (n):** A relationship centered on care and interdependence, characterized by loyalty, comfort, and quality time spent together.

Jesse and I were doing the usual mall madness with our boys during the Christmas rush. As we sat together, holding hands and watching our energetic little ones burn off steam in the play area, I couldn't help but notice a couple across the way. The wife (who had one of the prettiest rings I had ever seen, might I add) stepped out for coffee, and when she returned, her husband's face lit up with a smile and a rare kind of joy that caught my eye.

It was a brief moment, but his silent, heartfelt gratitude for her return was impossible to ignore; he let out a happy sigh, which—to me—seemed to indicate everything was right in his world, and he gently wrapped his arm around her waist.

I turned to Jesse, sharing the sweet moment I had just witnessed. I asked wistfully, "Do you think it's possible to feel that same gratitude to be in your partner's presence, even when you're both eighty-five years old?"

He nodded thoughtfully. "Yeah, but I think it's about a lot more than just love. It's building a relationship where you're each other's safe place and consistently relieving each other's burdens."

Our conversation was quickly interrupted when Saxon—true to the nature of a second child—leaped from a slide and body-slammed Sutton. Just another typical day in boy-mom life.

Jesse was right, though. A successful marriage is both companionship and partnership. Without companionship—that shared emotional connection—couples risk becoming roommates, business partners, or just friends.

When I think of companionship in a spouse, I think of a safe place to land.

We have a friend who loves touch. He considers himself overly physical, whereas his wife could go the rest of her life without being touched. They're best friends. They laugh together, run a business together, and talk regularly, but they can't get over the hurdle of physical affection.

Another friend longs for emotional connection, but her spouse only wants to talk about his hobbies or the next football game. No matter how hard she tries, he withdraws from deeper conversations.

Life, and sin, have a way of pulling us from the companionship that our marriages so desperately need.

Dr. John Gottman, in a foundational concept, states that

masters of relationships are highly skilled at one thing: turning toward each other instead of away. His work underlines the importance of responding to your partner's bids for attention.[1]

Have you ever heard of this? A bid for attention is any attempt by one partner to gain the attention, affection, or support of the other. It can be a simple gesture, a verbal request, or an emotional expression, and it's a crucial way to connect and communicate in a relationship.

The cool thing is that any response to a bid for attention is technically better than no response at all. But even better, recognizing and responding well to these bids quickly builds toward a healthy marriage. In contrast, turning away from each other happens when you ignore or dismiss a bid for attention.

Here are a few examples:

Request for Help:

"Can you help me set up for this party?"

- *Positive Response:* "I'm happy to help. I may not fully understand the need for this, but if it matters to you, it matters to me. What do you need me to do?"
- *Negative Response:* "Why can't you handle it on your own? You're the one who wanted to plan this elaborate event for a kid who won't even remember it. We don't need all this stuff."

Sharing a Rough Day:

"Today was awful. I feel drained."

- *Positive Response:* "I'm sorry to hear that. Do you want to talk about it? Let me know if you want me to help fix it or if you just want me to listen."
- *Negative Response:* Being dismissive of their feelings

or saying something like, "You have no idea what a hard day is. You should have seen how challenging my day was."

Seeking Affection:

A partner reaches out to hold hands.

- *Positive Response:* Partner responds by holding hands and turning to look at their spouse with a smile, saying, "I love being with you."
- *Negative Response:* Partner ignores the hand being held out, or says, "I'm doing something on my phone," or, "I need space."

Gottman emphasizes that while these interactions may seem minor, they are critical for a strong emotional connection. When couples consistently turn toward each other, they create an environment of trust and intimacy.

In what ways do you feel pursued or disconnected by your spouse's bids for attention? How do you feel when you make bids for connection with your spouse—ignored or genuinely received?

Take a moment to ask your partner what bids they make that you might not realize and how you could improve your response to them. What do they wish you noticed more often?

Togetherness

"They do everything together," my mom said as we sat on the couch during one of her visits. She shared in detail about the married couples she knows—couples in their sixties and seventies who are best friends and enjoy spending all of their time together.

I knew that's what I wanted in my future but also realized that if I didn't continue taking steps toward that now, it would be far more difficult to get there in the future.

This conversation triggered something in my heart—a mix of conviction, longing, and the feelings from lessons learned along the way.

Jesse and I had lost our togetherness for a season when our boys were babies.

I really noticed this loss for the first time at my sister Megan's house during a vacation. I had spent a lot of time with my sister and her husband, Tripp, before, of course, but something stood out during that particular visit. As I watched the two of them go about their day, I realized I had rarely seen a family so connected, so together, so intentional.

Grocery shopping, a quick run to pick up food, home projects, making sourdough (and handmaking the tools for their sourdough—don't even get me started on how creative they are), tending to their chickens (Meg definitely got the homemaker gene that I didn't get), playing on the floor with their son and daughter—you name it, they did it together.

Was it always more convenient to do things as a family? Absolutely not. Were there moments of toddler tears and tantrums? Absolutely. But they did it and they did it together, as a couple and as a family.

I envied them.

When Jesse and I had our two boys, we adapted to navigating life separately for the sake of convenience and comfort. Our plans started to sound like:

- "I'll go to the grocery store while you stay home."
- "I'll take the kids to a play date while you rest."
- "Let's just go to the gym separately; it's too much work to pack up both boys."

We became accustomed to living in the most convenient way, not in the way that was most together. Our routines became fragmented, filled with quick solo tasks instead of shared experiences.

While y'all know that I'm all about maintaining a sense of independence (because idolizing our spouses and their company can lead to dependency and a loss of individuality), it's equally important to recognize that oneness in marriage is biblical. A marriage lived separately can quickly become filled with temptation, loneliness, an unwillingness to be together, and a lack of desire for each other.

What are some areas in your marriage where you live separate lives?

Does one of you read at night while the other watches their own shows? Does one go out to buy clothes for the family while the other stays home? Do you often go out separately with friends instead of spending time together with other couples?

These separations may seem small, and they're completely fine and healthy in moderation, but they can lead to emotional disconnection over time. We were not created to live on an island. When we lose that sense of togetherness, it becomes easier to overlook the changes happening within ourselves and our partners.

At the beginning of this book, we discussed how much we change as individuals over the years. Have you ever considered how different you are now compared with three years ago, or even ten? So much has likely shifted within you—your fears, dreams, character, and stories. And the same goes for your spouse. You're both constantly growing and becoming, so learning about your spouse should be a lifelong pursuit. Knowing one another isn't something you'll ever master, but it's something you should perpetually remain curious about. I want to encourage you to never stop asking. Ask questions (even the ones you think you know the answers to) so that you get to know the new versions of your spouse as often as you can. This togetherness and time getting to know each other again will build your companionship like never before.

Are you willing to humble yourself enough to ask the questions?

Extinguishing Pride

Marriage is about choosing unity, even when everything inside of you wants to pull apart. And if there's one thing that can quietly unravel that togetherness, it's pride. Pride blinds us. It makes us focus on ourselves—our feelings, our hurts, our perspectives—at our spouses' expense.

If you're honest with yourself, the question isn't whether you're a prideful person. Scripture makes it clear that pride is deeply ingrained in the human heart, even in ways we likely don't recognize or acknowledge. Jeremiah 17:9 reminds us, "The heart is deceitful above all things, and desperately wicked; who can know it?" So rather than asking whether you are prideful, a more revealing question is to consider where pride is taking root and how it's showing up in your actions and attitudes.

There's biblical evidence that few sins are more offensive to God than pride. Proverbs 16:5 tells us, "Everyone proud in heart is an abomination to the LORD; though they join forces, none will go unpunished." And James 4:6 reminds us, "God resists the proud, but gives grace to the humble."

If pride separates us from God, it will certainly separate us from each other.

In moments of conflict, our hearts tend to shut down. Instead of seeking connection, we protect ourselves. We build walls and close off, and in that tight, closed space, selfishness, stubbornness, and judgment creep in. Pride fuels this behavior.

It prevents us from being the first to apologize or extend grace because we're too consumed by the desire to win.

Doesn't pride have a way of making us ignore reason and another person's perspective altogether? It has only one end: self-exaltation. The proud person seeks to elevate themselves, not God.

Pride says, *Protect your ego, your name, your hurt*, rather than seeking to understand your spouse's pain, needs, or perspective. It says, *How can I point my finger at you?* rather than, *How can I make the most of us?*

What if, in our heated moments, we pause and ask, *Am I seeking self-exaltation right now, or am I seeking a holier heart and a healthier marriage?*

Proverbs 11:2 says, "When pride comes, then comes shame; but with the humble is wisdom."

Pride divides. Humility heals. And healing begins with an open heart.

Here's the reality, though: We cannot manufacture humility on our own. Our hearts are naturally bent toward pride, seeking our own interests and glory. Humility starts when we surrender to God, die to ourselves, and pursue the heart of Jesus. In moments of conflict or tension, it means pausing, praying, and asking him to soften our hearts and fill us with humility.

The Compatibility Blueprint

One of the most effective ways to prioritize each other's company is by doing exactly that: making each other a priority. You can begin by planning regular date nights. Please, please, please, go on dates! Don't neglect them; they are way too important.

I receive a lot of flak from people when I share the importance of weekly dates on my podcast or social media because they say they don't have the time or the resources to go on dates, go to the gym, or spend quality time together. I don't diminish the reality that having kids or demanding jobs can limit the ability to go on dates. But again, we make time for what we care about, and sometimes we have to become creative and flexible to make dates happen.

Try these ideas:

- *Take walks.* A date doesn't have to be fancy or require a ton of money. One simple idea? Go on daily walks together. The increased oxygen and blood flow help you communicate more clearly. The physical activity of walking can help distract from anxieties or nerves, making it the perfect way to work through disagreements or conflicts. It's also the perfect way to reconnect, calm down, and open up with each other. If your kids are homeschooled or not in school yet, bring them along a few steps behind. Sure, there might be some interruptions, but as you model that dedicated mom-and-dad time, they'll learn to play independently.
- *Living room dates.* Another fun option is to turn your living room into a cozy date-night spot. Grab some blankets, whip up some popcorn, and watch a favorite childhood movie together. You can even make it special with a simple dinner or dessert while sharing your favorite memories or dreams.
- *Cook together.* Turn cooking into a fun date night. Choose a recipe you both want to try, gather your ingredients, and spend the evening preparing dinner together. You can make it more special by setting up a cozy dining area at home, complete with candles and your favorite music.
- *Have a spicy game night.* Bring out your competitive spirit with a game night at home. Dust off board games, card games, or even video games you both enjoy. Make some snacks, set up a cozy space, and enjoy a fun evening of laughter, friendly rivalry, and maybe a little striptease, if you're lucky.

Fix the Misplaced Energy

Building a strong companionship with your spouse requires understanding each other's needs. But often we misplace our energy in ways that don't address our spouses' needs effectively.

For instance, when your spouse vents about feeling overwhelmed with household chores, you might respond by working longer hours to hire a cleaner. While this seems helpful, what they may really want is your participation in the chores—sharing the load together.

Similarly, if your spouse shares that they're feeling swamped with life and needs some company, you might rush to clean the house, thinking you're easing their burden. But while it may be easier for you to do that than to give emotional energy to your partner, what they really might be craving is a compassionate ear and your undivided attention.

Or maybe when your spouse mentions wanting to get out of the house more, you send them off on a solo outing, believing you're giving them space. But what they may be yearning for is time together.

These well-meaning actions often miss the mark because they don't stem from truly hearing your spouse's needs. They only reflect what you think needs to be done. Listen well. Clarify. Then work to meet the need.

The Six-Second Kiss

Have you ever heard of the six-second kiss rule?

During a kiss, sensations travel to the limbic system, the part of the brain linked to love, passion, and lust. As neural impulses move from the lips, tongue, facial muscles, and skin, a "love cocktail" is created in the body, resulting in a natural high. This cocktail consists of neurotransmitters and hormones like dopamine, oxytocin, serotonin, adrenaline, and endorphins.

Research by Dr. John Gottman shows that a six-second kiss triggers the release of oxytocin—the love hormone—into your brain.[2] And a decade-long German study found that men who kiss their wives for at least six seconds lived significantly longer than those who didn't.[3] Do you really need any more reasons to make out? One of the many reasons that we get married is to have someone to make out with and love on all the time. Remember, you don't have to. You get to.

Greeting Each Other at the Door

The small, daily practice of greeting each other at the door has been a game changer for our marriage, and also for many of the students in our courses.

Taking a moment to greet each other at the door tells the other person, "I prioritize you."

This practice can be difficult when you have children, but it is a necessary way to maintain the structure of your family. A child-centered marriage is not healthy for you or for your children. When you are able to put your children aside for a couple of minutes and greet each other at the door, they are able to see that you prioritize your spouse. You set aside the chaos of kids and daily responsibilities and it's like hitting the pause button on life.

This is more than just a routine, it's a choice to place each other first and create a sanctuary within the walls of your home.

Love Their Way, Not Yours

A love language is the primary way you express and receive love. Dr. Gary Chapman identified five distinct love languages: acts of service, words of affirmation, physical touch, gifts, and quality time.[4]

Jesse says my love language changes weekly, or that I need all five before noon. I like to call it being well-rounded.

It's honestly quite common for spouses to have different love languages than each other.

Jesse and I have figured out that our love languages are pretty different. He feels loved by acts of service—like when I take care of things for him—while I'm more of a words of affirmation person who thrives on encouragement and praise.

The problem is that we often twist this up. We love our way instead of loving each other's way. For instance, Jesse often shows his love by doing the dishes or tackling the laundry, thinking that will make me feel appreciated. Meanwhile, I try to lift him up with encouraging words, reminding him how amazing he is. We both feel grateful for these things, but it doesn't fill our "love bucket."

We've come to realize that to really connect, we need to love each other in the way we each feel loved. I've been working on showing my love through acts of service, like cooking Jesse's favorite meal or taking something off his metaphorical plate, while Jesse is working on telling me when he thinks I look beautiful and encouraging me as a mom and in my work.

Talk about your love languages with your spouse. How do they feel loved? How do you feel loved? Has this changed since you first got married?

When you strike the right balance between partnership and companionship, you create a relationship that not only boosts each other's growth but also creates lasting courtesy, respect, and love.

CHAPTER 12

RESPONSIBILITY TUG-OF-WAR

Sometimes the heaviest burden is not the
weight of the world but the weight of a
family carried alone.

—Unknown

Partnership

> **Partnership (n):** A dynamic in which power is
> shared and respect is inherent, enabling both indi-
> viduals to work together toward a unified vision.

"I am so tired of carrying the weight of our family with so little
help from my spouse." I've heard this sentiment expressed by
countless people we've spoken with over the years. Often one
spouse ends up bearing the majority of the burden—doctor's
appointments, school lunches, chores, childcare. Many feel they
lack an equal partnership and shared responsibilities.

I have found that a large number of marriage relationships falter because of an imbalance of partnership and companionship.

While anyone can share a Netflix binge or grab coffee with you (even a dog can be a great companion), it's partnership that transforms a house into a home. A good partner provides support and effort toward shared goals.

When you walked into your marriage, you and your spouse brought your unique ideals, visions, and dreams into the relationship. When you said your vows, you were still holding tightly to your own aspirations for the future. (Note: This is a good thing. I want this for you! It means that you still have your individuality and sense of self, which are important for a healthy marriage.)

Take some time to come together and draw a Venn diagram. In one circle, you'll have "my values and goals," and in the other, "your values and goals." Then right at the center where the circles overlap is "us," where our dreams and commitments come together.

Take the time as a couple, if you haven't already, to determine your family's core values. What matters most to you? What legacy do you want to leave behind? Fill in the Venn diagram and place it somewhere in your home where you can view it regularly.

Jesse and I often repeat our core family values, and we love chanting all, or some, of them with our boys: "The Maestas family is generous to those in need. We are kind. We care for our minds and our bodies. We love God and people more than we love items or money. We believe the best in others and in one another. We never let anyone sit alone. We reflect God's love to others." You get the idea. It sounds a little cultish written down like this (ha!), but I promise it's less weird than it sounds. We do it naturally, especially after a moment of discipline or a family meltdown when we need to remember who we are. It's a fun way to reinforce what's important to us and keep those values front and center in our daily lives.

These values started with us as a couple and have since

solidified into the foundation of our family. We remind the boys that every time they walk out the door, they're representing our family—and we are too. It's a constant reminder that our actions reflect who we are and what we stand for.

Whether or not you have children, it's really helpful for you as a couple to identify your core values and beliefs, both as individuals and as partners. This clarity forms the foundation for supporting each other's needs and helps you grow closer in your relationship.

But don't make the mistake of failing to create a vision for your relationship that is bigger than your individual desires. Without a shared vision, a marriage often tips out of balance, leaning too heavily on personal wants than on a connection that honors both partners.

Think about the dynamic of your own relationship: Is it balanced, or does one person's needs or schedule always seem to take priority? When was the last time you and your spouse dreamed together? Not just about the next vacation or renovation but about the kind of legacy you want to leave, the values you want to live by, or the impact you want your marriage to have.

This lack of dreaming or setting goals together can start a negative domino effect. One person's dreams and goals may overshadow the other's, hobbies may take precedence, or someone may feel entitled to more downtime or personal space than the other to pursue their own interests. When you're laser-focused on your individual goals, you miss the chance to build a vision for your marriage that encompasses both partners' dreams.

And that's when division creeps in, often leading to resentment. It becomes all about "me" instead of "we," and suddenly God finds a place at the bottom of your priority list rather than at the center of your marriage. That's when you shift from being us-focused to self-focused.

I get it: This is all great in theory. But what happens if your core values don't align, especially as you grow older, making it feel impossible to be partners?

You're bound to face differences in your values and decisions—and that's normal.

One of you might value financial security, while the other dreams of quitting their job to start a business.

One of you might crave structure and routine, while the other thrives on spontaneity.

Maybe one of you is passionate about personal growth or faith, while the other seems content to stay the same.

These are core differences.

And while they can feel discouraging or even threatening to the unity you hoped for, they don't have to divide you. Sometimes we just need to remember not to villainize the fact that we are made differently. Nobody actually wants two of themselves in a relationship. That would be pretty exhausting. What we do want is a partner who listens, tries to understand, and is willing to grow together, even when it looks different for each of you.

Are We Even Compatible?

Scholar and theorist Lauren Berlant explores the emotional complexity of intimacy in *On the Inconvenience of Other People*, in which she unpacks a truth we don't always want to admit: The people we're closest to are often the ones who most disrupt our sense of ease. Deep connection doesn't come without friction. Being close to someone means brushing up against their habits, moods, and emotional patterns on a regular basis, and sometimes that's inconvenient. Love doesn't erase that. It magnifies it.[1]

One of the hardest parts of marriage, or any close relationship, really, is how we handle our differences. And let's be honest, we're all so incredibly different. Sometimes those differences are glaringly obvious, like our values, beliefs, or life goals.

Other times they're in the small things: how we manage our money, how we do the laundry, whether or not we exercise, or whether our kids should go to public school. Being in any close relationship forces us to face these differences head-on. Naturally, we respond with, "Are we really compatible? Who's right? Who's wrong? Who's better? Who's worse?" Some of us might approach it with curiosity, but for many, it triggers an alarm.

We start to question, "Can we even make this work?"

When we experience the everyday inconvenience of other people, like how they bump up against our space, our rhythms, and our expectations, it forces us to pause and evaluate what we're doing and who we're becoming. Those differences, even the small ones, can start to feel like intrusions. And over time, they can grow into bigger questions: What if we want different things out of life? What if our values don't align? What if we vote differently, raise our kids differently, or see God through a different lens? These are not bad questions. It's actually very fruitful to say them aloud versus stuffing your feelings or pretending that they're not a concern for you when they truly are. These are the conversations that stretch us; they test our patience, challenge our assumptions, and push us to negotiate.

As time passes, though, our appreciation for these differences can shift and grow. What once seemed like a deal-breaker can, with a change in perspective, become something you admire. What once felt like a massive wall between you can actually become an opportunity for growth.

Of course, some differences don't just go away, and compromise is sometimes unavoidable. The key is recognizing that not every difference needs to be "fixed." Some differences are meant to be worked through, respected, and navigated together.

You're unique, yes, but you're also united.

We often try to force our spouses into molds of ourselves, don't we? It's like trying to squeeze a chocolate Santa into a mold for a chocolate bunny. I'm a chocolate fiend, so I would eat it anyway, but predictably the Santa crumbles and breaks under the pressure because it was never designed for that transformation. It wasn't meant to fit that form. Similarly, our partners aren't meant to mirror our appearance or behavior or conform to a specific expectation.

Jesse and I are wildly different in so many ways—from our social battery levels to the way we handle conflict. And if I'm honest, there are still moments when those differences scare me. I sometimes wonder whether they'll always be the thing that causes friction between us. But I don't want to live there. I don't want to shape Jesse into the version of him that I think he should be.

Even better, I get to walk beside him as he becomes the person God created him to be, and I'm more grateful than ever that I've been entrusted with that role. He gets only one heart. I want to treat it well.

But disagreements are a part of life. Compromise will always be necessary in any relationship, no matter how healthy. So what do you do when two people disagree and neither is happy with the decision made? Who gets to win? How do you find a compromise that truly works for both of you?

Compromise or Collide?

One afternoon I sought counsel from an older couple who had been married for more than forty years. They shared a concept that profoundly impacted me and the future of our marriage: "Lindsey, you both need to choose your hard. You can either compromise or you can collide. It's hard to compromise, but it's equally hard to collide. Which hard will you choose?"

Game. Changer.

It's not like this revelation made everything cut and dried.

Marriage is sanctifying—it pulls the dirt and mess out of our hearts and exposes our vulnerabilities to someone we want to show our best selves to, especially when we really want something. It's humbling. It's hard. We want what we want, and compromise can feel as uncomfortable as stepping on those little Lego landmines that our kids leave scattered everywhere.

Are you in a situation where one partner is a peacemaker who tends to shut down during conflict, while the other feels the need to talk through every issue? Do you compromise or do you collide?

Does one partner desire to attend church and pray as a family, while the other may feel less strongly about those things? This can lead to tension, especially if one partner feels abandoned in their faith journey or is forced to become the sole spiritual leader of the family. Do you compromise or collide?

You might have differing views on how to raise your kids— what they should watch and listen to and how they spend their time. Do you compromise or collide?

Choosing your hard means recognizing that every choice we make has its challenges. You can either choose the hard work of compromise, which involves communication, negotiation, understanding, and maybe discomfort, or choose the hard that comes with collision, which leads to fights, resentment, emotional distance, and likely no resolution to the problem.

So how do you move forward in a marriage when you both want different things? Here are some tips that might help:

1. *"Please help us!"* I'll say this until I'm blue in the face: It's a good thing to ask for help. It's so immensely beneficial to regularly receive a fresh, outside perspective on your marriage. Have you considered talking to a counselor or a couple close to you? Even our messiest fights aren't hidden from our closest people. Sometimes getting a

different perspective can really help you see things in a new light.

2. *Lay out the facts.* Take a moment to assess what you both want, why you want it, and whether it makes sense. Is this decision beneficial for your family? Is it financially wise? Is it impulsive, or well thought out and prayed through?

3. *Compromise.* In marriage, leadership is all about guiding each other with love, not about calling the shots or forcing decisions. Think about Ephesians 5, which teaches us that the goal is unity, not using leadership to gain power over your partner. You choose to work together, not to step on each other's toes. How can you support each other in a way that feels collaborative and respectful?

4. *Take inventory.* Can you try to soften your feelings about your partner's values? Instead of focusing on what they might lack, take inventory daily of what they bring to the table. Deciding to set your attention on the positives can really change your perspective and help you see the good in each other.

5. *Is this really a big deal?* Ask yourself whether this issue is truly significant to you. Are you choosing your battles wisely? Sometimes letting go can lead to a more peaceful relationship. Take some time to journal about the things that feel overwhelming, and rate each one on a scale from one to ten. If you lost your partner tomorrow, would this issue still feel as significant? You might realize that those small decisions or character flaws aren't as big as they first appeared.

6. *The safety net.* I often envision falling off a building into a foam pit, like the ones you see in a gymnastics facility, when thinking about how I want to feel when I come to

my partner about topics that matter to me. I want us to feel we're in a safe and cushy and open space that offers a safe landing when we freely express ourselves. If you immediately react out of anger or become defensive, your partner will avoid coming to you again. You will teach them that vulnerability is not safe. Try to avoid hard and fast rules. Nothing needs to be black and white. There's nearly always room for middle ground.

7. *Respect each other's needs.* It's important to genuinely care about what matters to your partner. Are you at least attempting to see the situation through their eyes? Are you being understanding, or are you being stubborn?

But What If We're Damaged for Good?

If you're anything like the people in my sphere, you're probably fascinated by personality tests like Myers-Briggs or the Enneagram and their ability to give a generalized level of compatibility that you share with your friends or partner. I can't begin to tell you how many texts I've received from people who say something like, "Oh my gosh, Linds. It says my husband and I are completely incompatible! Are we doomed?" or "I knew we were friends for a reason; look how compatible we are!"

Listen up, friends.

A personality test is great and can help to determine certain facets of a relationship that may cause some difficulty or bring joy, but they're not the final word. These tests don't account for sanctification, growth, or the miraculous ways God can restore and transform hearts over time. Please take the results with a grain of salt; don't allow a quiz to tell you that you're a terrible match for each other.

Maybe you don't take these tests but you've convinced yourself that you and your spouse are too different, or you've both changed too much. You've thrown your hands up and are ready to call it quits. If you're feeling incompatible, discouraged, or even broken, hear this: You are not stuck. Our God is a God of redemption, of restoration, of growth. Sanctification is a lifelong process, which means our personalities, along with our capacity to love, are always evolving through his grace. A deeper compatibility between two people who are less compatible simply takes consideration, compromise, and humility.

Okay, sure, maybe you have more issues than others in your circle (or more perceived issues because they don't tell you everything that actually goes on in their marriage), but do you realize that you also have the power to shape or to completely rewrite your relationship's narrative?

I love this verse: "For where envy and self-seeking exist, confusion and every evil thing are there. But the wisdom that is from above is first pure, then peaceable, gentle, willing to yield, full of mercy and good fruits, without partiality and without hypocrisy. Now the fruit of righteousness is sown in peace by those who make peace" (James 3:16–18).

God's love is pure. It's peaceable, gentle, willing to budge, merciful, and fruitful. It's fair, equal, and not hypocritical. It's respectful and considerate. Peace comes to those who make peace.

The concept of being "without partiality" is important here.

In a fractured relationship, you may have a tendency to judge each other based on past behaviors or current frustrations. Do you ever find yourself focusing on your partner's mistakes while ignoring their strengths, allowing that negative lens to define your interactions?

Sometimes you have to strip the peeling paint, pull up the burned floorboards, and reinforce the foundation. You have to do the dirty work. Not because the whole house needs to come down but because it's worth saving.

If your marriage has been built on blame, silent resentment, performance, or past mistakes, you will not move forward if you don't clear the rubble. Because the truth is that you can't keep going in circles about who did what and when. The endless arguments, the scorekeeping, the stubborn refusal to shift your own behavior while demanding change from your spouse is exhausting, and it's dangerous.

The Enemy thrives in this kind of environment, and it can quickly become spiritual warfare.

In one of my favorite books of all time, *The Screwtape Letters*, C. S. Lewis paints a fictional picture of spiritual attack through a series of letters from a senior demon to his apprentice. At one point, he writes, "It is funny how mortals always picture us as putting things into their minds: In reality our best work is done by keeping things out."[2] That's the power of deception. The Enemy doesn't always scream lies; sometimes he simply distracts you from truth. He keeps conviction out of your mind. He numbs you to the Spirit. He keeps you focused on the other's faults, not your own. He convinces you that you're the victim, that they are the problem, and that starting over would be easier than staying.

He'll also whisper that humility is weakness, that grace is optional, and that being offended is your right. He'll tempt you to stop praying, to choose pride over surrender. And before you know it, he's gained a foothold in your mind and in your marriage.

But here's the truth the Enemy hopes you forget: "Most assuredly, I say to you, whoever commits sin is a slave of sin" (John 8:34), but "you shall know the truth, and the truth shall make you free" (v. 8:32). You don't have to live bound by bitterness. You don't have to keep dragging the destruction of the past into the new construction zone God is calling you into.

The fear of God is the beginning of knowledge (Prov. 1:7), and trusting in him is your safety net. So stop declaring defeat over your marriage. Start proclaiming freedom. Not the kind the world offers but the kind that comes from surrender. From humility. From the courage to rebuild with Jesus as the cornerstone.

The words you speak, belief systems you hold, and actions you take have the power to make or break your future.

As author and mental health expert Dr. John Delony often says, "Behavior is a language. What are they trying to tell you?"

Why I Almost Called Off Our Engagement

Jesse and I experienced a lack of alignment early on in our relationship. I remember being at the park across the street from my sister's house with Jesse. It was the day I almost called off our engagement.

We hadn't been engaged for long, and I was eager to move out of our hometown right after we got married. We were swinging on the swings next to each other, playfully talking about our upcoming wedding. Dreaming of our future, I asked him, "Where should we move?" Followed up excitedly by, "After the wedding, how soon can we pack up and go?"

Jesse looked at me, confused. I was shocked (flabbergasted) when he said, "I don't have any plans to leave here. My whole family and my entire life are here."

I immediately panicked. I abruptly stopped swinging and looked into his eyes, "Wait, what do you mean?" I asked. "I've wanted to move out of this city since I was ten years old. Not leaving isn't really an option for me."

We had completed an entire session of premarital counseling. How on earth had we bypassed this massive discussion? I wanted him to be my husband, but the thought of staying in my hometown for even another day felt suffocating. As we continued the discussion, it was evident that we were on entirely different pages. It was jarring to realize how different our visions for the future were. I had assumed the entire time that we had been dating that Jesse felt just as I did and wanted to experience a new city after graduation.

I blurted out that I didn't know if we could get married anymore. He listened patiently and told me to sit with it for a while.

For weeks upon weeks, I prayed and talked with the women I respected most in my life. I was so torn. A move for me wasn't just about new scenery; it meant more opportunity, exploration and adventure, getting outside of my comfort zone, advancement in my career, and immense personal growth. I didn't want to give it up.

At the end of a long, overly dramatic conversation about what felt like a full-blown life crisis at the time, my friends looked at me and asked, "Linds, what do you want most? Do you want Jesse, or do you want the dream of living in another city? Do you trust that God will do what's best for your family, but in his timing and not yours? If he wants you to move, he'll make that path clear. Maybe that time just isn't right this second. But you also have to face the possibility that it might never happen. At the end of the day, you still have free will. If you genuinely believe that this marriage isn't what God is calling you to, then you have a decision to make. But you need to get honest about what matters most."

I was fully aware that Jesse was irreplaceable. (Let's be honest, I definitely married up, and that would have been the biggest mistake of my life. He's a ten thousand out of ten.) When my mind was clear, I knew I wanted to be with him, and I didn't question whether I would choose him. I just had to let go of a dream I'd had for a very long time.

In the weeks that followed, Jesse and I had countless conversations. We agreed to remain in our hometown until, or if, we both felt a clear calling to move. I learned to express my feelings while respecting Jesse's stance. I realized pretty quickly that if

I spent all my time begging and pleading for him to move, and even if he agreed just to make me happy, that kind of pressure could quietly grow into resentment. If things didn't go well, it wouldn't feel like our decision, it would feel like mine. I didn't want him to resent me, and I didn't want him to move just to appease me. I wanted him to choose it because he believed in it too.

Still, those little bits of frustration would surface whenever I thought about his reluctance to budge. It made me question how to balance my longing for experience and opportunity with the reality of our partnership. How could I honor my dreams while respecting his feelings?

Your Waiting Isn't Wasted

I believe that God says one of three things in response to our prayers: yes, no, or not yet.

I realize now that the answer to my prayer often felt like a no for all those years, but in actuality, it was *Not yet, Lindsey.* As I look back now, I'm able to see how little of the picture we actually see when we're praying for something. It's a gentle reminder to me that God's timing is always perfect, even when we don't understand, and that waiting often leads to unexpected blessings.

Had we left when we got married, we would have missed so much that I couldn't have foreseen: our family surrounding us during the births of our babies, the incredible village that helped us to raise those babies, and the successful businesses that Jesse and I built, which thrived because of the support from the people in our hometown.

We wouldn't have had those deep conversations while crammed onto our friends' couches—the friends we'd known since childhood—with coffee in hand and tears streaming down our faces, our lives seemingly being held together by a thread.

This period of patience taught me that growth often comes in the waiting.

Can I remind you today that your waiting is never wasted when God is involved? Neither is the reliance you have on him or those heavy prayers lifted to him when things don't look like they're "supposed to."

Your waiting isn't wasted when praying for your partner's salvation.

Your waiting isn't wasted when adjusting to changes in intimacy.

Your waiting isn't wasted when longing for children.

Psalm 27:14 says, "Wait on the LORD; be of good courage, and he shall strengthen your heart."

If you're in a season of waiting—on restoration, on healing, or on a desire that hasn't yet come to pass—I want you to think of Joseph, who sat in a prison cell for years for something he didn't do.

He couldn't see it then, but God was positioning him for purpose, shaping his heart to hold what was coming. What very likely felt like abandonment to him was actually alignment for a future good. But it's so hard to see hope when we're stuck in the fog, isn't it?

God hasn't forgotten you. He isn't punishing you or withholding blessings until you prove yourself worthy. Scripture shows us over and over that he's a loving Father who delights in giving good gifts to his children, not because they've earned them but because he is good through and through.

He's not uncertain or indifferent when it comes to your life. He's steady, patient, and near, even when you can't feel him. In the silence, he is preparing the way and strengthening your heart for what's ahead. "And we know that in all things God works for the good of those who love him" (Rom. 8:28).

Faith isn't the guarantee of your desired outcome; it's the

quiet confidence that the heart of God, even in your uncertainty, remains kind, always working toward your ultimate good and his glory.

Even in the friction and unmet expectations, Jesus has a plan for your life. You may not see it yet, but I believe that one day you'll look back and recognize his fingerprints all over your story.

And Jesse and I were finally able to see them on our own.

Fast-forward ten years—yes, a full decade!—and we were driving down some random road when Jesse turned to me and said, "This doesn't feel like home anymore. I'm ready to move if you are." I gasped, laughed out loud, and said, "Oh my gosh. Yes! Let's leave today! Where should we go?" It felt like the weight of those years had shifted in an instant as we began talking and praying about that next life transition.

We knew that God had kept us home for a season. There was so much refinement that happened in our hearts as he prepared us for the time when we would be ready to step out on our own. Looking back now, I genuinely don't think we would have been as ready or as equipped as we were that day if we had left any sooner.

The reality is that major decisions, and even minute, daily decisions, look different for every couple. I often wonder how our lives would have played out if the moving conflict had arisen after we had already gotten married. I deeply want to support my husband and be a true helpmate in the biblical sense, walking alongside him with strength and purpose, but that doesn't mean I'm a silent partner. I have dreams too. And sometimes those dreams don't align perfectly with his. Many couples find themselves chasing two very different goals and envisioning two very different futures.

Here's a little activity for you to try. Set aside an hour with your spouse this week without phones or distractions. Ask each other this: "What's something you feel like you're missing in your life right now? Is there a dream you've set aside or a part of yourself you've been ignoring? How can I be a part of helping you fulfill the dreams God has placed on your heart?" Then really listen. Don't interrupt, defend, or fix; just hear them out. Take notes if you need to. These quiet longings often hold the key to deeper connection, healing, and understanding. From here, explore the idea of compromise, not as a concession but as a collaboration.

This is the essence of partnership: working together even when your paths seem divergent.

Spiritual Leadership and Submission

In our home, Jesse is the head of the household. I know that our society scoffs at this idea, but hear me out. His leadership is not something that crushes me, it uplifts me. It empowers me. It softens me. It makes me better because it's done out of love, not out of control.

Let's begin by touching on what leadership and submission are, as they can seem like dirty words in today's society.

First Corinthians 11:3 shows us that the ultimate design for leadership is that of the relationship between God and Jesus, which is an example of love, sacrifice, and commitment. The verse says, "The head of every man is Christ, the head of woman is man, and the head of Christ is God."

This is not a big, magnificent God standing above you and demanding you to "obey your husband, no matter what he does, how he treats you, or how he views God." Instead, he is a loving, gracious God who desires good for your life, reminding you that his first desire is to be the God of your husband, that his sights will be set on Christ, and then he will lead you.

Ephesians 5 is a chapter that helps us to understand this in a deeper way. In verses 1–2, the apostle Paul reminds us to walk in love: "Therefore be imitators of God, as beloved children. And walk in love, as Christ loved us and gave himself up for us, a fragrant offering and sacrifice to God" (ESV).

Paul continues by calling husbands to be this kind of man to their wives:

> Husbands, love your wives, just as Christ also loved the church and gave Himself for her, that He might sanctify and cleanse her with the washing of water by the word, that He might present her to Himself a glorious church, not having spot or wrinkle or any such thing, but that she should be holy and without blemish. So husbands ought to love their own wives as their own bodies; he who loves his wife loves himself. For no one ever hated his own flesh, but nourishes and cherishes it, just as the Lord does the church. For we are members of His body, of His flesh and of His bones. "For this reason a man shall leave his father and mother and be joined to his wife, and the two shall become one flesh." This is a great mystery, but I speak concerning Christ and the church. Nevertheless let each one of you in particular so love his own wife as himself, and let the wife see that she respects her husband.
>
> **—Ephesians 5:25–33**

That is a high calling—a calling that, in my opinion, would be an honor to follow. And most husbands are likely not fully living this out because they were not created as perfect men or perfect husbands. They are Christ's workmanship, being molded and sanctified every day to become complete and lacking nothing—just as wives are. But the goal is to work toward it.

Men, are you active, or are you passive? Are you active at work but passive in your home? Are you active with your kids but passive with your wife? Loving your wife as your own body is not a passive act. It's active. It's intentional. It's about showing up physically, emotionally, and spiritually.

The Bible also gives women a high calling in Ephesians 5:22–24: "Wives, submit to your own husbands, as to the Lord. For the husband is head of the wife, as also Christ is head of the church; and He is the Savior of the body. Therefore, just as the church is subject to Christ, so let the wives be to their own husbands in everything."

Again, as we look at this text, we see that this is not a call to submit to harmful or abusive dynamics. God sees this perfect design as one where a godly man who loves his wife more than his own body cares for her and leads her through life.

I absolutely love this terminology: "Husbands ought to love their own wives as their own bodies." We all take care of ourselves, don't we? If we are hungry, we grab a snack. If we need a break, we take one. If we need a shower, we make time to take one. A man is called to care for his wife in the exact same way that he takes care of himself.

True biblical submission as a wife is a posture of love, strength, and support. It means seeking unity, not uniformity, and asking, *How can I build my husband up instead of tearing him down? How can I support and trust his leadership with grace while still being honest, bold, and wise?*

In Genesis 2:18, when God says, "It is not good for man to be alone. I will make a helper suitable for him" (NIV), the Hebrew word used for *helper* is *ezer*, which is the same word used throughout the Old Testament (Ps. 33:20; 70:5; Deut. 33:29) to describe God as a powerful source of help, strength, and protection. This tells us that the role of the woman is not one of weakness or lesser value but one of vital strength, designed by God for partnership and purpose.

And just as the husband is called to do this, we see through Scripture that we as Christians are called to selflessness in the same way.

Philippians 2:3 says, "Let nothing be done through selfish

ambition or conceit, but in lowliness of mind let each esteem others better than himself."

Jesse is someone who, by choice, prioritizes my well-being above his own. He doesn't put himself first; he leads with humility and intention. He has learned that when his wife and children feel secure and cared for, peace and joy overflow into every corner of the home. As the primary nurturer of our boys, I feel protected, supported, and steady because of the way Jesse leads, and my boys are able to reap the benefits of that leadership. Unfortunately, many men today reverse this model—prioritizing their own comfort, emotions, or desires over their family's needs—and then wonder why their homes are in turmoil.

I'll be completely honest with you. If someone who argued against the concept of submission walked into my home and said, "I free you from this construct, Lindsey! You can leave now. You've been brainwashed," my first thought would be, *Oh, heck no. I don't want to be freed. My marriage is my freedom.* Because that's my reality. Jesse's leadership is not oppressive to me. It makes me stronger, more empowered, freer, and more resilient. I haven't built my career or audience or published a book from the ground up because I'm stuck under his thumb; I've done all of this because he has lifted me up on his shoulders the entire time. His belief in me (sometimes unfounded), his refusal to let me quit when I fall, and his willingness to take over anything and everything in order to help me build my life and my dreams has helped me grow into the woman I am meant to be.

I've responded to Jesse's leadership by choosing to respect him, rather than trying to control or correct him through manipulation, criticism, undermining, or comparison. I've learned that respect, both in words and actions, speaks deeply to a man's heart. It communicates value, trust, and honor. When I treat Jesse with disrespect, even unintentionally, it can feel deeply emasculating and wounding. Over time, this posture of mutual respect (and honestly, a lot of trial and error) has built a lot of trust between us. Jesse regularly seeks my input and has always told me that my voice is the most important one in his life. That mutual trust brings a sense of peace when he leads our family because I know we're both doing our best to walk with God at the forefront and with both of our hearts in mind.

When lived out well, leadership and submission can be a gift to a home.

And let's be real: These roles in marriage often look different than we expect. My husband is a quiet, intuitive leader, while I'm vocal and full of ideas. Submission hasn't come easily for me, and I know many of you might feel the same way. This dynamic will likely look different in our home than it does in yours because we're all unique. Leadership and submission aren't one size fits all. I lead my boys in Bible study, speak up more than Jesse in community groups, and am usually the one heading our attendance at church because that's a strength of mine. For a time, I resented it, but I've come to realize that Jesse leads them in ways I can't match. His character, quiet wisdom, and one-on-one man-to-man conversations he shares with our boys are irreplaceable. It's a reminder that leadership doesn't always look the same in every home.

First Peter 3:1 reminds us wives to maintain our faith, even when our partners may not share it. Even if one partner doesn't attend church, you can still remain faithful to what God has called you to, setting a strong example of faithfulness for your kids.

The reality is that most husbands or wives won't perfectly embody these ideals. Grace upon grace. We're all works in progress.

But what if the spiritual aspect gets thrown to the wayside because you're so weighed down?

The mental load, the behind-the-scenes work of managing

not just tasks but feelings, expectations, and relationships can quietly build over time. And when it falls unevenly, which it often does, it doesn't just exhaust the one carrying it; it shifts the balance of the entire relationship.

Who Bears the Emotional Burden?

I discuss emotional labor regularly in my work because it has an immense impact on so many aspects of a marriage, such as intimacy, bitterness, partnership, and even how seen or valued each person feels in the relationship. Emotional labor is the work of keeping things running smoothly in the household. It's the mental load of planning, anticipating needs, and resolving issues. It's also the invisible work of maintaining a positive emotional climate in the home.

When one partner is constantly managing the mental and emotional logistics of family life, it can lead to deep resentment, exhaustion, and a sense of being alone in something that was meant to be shared. Over time, it doesn't just affect how much someone is doing, it affects how connected they feel. The person who carries the majority of the emotional load is the one who tends to remember birthdays, makes sure their parents and in-laws are contacted regularly, schedules medical and dental appointments, buys holiday gifts for teachers, plans time to spend with friends, and buffers the family from external stresses. They're the emotional thermostat, always adjusting the temperature to make sure all is right all the time.

This is a heavy burden for one person to carry.

Who carries the majority of the emotional load in your home? Research indicates that couples with an equitable division of emotional labor report higher levels of satisfaction and stability. An imbalance in this area is a red flag and is bound to create some burning flames in the foundation of your home.

But when both partners feel that their time and effort are seen and valued, the flames are quickly extinguished.

Emotional Labor and Your Sex Life

I mentioned that emotional labor directly impacts intimacy. This is one of the most common and constant complaints I hear from the people in my community. My inboxes are filled with messages like, "My partner never helps with anything; it's like I'm parenting another child. I don't understand how they can expect sex after I've been whined at, poked, and prodded all day."

Nobody wants to have sex with someone they feel like they're having to parent. Few things are more unsexy, am I right? They want a partner. A teammate. Someone who gets ahead of the needs of the household without having to be told what to do.

You can probably relate to feeling less desirous of physical affection when you feel emotionally depleted from all of the day's tasks. Naturally so. Your sex drive didn't die; it has been buried beneath a pile of laundry, unanswered texts, and sticky toddler fingers. It's hard to feel open to physical affection when you're overwhelmed and exhausted by the demands of parenting and household management. Addressing this imbalance can alleviate the strain that affects your intimacy.

So how can you bridge this responsibility gap so that you can get your sexy libido back and also be less stressed out? The answer: task lists.

Step 1: Make your task lists. Each partner takes fifteen minutes to quietly reflect on the past week. Write down all the tasks you handled, both big and small. Consider chores like cleaning, laundry, grocery shopping, and meal planning. Don't forget about things like scheduling appointments, planning family events, and managing finances. Also, include the emotional labor you've done, such as listening to your partner, offering support, resolving conflicts between siblings, and helping manage kids' emotions. As you list these tasks, note how each one made you feel, whether it was stress, frustration, joy, or satisfaction.

Step 2: Discuss the lists without defensiveness. Once you've made your lists, share them with each other in a supportive way. Don't assign blame and don't allow defensiveness into the conversation. Discuss the tasks you've both handled and focus on a few key points: Which tasks are shared equally? Which are taken on most often by only one of you? It's also helpful to talk about the emotional impact of each task so you can better understand each other's perspectives.

Step 3: Balance the workload. Next, think about the tasks that one of you consistently handles and the emotional weight those tasks carry. Discuss how you can redistribute responsibilities more fairly. Brainstorm together and create a concrete plan for sharing tasks, including specific actions and deadlines to keep you both accountable.

Don't forget to check in with each other! Agree on a system for checking in, ideally once a week or during your Sunday Meeting, to see how things are going and to make any necessary adjustments.

In partnership, the road is bound to be occasionally bumpy. You will have disagreements, differences in perspective, and moments when it feels like you're not on the same page. But that's where the strength of your commitment lies.

Balance may not be possible, but harmony is. So keep choosing to walk forward together. She is your woman, he is your man. God didn't make a mistake when you chose one another and committed for life. True partnership isn't about never facing difficulty or conflict but about choosing to repair it together with trust, patience, and love as your anchors.

CHAPTER 13

MONEY IS A SPIRITUAL ISSUE—AND A DIVORCE ISSUE

If you worship money, it will eat you alive.

—John Mark Comer

When I moved to Franklin, Tennessee, I was hit square in the face by the wealth all around me—maybe *punched* is a better word. I didn't realize how much something like money could affect the state of my heart and my spiritual health. Many days I felt knocked breathless by my desire for more and a gnawing sense of inadequacy.

In those moments, I found myself thinking, *Lindsey, you came here for quality of life. To build community and invest in your family. Not to hustle endlessly. Not to compare your worth to others' or chase after every material possession. You came here to live.*

We had more than we'd ever had in our lives, but every time

I caught a glimpse of someone who had what I wanted, it suddenly felt like what God had already given us wasn't enough. My soul was being battered by my own wants—my desperation to live in that neighborhood, to drive that car, and to have a home that looked like that.

Gross, right? But as ungrateful as I knew I was being, I couldn't shake it.

I wanted it too badly.

I vividly remember one evening when I was desperate to crawl out of my skin, overwhelmed by the weight of this struggle. I jumped into a scalding hot shower and prayed, *Remove this from me, Lord. Enough has never been enough for me. I'm always seeking, always chasing, always striving, always wanting. I want you to be enough. I want to be content. Rid me of this unfulfilling desire, this need for control and the anxiety it brings. I don't want it.*

And yet just a few hours later, I found myself mindlessly scrolling on my phone, yearning for a car that looked nicer than the new one I'd bought just weeks before.

Jesse and I both found ourselves caught in a cycle of obsessing over our wants, fixated on growing our savings, and constantly chasing the idea that just a little more would finally feel like enough. It wasn't always the material items, either. Sometimes it was just the desire to pad our bank account, hoping that more security would bring more peace. We poured ourselves into working longer hours and adding to our investment portfolio, but instead of bringing peace, it only created more tension and pressure between us.

We quickly realized that enough would never feel like enough if we continued treating money like our god.

For many in today's society, this relentless, persistent pursuit for money or success only leads to wanting more. Once we get one thing, we find ourselves wanting another. The thirst is never quenched.

The Hedonic Treadmill

Have you ever heard of the hedonic treadmill? This psychological theory was first proposed by Canadian psychologist Philip Brickman and American psychologist Donald Campbell in their 1971 paper "Hedonic Relativism and Planning the Good Society."[1]

It has completely changed my life and the way I perceive my needs and successes, so I hope it changes you in the same way. This concept suggests that a person's level of happiness tends to return to its baseline after experiencing major changes, regardless of whether they are positive or negative.

Also known as "hedonic adaptation," the theory suggests that even when we achieve something we've long desired, such as a raise, a new home, weight loss, or a personal milestone, we will be happy for a short time but will eventually go back to the same level of happiness we started with.

In relationships this plays out when we tie our happiness to external events or accomplishments, thinking that once we reach that next goal, we'll feel more fulfilled. But the truth is, we often return to our original emotional "set point" after a period of adjustment. We're still left searching for that deeper, lasting satisfaction.

As economist Henry George once said, "Humans are the only animals whose desires increase as they are fed."

Unlike other creatures that seek to meet their basic needs and then find contentment, we humans have an insatiable appetite for more.

This cycle raises a critical question: Are you better off when you get that thing, or are you caught up in a never-ending pursuit?

Maybe you're waiting for your tax return to help you reach your emergency fund goal, but before it even arrives, you spend it all. Or there's the scenario where you receive a check that boosts your account to $10,000, and your immediate thought is, "Okay, now I want $15,000."

The issue is that we often look to money as our source of happiness and peace. The hedonic treadmill is proof that money will never satisfy that need. But when we find ourselves lacking or feeling out of control, that seriously harms our marriages.

Consider how this relentless desire shapes our lives. We spend countless hours and resources striving for things that promise happiness but often leave us feeling emptier. This phenomenon not only pertains to material possessions, it also seeps into our relationships, ambitions, and self-worth. It's often why we find ourselves comparing our lives with others', feeling inadequate because someone else seems to have it all figured out.

The Number-Two Cause of Divorce

Finances hold immense power in marriages, and not only because they provide your livelihood.

1. Finances reflect your deeper values and priorities. Disagreements about spending, saving, and financial goals often reveal the fundamental differences in how you view your life together. For instance, one spouse may prioritize experiences like travel, while the other focuses on retirement savings. This clash of values can lead to conflicts that extend far beyond money.

2. Financial stress is a major source of anxiety. Financial difficulties, like debt or unexpected expenses, breed a sense of insecurity, which often manifests as frustration, resentment, or blame, preventing fruitful communication.

3. Money-related issues can create a power imbalance. One partner earning significantly more than the other can create feelings of inadequacy or dependence. The financial imbalance often leads to tension and resentment, with the less financially secure partner feeling marginalized or controlled.

4. The fear of financial instability can lead to avoidance and further problems. When couples face financial uncertainty, the fear can feel suffocating. To cope, they might stop talking about money altogether, thinking that ignoring the issue will make it disappear. But that avoidance usually backfires. It creates a wall of silence that breeds mistrust instead of resolving the problem.

Without honest conversations, misunderstandings pile up. One partner might feel frustrated that the other is overspending on things like takeout or new clothes, while the other feels unfairly judged. This silence can lead to anxiety and resentment as each person struggles with their fears alone.

5. A lack of support in managing finances creates strain. Handling all the budgeting or keeping track of finances can be a lot for one partner to carry on their own. This imbalance often causes stress and leads to frustration or resentment because the person managing it all feels the pressure piling up.

At the same time, the less involved partner might feel out of the loop or unsure about where things stand, which can create its own anxiety. It's like trying to carry a heavy bag solo: It's exhausting and eventually wears you down. Sharing the weight makes it easier on both of you.

6. Imbalanced power dynamics cause harm. When partners don't share a bank account and one person controls the finances, it creates a power dynamic that can seriously undermine trust. Y'all, if you're sharing a life and a bed, you should definitely be sharing a bank account. Regardless of whether one or both partners work, having equal access to your finances is important. Anything less can tip into financial abuse.

In this situation, the partner with limited access may feel sidelined in important financial decisions, leading to a sense of powerlessness. This lack of transparency can erode the teamwork that's crucial for a healthy relationship, resulting in heightened anxiety and tension around money.

The reason all of this matters is that finances are deeply intertwined with emotions, values, and trust. Couples who aren't communicative and don't share mutual respect regarding money often find themselves on a path toward division.

Financial strain is one of the most potent destroyers of marriage.

There's a reason finances are the number-two cause of divorce in America and the leading source of conflict in relationships. It's not just the stress that money issues create, it's also the heart issue. Money can drive a wedge between partners faster than almost anything else.

If we don't learn to manage our hearts and attitudes toward money, we risk losing control not just of our finances but of our relationships too.

Here's the truth about the love of money and material things: You'll thirst for them endlessly unless you let the grace and power of God quench that desire. The Bible is clear that "no one can serve two masters; for either he will hate the one and love the other, or else he will be loyal to the one and despise the other. You cannot serve God and [money]" (Matt. 6:24).

Have you felt this truth too? It may hit you as you walk through your city, passing those shiny cars.

It may happen as you scroll on your phone screen and see that "perfect" kitchen.

Or maybe it feels heavy when you look over the fence at friends enjoying extravagant vacations and piles of Christmas presents, or see the ease with which they enroll their children in camps and sports.

You may be a husband feeling like you're not living up to the standards set by other men, or a wife grappling with feelings of failure because you aren't contributing financially.

Here's the truth: There will always be someone out there doing better than you—a wealthier friend, a family member with fewer struggles, or someone who seems to lead a life of abundance.

(They could also just be in an enormous amount of hidden debt, so be cautious about who you compare yourself with!)

You cannot buy your way to peace, and no amount of savings will guarantee your happiness.

The reality is, if your castle—your success, your home, your reputation—remains the main thing, it's bound to burn down eventually. God must always be the main thing, and when he is, it brings freedom.

If God Says Something Two Thousand Times

A while back, I popped into an estate sale with my sister. Cars lined the street, so we figured it was worth a look. As soon as we stepped inside, we were met by a house overflowing with stuff—so, so much stuff.

I learned this was the home of a woman who had spent her lifetime collecting earthly treasures, treasures she had spent decades caring for, doting on, cleaning, and tidying up. Now her time on earth was over, and her home was swarming with strangers sifting through her beloved possessions, bargaining over what once held great meaning in her life.

Matthew 6:19–20 tells us, "Do not lay up for yourselves treasures on earth, where moth and rust destroy and where thieves break in and steal; but lay up for yourselves treasures in heaven, where neither moth nor rust destroys and where thieves do not break in and steal."

When we take a moment to reflect, it becomes clear that we often allow our marriages to be jeopardized by things that will absolutely, without a doubt, disappear.

We've all heard it before, but it bears repeating: On our deathbeds, we will absolutely not be wishing we'd had a bigger house, prettier clothes, a longer list of awards, or more cars.

The struggle doesn't revolve solely around wanting to be wealthy; it's also about relieving stress related to money and the desire to be comfortable. But paycheck-to-paycheck living often happens because of lifestyle creep, which occurs when we adjust our spending to match our income. As our earnings rise, so do our expenses. Freedom comes when we keep our spending in check regardless of how much our pay increases.

Did you know that one out of every ten verses in the New Testament addresses money? I was blown away the first time I learned that. A staggering 25 percent of Jesus' teachings focus on financial resources.

For a little perspective, in Scripture there are more than five hundred verses about faith and five hundred about prayer.

Guess how many verses there are about money? More than two thousand.

If God mentions something two thousand times, clearly he wants us to pay attention.

In a sermon by Pastor Matt Chandler, a teacher I've followed for more than sixteen years, he points out that while Jesus spoke extensively about money, he never asked for any. Jesus didn't request offerings or try to leverage generosity for personal gain. Chandler humorously notes, "Jesus didn't say, 'Hey guys, I could be so much more effective in my deity if I just had a chariot that would take me to the outer reaches.'"[2]

Can you imagine? What a different tone that would have set.

Instead, Jesus walked alongside the people, showing that true power and purpose don't come from status or luxury. He prioritized connection over comfort. He wasn't after people's resources, he was always after their hearts. Yet today many prosperity-gospel pastors seem to think they need private jets, lavish mansions, and designer suits to spread the Word. They urge congregants to sow "seeds" of faith, often in the form of hefty donations, with promises of abundant returns.

It's all a heart issue.

In the same teaching, Pastor Matt goes on to say, "In the Sermon on the Mount, Jesus is ruthlessly addressing the heart, not just the action. He wants your heart, because the fruit of a transformed heart is true action."

God goes beyond surface behavior and dives into our motivations. He wants our hearts, because that's where change begins. The Christian life is not about merely avoiding sin or performing good deeds as an act or a show, it's about cultivating a heart that reflects God's love.

Money intertwines with our lives in ways that can be either toxic and destructive or liberating and life giving.

The choice is ours to make.

Show Me Your Bank Statements and I'll Show You What Matters to You

Matthew 6:21 reminds us, "For where your treasure is, there your heart will be also."

If you think about it, no one is as dishonest with you as you are with yourself. Nobody lies to you as frequently, as perfectly, or as insistently as you do. You might be able to talk about your values, what you treasure, and what you're passionate about, but this verse in Matthew essentially says, *That's all great. Now let me see your credit-card statements.*

Tim Keller says, "Money flows effortlessly to that which is its god." Your money will flow easily to whatever you worship. The way we handle our money reflects the state of our hearts. Our spending patterns reveal what we value most. So when you look at your budget or monthly spending, where does the majority go? Is it on food, clothes, beauty, generous gifts, tithing, or dining out? These choices indicate your priorities; they highlight what matters most to you.

If you haven't done so lately, I encourage you to sit down with your spouse and review where your money is going. What do your statements reveal about what matters to each of you? Jesse and I each use reloadable cash cards for our personal spending so we can track our habits and hold healthy boundaries for ourselves. We look through the statements at the end of each month, and oftentimes we see the things that we are prioritizing, or even idolizing, in that season of life. Do our habits align with what we say matters most?

Is there a shift that needs to happen in your home?

As you consider having these conversations, remember that living in alignment with God's calling extends to how we handle our finances. Proverbs 11:25 reminds us of this: "A generous person will prosper; whoever refreshes others will be refreshed" (NIV).

Generosity: The Antidote to Financial Anxiety

Generosity has played a huge role in our lives. In our first year of marriage, right after I graduated from college, we were living in a modest thousand-square-foot home and just scraping by. But as we looked around, we noticed others who were struggling even more. It weighed heavily on my heart to help them, to offer some relief, but honestly, I didn't know where to begin. So I started praying.

As time passed, I felt a growing excitement about a ministry idea: blessing families in need during the holidays or when they were facing financial struggles. I hadn't felt that kind of enthusiasm in a long time, so I turned to Jesse and asked if he'd join me.

We started brainstorming and eventually crafted a plan. Our mission was to anonymously deliver groceries, gift cards, and essentials like toilet paper and toothpaste, and to always include a toy or two for the kids. It felt incredible to take that step and spread a little joy and relief where we could. We began with a budget of $100 every few months and gradually increased it from there.

We had never been as broke as we were then, but our desire to give only grew stronger. We had to make sure we didn't go broke in the name of generosity (and we definitely pushed the limit a few times!), but God opened the door for friends and family to join us. They started contributing, whether financially or with their time, and it turned into a beautiful opportunity for both ministry and connection.

Let me tell you something: This ranks in the top five most life-giving experiences in my life. No competition. It completely changed my perspective on money. The more I earned, the more I wanted to give. And I've found that the more I give, the more the Lord provides.

Generosity is a powerful antidote to financial anxiety. Tithing is a wonderful starting point, but it's just the beginning. It may seem paradoxical, but the act of giving, even when funds are tight, creates a shift in our lives, an others-centered mindset.

Giving money away doesn't always feel like the obvious choice. Sometimes I hold mine with such a tight fist that God has to gently pry it open through conviction. Growing up, I had a scarcity mindset about money, even though my dad modeled generosity for me. (I watched him actually give the clothes off his back more times than I could count when I was a young girl.) The only thing that truly changed my heart was the love of Jesus. The older I've gotten and the more I've accumulated, the more I've realized how empty it all really is.

Like actor Jim Carrey once said, "I think everybody should get rich and famous and do everything they ever dreamed of so they can see that it's not the answer."

What would your life look like if you began to loosen your

grip on your successes and the external validation that comes with them? What if you reject the idea that material things define your worth and instead focus on giving more and more each year?

Imagine redefining your success not by what you own but by what you share.

The impact generosity has on a family is powerful. It draws you closer together, softens the edges of stress and striving, and reminds you every day that everything you have in life isn't even yours. It's God's. We've experienced firsthand that when you invite your children into that lifestyle of giving, their hearts start to expand too. God has entrusted what we have to us, and with so much need in the world, who are we to hold it all tightly to ourselves?

Take a moment to think about whether you have the capacity to bless others. I'm fully aware that a paycheck-to-paycheck lifestyle doesn't leave much wiggle room for generosity, and I don't want to minimize that reality. But it's also worth asking: Are there choices in your life that are quietly crowding out the opportunity to give? If you're living in a house you can't afford, driving a car that stretches your budget, taking daily trips to Target, or buying seven-dollar coffees every day, it's important to reflect on what those choices say about your financial priorities. Generosity doesn't have to be a hundred-dollar gesture; it's less about the amount and more about your heart behind it.

Also, please hear my heart, y'all. I'm not here to knock your coffee habit, primarily because then I'd have to confront my own, but also because you likely work very hard for the income you have. My weekly (okay, sometimes daily) latte run is life giving. I just want to encourage you to regularly reevaluate what matters. My heart behind all of this is simple. I care about your growth. I care about your healing. I care that, at the end of your life, you can look back and feel proud of the life you lived. And my hope is to keep nudging you toward becoming the best version of yourself, one choice at a time.

A few simple ideas for starters: As a small act of love, could you send the money you'd spend on a coffee to someone who needs it more than you do today? Could you sell your car or minimize the things in your home to afford more opportunities for generosity? Downsizing could not only lighten your load but also free up funds that can be used to help others.

Our treasures are meant to be stored up in heaven, not on our shelves or in our drawers.

In Ecclesiastes 2:10–11, Solomon says this: "Whatever my eyes desired I did not keep from them. I did not withhold my heart from any pleasure, for my heart rejoiced in all my labor. . . . Then I looked on all the works that my hands had done and on the labor in which I had toiled; and indeed all was vanity and grasping for the wind. There was no profit under the sun."

Solomon had wealth, wisdom, and power, and yet he still wasn't satisfied. Today, even if you earn just two dollars a day, you're already doing better financially than more than 650 million people around the world. Let that sink in. If you have food, a roof over your head, and even a little left over, you're among the wealthiest percentage of the global population. And yet like Solomon, so many of us are still aching for more.

Gosh, how quickly it all fades away. I look back at some of my most expensive purchases from the past, and I don't even own most of those items anymore. Or they're stuffed in the back of my closet. Jesse and I argued repeatedly over many of those purchases early in our marriage, only to find ourselves pushing each other away over things that decay.

We made countless mistakes with our finances early on. As we started our careers, we were allured by money and fell into debt chasing shiny things. We took out loans for cars instead of paying cash and bought new gaming systems, TVs, furniture, and more. At the time, we didn't consider the consequences; we considered only what was right in front of us.

But this behavior only increased our stress and left us feeling more disconnected.

Financial strain is a significant contributor to mental-health issues as well, including suicidal thoughts. A study analyzing 34,653 US adults reported that individuals experiencing significant financial stressors, such as debt, unemployment, homelessness, or low income, were up to twenty times more likely to attempt suicide than those who didn't face any of these challenges.[3]

Financial strain isn't to be taken lightly.

Let's Talk Debt

"Owe no one anything except to love one another, for he who loves another has fulfilled the law" (Rom. 13:8). We aren't encouraged toward a debt-free lifestyle to punish or constrain us. It's meant to set us free.

Have you ever met someone in massive debt who feels even a hint of freedom? Probably not. They're trapped, and if you've experienced financial struggles yourself, you know this sense of enslavement all too well. It breeds anxiety, discord in relationships, and a constant weight of overwhelm and stress. This bondage suffocates everything.

And so many people in today's world are in debt or living paycheck to paycheck simply because of the desire to "keep up." And yet what does that do? It only puts them behind for their future.

We cannot serve both God and money. We will hate one and love the other (Matt. 6:24).

When our minds and lives are consumed with controlling every penny or chasing after more, we lose sight of our reliance on God. We forget that he gives and takes away, that he is the source of all good things. He can be trusted to care for us, but we aren't meant to take advantage of his provision.

Financial strain causes us to feel lost with no way out. We grow more and more overwhelmed by the bills coming in, the medical emergency we now have to pay for, the car that we shouldn't have purchased. You get the gist. Eventually, we grow weary of the stress, unable to contain it, and take it out on the people we love the most—usually our spouses.

The gravity of this situation prompts an important question: If you have debt, are you willing to wage war on it for the sake of your relationship?

This challenge goes beyond sticking to a budget; it requires owning up to the habits that have led you here. Think about those little purchases you laughed off or the sales you "couldn't resist." They're all part of a tangled web that pulls you deeper into financial strain. "Babe, it's five thousand dollars, but technically, it's only $208 a month if I pay it for the next two years of our lives. You only live once!"

But you're spending money you don't have.

The real danger of this type of financing, or any debt, is that you're assuming you'll be in a better financial position six months from now than you are today. But you're actually putting yourself in a worse position.

Being in debt, no matter the amount, robs you of hope for the future.

Consider this: America is one of the wealthiest countries in history, yet we are also the most in-debt and, troublingly, the most depressed. Depression is often rooted in a loss of hope.

I've been able to witness firsthand the joy that can come when living well financially. I was incredibly fortunate to be raised by a mom who stewarded her money with wisdom and purpose. From as early as I can remember, she taught me to spend only what I had—never more. She always knew exactly where every dollar was going and made decisions with intention and the goal of honoring God and her family. Her intentionality has paid off because she is now completely debt-free and, more important, free to focus on what truly matters most in her life.

There's nothing wrong with treating yourself to nice things. But when you're able to pay for them in full, without added stress or overwhelm, it brings a sense of peace and hope—rather than the heavy feeling of always playing catch-up.

Delayed Gratification

As parents, we have the important role of teaching our kids about delayed gratification, but we must also be willing to practice it ourselves. When we don't get something easily or quickly, we often develop a deeper appreciation for it when it finally arrives. This leads to genuine joy in the things we've waited for or worked hard to earn.

For example, we recently took Sutton and Saxon to downtown Franklin for dinner. After we finished eating, we saw the waitress delivering a dessert to the table next to us. It wasn't a dessert the boys were particularly fond of, but they immediately started asking for it simply because they knew they could have it right away.

I reminded them that we had just picked up their favorite ice cream from our local custard shop and that it was waiting for them at home in the freezer. They looked at each other, calculating and plotting, eyes filled with sugar temptation, and said, "We'll just get this dessert!"

I reminded them—again—of one of our regular lessons about delayed gratification. Just because something is available right now doesn't mean it's the better option. Still, the choice was theirs. They chose the restaurant dessert. And as soon as they took their first bite, they sheepishly looked up and said, "This isn't even that good."

We told them we understood, but they had to stick with the dessert because it was the choice they made.

When Jesse and I got home, we ended up eating the ice cream ourselves (savage, I know), and the boys were so bummed. They realized that the restaurant dessert wasn't worth it. It was just a quick fix.

That night, we talked more about how quick decisions can feel exciting in the moment, especially when they promise instant satisfaction. But that doesn't mean they're the best choice. I reminded them that what we really want—what's truly worth it—usually takes time. Whether in relationships, goals, or our walk with God, the things that matter most are very rarely on the quickest or easiest path.

That moment at the restaurant reminded me how easily we can fall into the same trap, even as grown adults. We chase what's right in front of us simply because it's available, not because it's what we truly want.

The issue of covetousness is significant here. Coveting can be defined as "an overwhelming desire for something that consumes us until we possess it." I'm sure you can recall that one thing you desperately wanted—like it owned you until you could finally own it.

I remember telling a friend that I hadn't even known some products existed until I came across them on social media, and then I felt like I couldn't live without them.

Gingerbread slippers for Christmas? I've never needed anything more.

Snail mucin eye cream? If it's from a snail and snails are slimy, it's got to be good enough to achieve glassy skin.

A fabric shaver? So satisfying. TikTok made me do it.

Tell me I'm not alone here. I keep buying these ridiculous things I never knew I needed just because they're right in front of me or because someone else has them.

But we have to draw the line somewhere. We don't have to settle for unhealthy habits just because they've become familiar. Impulse purchases, or those that leave us in debt—especially when we know, deep down, they're wasteful—are a clear example of not stewarding our money wisely. Not only does debt burden you but it also burdens your marriage, creating unnecessary tension and stress that takes away from the peace and partnership you're working to build.

Colossians 3:5 urges us to "put to death therefore what is earthly in you" (ESV), reminding us that covetousness is idolatry. When we allow possessions to become idols and let others dictate how we spend our money, we're straying from what God deems good and true.

If you lean into even 10 percent of what God says about managing money, your life will likely move toward financial freedom. God doesn't want your marriage to be suffocated by financial burdens, and that's exactly why you need to reclaim your hope and take back control.

So how do you do that?

1. Live Below Your Means

Jesse and I joke all the time that out of thousands of years and countless ancestors, not one of them managed to get it together enough to make us multimillionaires. What the heck! Ha! But in all seriousness, maybe that's part of the beauty of where we are. We weren't handed financial ease; we're building it together. We're learning how to steward what we've been given, not just for ourselves but for our kids and their future.

You may not be working with a family trust fund either, and may find yourselves living above your means because you've become discontented with what you have, drifting away from the life God intends for you. Instead of appreciating his provision, you chase after more—more space, more money, more status—rationalizing your choices along the way.

Thoughts may swirl in your mind: *If only I had a bigger house. If only I didn't have that bill. If only I could drive that nicer car.* Yet you quickly realize these desires don't bring the satisfaction you seek.

Nothing changes, and you remain trapped in a cycle of discontentment.

The idea that you just need to make more money is a distraction. The reality is that, at least for now, extra income isn't a certainty. What you can control is your contentment and your spending habits.

When we embrace gratitude for what we have and live below our means, we experience a lot more peace and rest.

2. Grit Your Teeth and Do It Together

If you're struggling financially, it's essential to recognize that money affects both partners differently. For many women, money represents security, while for men, it often relates to self-esteem. This difference can either tear you apart or build you up during what may be some of the most challenging moments of your lives.

Wives: Many men carry a quiet but heavy sense of responsibility when it comes to providing for their families. Even if they don't express it out loud, financial struggles often hit their pride and sense of purpose deeply. If your husband is trying, even if progress feels slow, he likely doesn't need reminders of where things are falling short. He already feels it. What he may need more is your belief in him. Encourage him. Remind him that he's capable and that you're with him, not against him.

But I also want to say this: If your spouse is neglecting responsibility—if he has become complacent or careless with his role in the home—it's okay to lovingly name that. Encouragement doesn't mean enabling, and God has called you to be a helpmate. Your wisdom and discernment matter. You can both challenge and support one another. Speak life into who he could be while still being honest about what needs to change. That's what partnership looks like.

Husbands: It's important to understand that when money feels tight, women can often begin to feel anxious and unsafe. There's often a deeper fear underneath financial stress: *Are we going to be okay? Can I trust that you see this and won't leave me to carry the weight alone?*

In moments like this, consistent emotional and physical reassurance matters. But more than that, what she's really looking for is presence and partnership. She doesn't need perfection or instant solutions, she needs a spouse who's in it with her.

It's likely that the financial strain isn't entirely one person's fault. The primary question remains: Who's going to lead your family forward now?

If you haven't already, you both need to eliminate finger-pointing and commit to working together toward shared responsibility. Ask God for wisdom, for provision, and for clarity. Tithe faithfully, even when it feels uncomfortable. Trust that God will care for you, just as he cares for the sparrows and the lilies. And take action. There's no benefit in ignoring the issue or numbing out. Peace and clarity come from doing the work and paying attention.

So hold hands, grit your teeth, and resist the urge to tear each other down. Don't throw fuel on the fire. Remember, you're on the same team.

3. Create a Plan

Creating a budget that accounts for every dollar won't change your debt, but it will give you a plan to go to war on your debt.

Start by assessing your situation. List all income, bills, and debts, and track your spending for at least a month to see where your money goes. Next, categorize expenses into those that are fixed (like a mortgage and utilities) and those that are variable (like entertainment and dining out). Set realistic goals for each category and adjust as necessary.

Start by trimming unnecessary expenses such as a Netflix subscription or an expensive gym membership. Sacrifice in a season of financial trial is necessary and important.

Sometimes the reality is that you simply need help. When you confront your financial reality, asking for help can feel awkward or even shameful. Talking about money can feel so taboo, especially if you were raised never to discuss it with others. But keeping silent often leads us to believe that we're alone in our struggles. When we reach out for support, we're most likely to encounter grace, accountability, and a desire to help us improve our situation.

Shame has no place in a life dedicated to growth.

We live in a time filled with endless opportunities to earn money online, leveraging the gifts and skills we already have. Taking action as a couple will not only boost your self-esteem but also strengthen your confidence in yourself and in each other.

There's more at stake than just your money. Your financial choices reveal what you're truly placing your faith in and what you're prioritizing. But even more than that, they reveal the condition of your heart and the unity, or division, within your home.

The path you choose begins with awareness. It continues with humility. And it flourishes through the act of coming together, praying together, and the daily decision to wisely steward what you've been given. Acting wisely isn't solely for survival but is for the legacy you're building together as a couple and as a family. Because when your heart is aligned with God and your priorities are aligned with each other, even your bank account can become a place of worship, restoration, and growth.

CHAPTER 14

GUARDING YOUR GLASS HOUSE

SECRETS, SEX, AND RADICAL TRANSPARENCY

> Vulnerability is the first thing I look for in you,
> but it's the last thing I want you to see in me.
>
> —Brené Brown

Intimacy, whether emotional, spiritual, or physical, requires great vulnerability.

When Jesse and I were still friends, he said something to me that I had never heard from a man before. It was the one sentence that made me truly lean in and believe his many claims that we would get married one day.

His words were profound. "Lindsey," he said, "my life is a glass house when it comes to you. I don't have any secrets from you. You can ask me anything that's on your mind, anything that feels confusing or unclear, and I will tell you the truth."

I had never been offered that level of transparency before. Even now, in my thirties, I'm amazed that a nineteen-year-old was so willing to be transparent, honest, and vulnerable.

I spent a lot of time reflecting on that idea of a glass house. Having been in many toxic relationships before—full of dishonesty, cheating with far too many of my "friends," and jam packed with secrecy, locked phones, and hidden lies—I had never experienced such openness. Most of this was before social media, and I can't imagine how much more complicated it would have been had that been as prevalent when I was in high school.

I was ready for something different.

A glass house in marriage represents a relationship built on transparency, openness, and honesty. It leaves nothing to the imagination, and in the same way, a healthy marriage should be just as crystal clear. No secrets, no silent resentments, no deception hiding in the corners.

In a glass-house marriage, trust is built through daily transparency, as both partners are open about their thoughts, feelings, and actions, eliminating doubts and suspicions. Is it too bold to say that you may never truly experience deep intimacy or trust in your marriage if you don't have radical transparency? I don't think so. I believe it with my whole heart. Secrets are one of the Enemy's most effective tools; he will use them to destroy even the best things by eroding connection, sowing division, and making room for shame to take root. Whether you're rebuilding some rooms in your marriage or you're newly married, honesty is not optional. It's not a punishment to live honestly, it's freedom.

When everything is out in the open, you aren't having to walk on eggshells, making assumptions, or constantly wondering if your spouse is telling you the truth. It's exhausting to live that way. Transparency creates a safe place for hard conversations, for growth, and for grace.

Let me ask you this: Does your spouse need more respect than you're showing them right now? Are you loving them in the way God has called you to love them, with selflessness and sacrifice? Are you honoring the Golden Rule that we all learned in our elementary school classrooms and treating them how you would like to be treated? At the office? On your phone? When everyone is sleeping? Are you honoring them in private, just as you should in public?

If you're praying and working toward restoring a godly relationship, you have to ask yourself, *Do I have secrets I need to confess or wounds I need to address?*

As I've continuously worked toward building stronger character in my own life, I've come to understand that integrity is about being honest even when it's really difficult and, honestly, sometimes seemingly impossible. It's about living truthfully, not just when others are watching but behind closed doors and in the quiet moments when no one else is around.

God doesn't call us toward convenience or comfort, he calls us toward holiness. And that means telling the truth even when it costs you something. I do realize that the cost of honesty could be monumental for many of you. However, whether or not you choose to be honest shouldn't depend on how much you think your spouse deserves it or whether you feel ready to take the risk. It's living in a way that aligns with your values and your integrity and living a holy and blameless life for the glory of God, even when it's hard.

And just as a glass house needs regular maintenance to stay in top shape, so does your marriage need consistent attention. If you let things slide, it's like allowing dust to settle on a beautiful glass surface; over time, it clouds the view, making everything look foggy and unclear. The Windex of Life (give me some grace on this analogy, okay?) is honesty. And it keeps those windows sparkling clean; you have to regularly polish up your communication, vulnerability, and honesty.

Living in a glass house means that every action and word contributes to a sense of safety and trust. It allows your marriage to become a safe space.

If I could put my foot down on one stance that I believe transforms a relationship, it would be this: The feeling of safety is one of the most healing aspects of marriage. It is also one of the primary keys to a fulfilling relationship. In a safe marriage, living out your God-given roles is a joy rather than a burden.

Do you feel safe enough to soften and lean into your relationship?

Write down the areas within your relationship where you feel safe.

Write down the areas where you feel unsafe.

When your house is glass, when secrets have been voiced, when repentance is active, when humility and God remain at the core of how you live, you clearly see the beauty of marriage and the joy you have in each other. Transparency is the house where trust can live.

Digital Boundaries in Marriage

Digital boundaries play a huge role in establishing safety. In today's world of online distraction and temptation, keeping our phones open and accessible is a big part of feeling emotionally safe. When transparency and trust are the standard, sharing access to each other's phones helps to ease worries or doubts.

Social media often plays a role in many divorces today, with some people admitting that they often look online for signs of their partner's unfaithfulness.

Here are a few practical steps you can take with your phones to cultivate an environment that honors both God and your spouse:

What's Mine Is Yours: Phone Accessibility

A healthy marriage rests on a few foundational pillars: a strong base, trust that is consistently grown and strengthened, open communication, honesty, and intimacy. However, I've found that all these wonderful things can be quickly brought down by one simple yet destructive force: phone secrecy.

In our increasingly connected world, where technology plays a central role in our lives, secrecy has found new avenues to creep into relationships. I recently searched phrases like "husband phone" and "wife phone" on a few search engines, and the most popular queries were alarming:

- "I want to spy on my wife's phone without her knowledge."
- "I snooped on my husband's phone."
- "How can I read my wife's texts without touching her phone?"
- "What app can I use to track my husband's location without him knowing?"

These questions weighed heavily on my heart. It's a stark reminder of the struggles many couples face today. The issue here isn't necessarily that these individuals may be irrational or paranoid (though that can sometimes be the case) but that there is a serious lack of trust and communication in their marriages. It's a significant red flag when husbands and wives feel the need to turn to the internet, rather than their spouses, to inquire about their partners' phone or location.

In marriage, oneness is central: What's yours is theirs, and what's theirs is yours.

When you hide email and social media passwords, delete internet histories, or erase messages and phone calls, you're not just keeping secrets, you're eroding trust and opening the door for temptation and sin to enter your relationship.

My heart sinks when I hear stories of a wife asking her husband for his phone, only for him to become defensive or label her as crazy. Or when a husband reaches for his wife's phone and she clings to it as if it were a lifeline. Technology is a massive part of our daily lives. Shouldn't we be eager to share that aspect of ourselves with the person we love most? This isn't about snooping or controlling your marriage, it's about transparency and embracing a glass-house mentality with your spouse.

For some, the idea of sharing phone access with their spouse might not be a big deal. But you may be surprised at how offering the simple words "You can look through my phone anytime you want" can provide your spouse with a sense of freedom and security that they didn't even realize they needed.

Jesse and I, along with the majority of our friends and family, have chosen to keep our phones open and accessible in marriage because accountability and vulnerability are important in our relationships.

We have no fear of leaving our phones face up on the counter or in the living room while we're taking a shower. When there's nothing to hide, there's nothing to fear, and no need to guard anything. It creates a space where trust flows freely, making it unnecessary to constantly invade each other's privacy or scour through one another's phones, simply because the accessibility is always there. Trust builds upon trust.

When we take steps to protect our marriage because the sanctity of our relationship is far more important than our personal comfort or selfish desires, we both win.

Protecting Your Marriage Through Clear Communication

Here are a few ways to create clarity and safety in how you communicate, especially when it comes to interactions with the opposite sex. These practices aren't about policing one another;

they're about building trust, protecting connection, and honoring your marriage through transparency:

1. *Discussion about boundaries.* Start by having an open conversation with your spouse about what boundaries feel necessary for both of you. This could include agreeing not to have private conversations or meetings with someone of the opposite sex unless it's work related or in a group setting. This isn't about controlling each other but about creating a safe space where both partners feel secure.

2. *Shared communication and social media access.* If a situation arises where you need to communicate with someone of the opposite sex, consider using shared communication channels. For instance, if you need to send an email or a text, copy your spouse or include them in the message. This ensures transparency and eliminates potential for misunderstandings.

3. *Regular check-ins.* Make it a habit to check in with each other about interactions that might involve someone of the opposite sex. This could be as simple as mentioning a lunch meeting with a coworker or discussing concerns that might arise from these interactions. Regular communication keeps both partners informed and reinforces trust.

4. *Social standards.* Agree on how you will handle social settings where you might interact with someone of the opposite sex. Whether it's deciding to avoid certain situations or choosing to attend social events together, having a plan in place helps prevent issues before they arise.

5. *Accountability partners.* Many couples find it helpful to have accountability partners—trusted friends or mentors who support both partners in maintaining boundaries. This external layer of accountability can

be especially valuable in situations where temptations might be stronger.

6. *Website blockers.* Implement website blockers or filters on smartphones and other devices to restrict access to harmful content. Website blockers are tools that restrict access to certain websites or content categories to protect your emotional and psychological well-being. They help reinforce personal and relational boundaries.

7. *ANTHEM.* Pastor John Piper uses this acronym to help Christians resist temptation, and it is one that Jesse and I have committed to memory.

> *A:* Avoid as much as possible.
> *N:* Say no to tempting thoughts immediately, with the authority of Jesus Christ.
> *T:* Turn your focus to Christ as your ultimate satisfaction.
> *H:* Hold on to the promises and pleasures of Christ.
> *E:* Enjoy that superior satisfaction.
> *M:* Move into a useful activity.

Sex and Vulnerability

Years ago, a friend of mine confided in me that she was struggling with her sex life. She was rarely intimate with her husband, but he pursued her every day. When they finally did have sex, she didn't feel connected to him in the slightest. It felt like an obligation rather than something she looked forward to doing. This obligatory sex mindset can cause a lot of damage in a relationship.

Jesse and I spent a lot of time with this couple, and because my friend had asked for help, I sat back and evaluated what I could see of her day-to-day relationship with her husband. It didn't take long to see what some of the issues could be: They were expecting sex to begin inside their bedroom, rather than outside, and showed very little affection or vulnerability outside of it.

When they sat on the couch, they sat on separate sides. When sitting next to each other in the car, they didn't hold hands or touch. Greetings at the door had become a formality, a hollow "hey" replacing the warmth of eye contact and a kiss. Days unfolded in a monotonous cycle of work, chores, and childcare, devoid of playful texts or stolen kisses. When he cooked, she remained engrossed in her phone. When she cleaned, the silence was punctuated only by sighs of exhaustion. She complained often that she felt like she was carrying the emotional load of the home, while he perceived her as distant and withdrawn.

Their lives had become a series of parallel lines. They did life separately and rarely showed affection.

When I finally spoke with them, I said this: "The beauty of it is that this is a relatively easy shift for both of you, but the discipline may take a lot of practice. You're expecting to experience the fullness of intimacy and touch in the bedroom, but you don't touch throughout the day. The lack of buildup likely makes the vulnerability that much more acute when you get into bed at night.

"You need to touch without any sexual expectations. You get to kiss, so kiss! Make out like teenagers. You need to talk and connect. It may be unfamiliar at first and you may feel pretty vulnerable, but sex is a vulnerable thing. You can't expect to be comfortable while fully naked in front of someone, allowing them to see all of your beauty, flaws, and shortcomings, when you haven't even touched fingertips all day. It's not realistic."

The buildup matters. You can neglect everything if you have to, but never neglect each other. Foreplay isn't just touch, it's phone calls, it's flirtatious texts, it's "let me get that for you," it's snacks you bring home because you thought of the other person.

Foreplay and connection begin outside of the bedroom.

Once the lights go down, the touch, longing, teasing, and serving each other matters.

I'm a firm believer that it should not be a rarity to have one or two hours of foreplay before penetration even happens. I'm laughing out loud as I write this because I feel like I can already hear some of you gasping at that idea. My friends have done the same when I share this concept because it seems so very foreign to them. But time flies when you're having fun, doesn't it? Just like you don't count down the minutes at a theme park and you soak up every moment and ride as much as you can, you shouldn't rush through foreplay either. God created our bodies with purpose. The clitoris alone has around eight thousand nerve endings—double the number in a penis. That design reminds us that arousal takes time and attention. Foreplay isn't extra; taking time to delight in your partner is how we honor one another's needs and build true intimacy. Enjoy the thrill and the fun. Make time for what actually brings you closer.

We make time for what connects us.

A harmonious sex life, the kind that leaves you breathless and wanting more, is built on a foundation of emotional intimacy. Shared tasks, sweet compliments, guilt-free hobbies, the act of softening toward one another, spur-of-the-moment compliments, and a whole lot of nonsexual affection strengthen your connection. Folding laundry together, respecting your partner's "me time," and peppering your day with lingering hugs or hand-holding can fundamentally change your experiences in the bedroom.

There are, of course, countless obstacles that can disrupt intimacy in the bedroom: postpartum struggles, lackluster foreplay, body insecurities, church trauma, emotional disconnection, feeling "touched out" by kids, pleasureless sex, and low libido. Life, circumstances, and even hormones can all work against us, making a fulfilling sex life seem elusive.

Because of these things, the hesitation to be fully vulnerable is common, especially for parents who are juggling the many complexities of life. It's difficult to tap out from parenting duties to shift into your best self.

But there are practical ways to reconnect with our vulnerability, ways to quiet the self-doubt and reclaim the freedom to love and be loved fully.

1. Ask your spouse to praise their favorite parts of you. This can be done both within and outside of intimacy, but be sure to ask your spouse to incorporate it in the bedroom, ensuring that you do the same for them. While in the middle of foreplay or sex, it can feel empowering to hear compliments about your body. These acknowledgments of your attraction to each other will help to remove the insecurities that keep you from enjoying one another.

2. Vocalize your insecurities. Talk to your spouse about the things you feel most ashamed of or embarrassed by, and let them know that it hinders you from pursuing intimacy. Ask them to reassure you in those areas during intimacy. Allow them into that vulnerable space with you. Tip: Neither person should respond with "Well, then you should probably work on that," because, obviously, that will cause more harm than good. Give encouragement where it's needed.

3. Get into the gym. This is an obvious one. If you feel uncomfortable, you have to take action. But honestly, this is just as much for your mental health as it is for your physical health. It usually takes me about thirty minutes in the gym before I feel like I've bulked up and hit some goals, even though nothing has changed at all. (Ha!) But truly, eating clean, exercising, and taking care of yourself is inspiring and boosts your confidence and sexiness.

4. Navigate past sexual pain together. For many people, intimacy is complicated by past hurt, abuse, or trauma. If this is part of your story, please know you're not broken and you're not alone. Healing takes time, and it isn't linear. Be open with your spouse about what feels difficult. Let them in. If you're able, seek counseling with someone who can help you rebuild safety and trust in your body.

Part of my testimony, which I have shared on my podcast, includes being sexually abused when I was fourteen. For years after marrying Jesse, I had to learn what it actually meant to be loved and cared for in the bedroom. Before that, sex felt transactional to me. It was something to be endured or performed, something owed to a man, instead of a mutually beautiful gift. But through prayer, counseling, Jesse's patience, and essentially living with a "shame off me" mindset, I slowly began to experience intimacy as something really sweet again—something safe, shared, kind, and pleasurable.

If you're the spouse of someone who's healing, know that it's okay to feel frustrated or confused at times, but your patience and gentleness matter more than you know. Your willingness to listen, to ask what helps, and to hold space without pressure can become part of the redemption itself.

And if you're the one who's still struggling years later, please hear this: You haven't failed. God isn't disappointed in you. He isn't timing your recovery or comparing it with anyone else's. He's still at work, patiently and lovingly helping you rewrite what love and safety feel like.

5. Let go. We are often our own biggest critics. There will likely always be things we don't love about our bodies, but when we remind ourselves that we are made in the image of God and that we are enough because God says we are, we can begin to let go of our obsession with appearance. If social media causes you to struggle with insecurity, take a break. If staring at yourself in the mirror makes things worse, step away. If you have a pair of jeans that never fit but you keep trying to squeeze into them, it's time to let them go. (And buy a pair that fit!) As Jess Connolly reminds us, "You are not a body, you are a soul with a body."

Release the things that harm you and your intimacy. By obsessing over your body and picking apart the things your spouse loves about you, you're robbing your intimacy as well as theirs.

From Parent Mode to Sex Mode

You may be thinking, *Okay, Linds, this is all great, but how do we even get there? We're so busy throughout the day. Switching from parent mode to intimacy mode can feel impossible.*

Incorporating some playful strategies can make a world of difference.

Starting your day by sending flirty texts to each other can create a fun anticipation. A "Can't stop thinking about how sexy you looked this morning" or "I can't wait to see you later" message, or something a little more scandalous if you choose, can create fun anticipation.

You can also write and spread little notes throughout the house (where tiny eyes won't see them), like one tucked into your spouse's lunchbox or stuck on the bathroom mirror, reminding your partner how much you desire them. This sets a fun tone for the day and builds excitement for when the kids are finally in bed.

Another approach, especially for couples who are more reserved, is to use an "intimacy scale." This scale is a laminated piece of paper with a dry erase marker hung up somewhere you will both see it. The one-to-ten scale has a space for both partners to place a checkmark next to the number that shows how ready they are to pursue intimacy at a specific time each day. This provides a discreet way to express your desire to make love. By checking in with each other this way, you can see whether you're on the same page and express your needs without the pressure of verbalizing them.

If this still sounds awful to you, have sex in the morning before you can get inside your own head!

You can also create a little intimacy ritual. Share a glass of wine or spend a few minutes quietly together, kissing, massaging, or touching, before diving into your "bed routine." Or switch up locations from your usual spot and get creative. The living room? Car in the garage? Kitchen? Honestly, guys, why not? This is your person. You married them. You signed up for access. Jesse and I always joke that one of the best perks of marriage is that we've given one another full permission to grab, admire, and enjoy each other whenever we want. Like, how lucky are we to ogle and manhandle our favorite body parts on demand? Marriage as a Christian is allowed to be both sacred and spicy. The more you're willing to explore your intimacy together, the stronger your bond becomes. That's where the growth happens: Vulnerability creates connection.

The Home Renovation

If your glass house is chipped all over the place and there are some areas that feel shattered and unfixable, you might find yourself trying to avoid the broken pieces. You tiptoe around the shards of glass and hope that small chips and nicks—such as criticisms, dismissals, or a lack of partnership—won't get worse.

If your marriage has been affected by betrayal, lies, inappropriate behavior, or the everyday stresses that lead to disconnection, this will likely be a familiar feeling. But just as glass can crack further under extreme temperatures or significant impact, unresolved issues and rehashed fights will only worsen if left unaddressed.

The process of repairing and fortifying your glass house needs to start now.

I know this isn't easy for everyone. We hear it all the time on shows like *The Bachelor* and *The Bachelorette*: "I have a hard time opening up." It's a line that has probably been said more than any other on those shows, and for good reason; vulnerability is hard.

The good news is that you're likely already in a safe, committed relationship. You're not competing with twenty-four other people for affection. (That would be my absolute worst nightmare, honestly.) But you may still be withholding vulnerability out of fear of being seen as inadequate or of risking more hurt.

Here are a few ways you can begin opening up and getting vulnerable:

1. *Share small truths first.* You don't have to dive into the deepest parts of your story right away. Start with lighter, everyday struggles or childhood memories to build confidence in expressing yourself.
2. *Ask open-ended questions.* Initiate conversations with your spouse that encourage sharing. Ask questions and show interest. It's easier to be vulnerable when someone is willing to share alongside you.
3. *Set realistic expectations.* Remind yourself that opening up is a process, not a single event, for both you and your spouse. Your spouse may not be fully comfortable right away, and growth is a process.
4. *Anticipate and accept discomfort.* It's normal to feel awkward or exposed when you start opening up. When you embrace this discomfort as part of the process, it can make it easier to reach your desired goal.

Be Clear About Your Needs

It's your vulnerability that makes you human and strengthens the connection with your partner.

I want to challenge you to recognize the courage it takes to show vulnerability in your marriage and to choose that courage instead of shame. Imagine if we, as a society, embraced vulnerability, openness, and honesty as normal, everyday expressions. I truly believe the world and our relationships would look radically different for the better. Sharing our secrets, worst-case scenarios, fears, and insecurities gives us the ability to change the trajectory of our marriage and develop the kind of relationship we've always dreamed of.

CHAPTER 15

DON'T GIVE YOUR SPOUSE YOUR LEFTOVERS

You should speak more kindly to your spouse than you do to anyone else in the world.

—Unknown

As I sift through the messages Jesse and I have exchanged in recent weeks, I'm struck by the weight of the struggles we've been facing. Sutton has pneumonia, which is already awful, but for an asthmatic it's absolutely brutal. And simultaneously, our youngest, Saxon, had his tonsils removed after fourteen bouts of strep this year. We haven't slept well in days. The financial and emotional toll of these ongoing illnesses feels like a heavy cloak, suffocating our peace. The worry is relentless, causing us to feel disconnected.

It's so easy to let the chaos sweep us away, to convince ourselves that it's just how life is. Busy, hard. Naturally, our relationship suffers.

But I want to challenge you to rethink this narrative.

Yes, life is hard, but life with our partners shouldn't add to that burden. Our spouses get to be our greatest allies, the ones who help relieve the pressure and remind us that we don't have to carry the load alone, and we get to be that to them. Amid chaos and uncertainty, we still have the power to choose each other.

A common understanding in relationships is that men typically desire respect while women typically desire love. When these core needs are met, a relationship thrives. For men, respect often translates into feeling valued and acknowledged for their contributions and efforts. On the other hand, women often seek love in the form of emotional connection, empathy, and affirmation.

When a man feels disrespected, whether through dismissive comments, lack of appreciation, or being overlooked, he may withdraw his love. This withdrawal is often a defense mechanism, a way to protect himself from further hurt.

When a woman feels unloved, perhaps because of a lack of affection, neglect, or emotional distance, she may respond by withholding respect. She may become less supportive, more critical, or emotionally distant.

The more the man feels disrespected and withdraws love, the more the woman feels unloved and withdraws respect.

None of us can avoid hardship in marriage, but we can learn how to communicate in a way that leaves our spouses feeling understood and seen. Communication is one of the greatest tools to redeem this cycle of brokenness and morph it into a thriving relationship. It allows partners' needs for love and respect to be consistently met.

I want to share twelve communication habits I've consistently seen in healthy, joy-filled couples. These are habits that I believe will both challenge and encourage you to show up as your best self in the relationship you've committed to for life:

1. Speak More Kindly to Your Spouse Than to Anyone Else

Familiarity leads to complacency. And my, oh my, how a complacent marriage quickly becomes a disconnected marriage.

We tend to reserve our best behavior for those outside our immediate circles. We often put on our best airs with neighbors, acquaintances, and business partners, while the people within our homes seem to get the worst of us. They receive our leftovers rather than a fresh meal.

In our home, leftovers night is considered an easy dinner night. It's a night of convenience when I don't have to think about cooking for (what feels like) the five hundred thousandth time that month. This leftover meal is a reprieve because it's easy, lazy, and lacks intention. It's great every once in a while, but I definitely don't want it all the time. I don't think any of us would be okay with a restaurant serving yesterday's leftovers, dressed up to look fresh, just because the chef gave the best meal to someone more important.

Who doesn't crave this same level of consideration in their relationships?

When we give our spouses our leftovers, we're handing over what's conveniently been reheated after we've given our best to everything and everyone else. It's the emotional equivalent of saying, "This is all I have left to give because I didn't reserve the best for you." While our relationship might survive this temporarily, it lacks the vitality and warmth it had when we gave it fresh servings of our time, energy, and affection.

I wish you spoke to me the way you spoke to them. Have you ever had this thought when hearing your partner talk to someone they admire? It's a disheartening feeling to know and see that they have that kindness within them but are unwilling or unable to show it to you.

How about you? Have you ever left a dinner party smiling at everyone, only to find yourself complaining to or being curt with your partner as soon as you get in the car? Do you exude warmth and friendliness with your neighbor, only to close the door behind you and speak harshly to your family members?

It's easy to blame those closest to you for bringing out the worst in you. But what if your treatment of your family reflects the inclination of your heart? Instead of blaming your mood or reactions on your spouse, consider that your behavior might stem from deeper emotions. If you didn't already harbor anger, resentment, bitterness, or misery within your heart, those negative feelings likely wouldn't reveal themselves in your interactions. What is in your heart will inevitably pour out in your behavior.

Or perhaps the problem seems more innocent: You spend hours endlessly scrolling on social media or immersing yourself in hobbies, but spending quality time with your family is an afterthought.

We even give leftovers in the bedroom when we postpone, avoid, or rush through physical intimacy because stress or self-neglect have sapped our desire and connection.

Instead of letting your relationship survive on what's left over, I want to challenge you to bring the best parts of yourself to your spouse every day. If the flip side is true that you aren't getting the best from your spouse, it might be helpful to have an open and honest conversation. Discuss your feelings without blaming or accusing. Focus on how you're feeling and what you need from the relationship.

Here's an example of how you might approach the conversation: "I've noticed that you sometimes speak to [other person] in a way that's really kind and gentle. It makes me feel a little hurt when I don't always see that same side of you with me. I'd love to understand why that might be or if there is anything I can do to make it easier for you."

When you and your spouse speak more kindly to each other than to anyone else, your home transforms into a place of grace.

2. Say Thank You (for Everything)

One of the best ways Jesse and I have learned to show respect and appreciation to each other is by expressing gratitude in our weakest and most exhausted moments. We say thank you for everything, even if it's a task we're expected to do. Doing this has changed how we view our circumstances, and each other, while providing a sense of reprieve in our relationship when everything else feels overwhelming.

I firmly believe that appreciation and gratitude are the antidotes to resentment and bitterness.

As I read through our recent text messages while writing this section, I smiled as I was reminded of our recent exchanges of gratitude:

- "Thank you for putting the boys to bed. Want to come into the kitchen and make s'mores cookies with me? :)" —Jesse
- "You're a great husband and a great daddy. Thank you for encouraging me to get out of the house and for always being so on top of things. I never need to worry or stress while I'm gone. I appreciate you." —Me
- "Thanks for sending me out to play pickleball today. I needed that time." —Jesse
- "Thank you for doing those dishes. They were overwhelming me, and the house feels soooo much better." —Me

Of course, we don't necessarily need permission to pursue hobbies, and household chores are the responsibility of both partners, but that doesn't mean we shouldn't show courtesy and appreciation for the smallest things.

Courtesy is often one of the first things to fade in a marriage once comfort sets in. Acts of courtesy throughout the day—kindness, friendliness, love—set the tone and establish a solid baseline in the home. Simple phrases like *please, excuse me*, and *thank you* go a long way. And you'd be surprised at how quickly some couples let those basic manners fall to the wayside.

Appreciation breeds more appreciation, so why withhold it?

Jesse and I didn't always appreciate each other. We were better at competing (and sometimes we still are), trying to outdo each other, but not in a positive way. We both wanted to prove that we were doing the most work or being the most helpful at home. The constant one-upping led only to annoyance and resentment and kept us from working together toward a shared goal—the upkeep of our marriage and our lives to the glory of God.

Throughout our marriage, we've discovered that saying thank you quickly and often has transformed not only how we view each other but also how we perceive our marriage.

We are a team, and just like any successful partnership, the key to effective communication is acknowledging even the smallest efforts. Those small gestures make a significant difference.

Say thank you excessively. Repeat it again and again. Watch how this simple practice can change your heart and relationship.

3. Get the Timing Right and Avoid the Fight

Conflicts are normal and as certain as the changing seasons. I might even dare to say that if you never have any disagreements or arguments, something is likely brewing beneath the surface, waiting to explode. But the timing and tone that we choose when navigating hard conversations can make a big difference in the health of our relationships.

When it's necessary to discuss a difficult topic, I have two rules of thumb.

1. Bring It Up When Emotions Aren't High

Many couples address issues when they're already at a level ten. They begin the conversation when they're triggered or feel hurt and are ready to fight. Sure, it feels easiest to do it this way, because when things are fine we don't want to rock the boat. But a conversation is far better than a blowout.

The best time to bring up concerns is while they're still minor and when we feel calm and relaxed. This approach helps prevent issues from escalating into larger conflicts. If you've already had the argument and need to continue the discussion, it's far more effective to wait until tensions have fizzled than to engage in a heated exchange when emotions are running high. You are more likely to have a kinder tone of voice, less defensiveness, and more patience with your spouse, which inevitably leads to a more conducive conversation and, hopefully, a solid solution.

2. Never Discuss It Late at Night

Regarding tough conversations, I often say, "Nothing good happens after 9:00 p.m." People are tired or emotionally drained late at night, which increases the risk of miscommunication and heightened emotions during hard conversations.

Mornings can be a great time to handle conflicts. We're usually more alert, focused, and less emotionally taxed, which helps us think clearly and solve problems better. And of course, after a good night's sleep, we often feel more balanced and ready to discuss things calmly.

4. Speak Words That Breathe Life

A common communication mistake is the tendency to correct our spouses when we see them doing something incorrectly. Not once, not twice, but all the time. This can easily lead to nagging, complaining, or criticizing rather than praising. While we may be well meaning, this approach can inadvertently make our partners feel incapable.

Even if you're right, instead of dwelling on their mistakes, try praising the positive aspects of their actions. Whether they've done something right 10 percent or 90 percent of the time, highlight their successes. When you acknowledge your partner's accomplishments, you're subtly encouraging them to continue doing more of what they're already doing well, no matter how small the achievement.

Conversely, constant criticism can make your spouse feel like they'll never meet your expectations, leading to frustration, disengagement, and even an increase in negative behaviors as they become more and more discouraged. Criticism not only makes you less compassionate toward them and erodes your respect for them but also diminishes their respect for you.

Praise one another, even for the small things, and watch as each of you feels motivated to contribute even more to the marriage.

One of my favorite illustrations of this concept comes from Jeremiah 18:1–6. In this passage, the prophet visits a potter's house and watches as the potter works with a lump of clay. The vessel the potter is shaping doesn't turn out as expected—it's flawed and spoiled. Instead of discarding it, the potter reworks the clay, reshaping it into a new vessel that meets his approval.

God uses this imagery to communicate a profound truth to Israel, saying, "Can I not do with you as this potter has done? . . . Like the clay in the potter's hand, so are you in my hand" (v. 6 ESV). This metaphor illustrates that just as the potter has the power and skill to mold the clay into something beautiful, so God has the ability to shape and refine our lives and the lives of our partners.

Our spouses' imperfections may feel wildly frustrating to us, but accepting them is part of the process of growth and sanctification. God is continually at work shaping and molding us, often through repeated trials and adjustments. Sometimes, like clay, we need to be reworked several times before we become who we're meant to be.

I'll never forget the day, early in our marriage, when Jesse gently asked me, "Do you ever wonder if all the effort you're putting into fixing me might actually be getting in the way of the work God is trying to do in me?"

He was right. I quickly realized that I needed to spend less time trying to change him and more time on my own self-reflection. If I expect my partner to change, I must also be willing to look at myself.

Do your values align with your own expectations of your partner? Are you living by the principles you preach? Or are your words hollow promises? When you see something in your partner that bothers you, is it a reflection of your own shortcomings?

If you focus on improving yourself—the only thing you can truly control—you'll likely see a decrease in negative behaviors from your partner. This is because your own sense of peace and emotional stability can have a positive ripple effect.

A 2008 study by James Fowler and Nicholas Christakis found that happiness is contagious. Positive emotions such as happiness can spread through social networks, similar to the way diseases do. This "happiness ripple effect" suggests that a person's happiness is influenced not only by their friends but also by their friends' friends and their friends' friends' friends.[1]

If happiness can ripple through large social circles, imagine the impact it could have on the few members within the four walls of your home.

Remember: The language you choose can either breathe life or spit poison. Your words can either uplift and encourage your spouse or push them down into feelings of inferiority and failure.

Find the little things they do and acknowledge them.

Did they load the dishwasher, even if it wasn't done perfectly? Praise them for making the effort.

Did they get the kids dressed, even if it's not the outfit you would have chosen? Praise them for taking care of it.

Did they attempt to manage the budget or finances despite limited experience? Praise them for their time spent.

Even if this feels unfamiliar or awkward at first, it's never too late to begin praising the small successes, acknowledging efforts, and providing support without trying to control or change your partner.

5. Avoid Weaponized Incompetence

Have you ever heard the term *weaponized incompetence*? It refers to someone pretending to be incapable of performing a task as a way to avoid responsibility or manipulate someone else into doing it for them. This tactic is often used in relationships or work environments to shift the burden of responsibility onto someone else while feigning helplessness.

For example, a partner might pretend not to understand how to manage household chores, forcing their spouse to take over those tasks. The goal is to evade effort or accountability while maintaining the appearance of incompetence.

Similarly, one partner might act as though they are incapable of handling routine childcare responsibilities, such as scheduling or attending doctors' appointments. They may feign ignorance or simply refuse to learn the details, leaving the other partner to manage these tasks alone. This behavior not only shifts the emotional burden of managing the child's health care but also neglects the shared responsibility of parenting.

Consider a scenario where it's your child's birthday and you ask your partner to help with a part of the party that matters to you because you're overwhelmed. If they respond with, "That's not necessary or important; you should just skip it," instead of helping, you'll likely feel disheartened and unsupported. There's no space for weaponized incompetence in a marriage that's built on love. When both people show up and do their part, it builds trust and makes life feel lighter.

In contrast, working hard to share burdens and face challenges together as a team is far more rewarding. Life feels better when we tackle tasks side by side. Even routine activities such as going to the grocery store together often feel more enjoyable than doing them alone.

Be competent together.

6. Heal Your Heart

If you've been hurt in childhood, past relationships, or even within your marriage, you probably carry some lingering pain. I'm careful with the word *trauma* because it's often overused or watered down. But many of us have walked through very real, deeply painful experiences as children, and those moments don't just vanish with time. They echo. They show up in our reactions, our insecurities, our arguments, and our silence.

Can I remind you of something important? You need to heal your heart so that you can hear what your partner is saying without filtering it through your own wounds.

It's easy to notice the negative in our partners, but when we're hurting, it becomes even easier to interpret their actions as malicious, misguided, or unloving, even when that's not the case.

If you don't take the time to care for your mental health through therapy, self-reflection, or other means, and evaluate the patterns that have developed from past experiences, you risk falling into the emotional traps and conflicts that arise in marriage. For example, you might find yourself reacting defensively to an innocent question because it triggers a flashback to an incident you haven't forgiven or worked through.

It's so important to take responsibility for learning how not to be ruled by your emotions. This means believing the best about your spouse, showing up for yourself in tough moments, and making an effort to view situations through a lens of clarity instead of one of hurt or confusion.

7. Apologize Well

Would you rather be right, or would you rather be married?

Every time you withhold an apology after a fight, you build a wedge within your marriage.

Every time you ask for forgiveness for any hurt you've caused, you're investing in the health of your marriage.

Which path do you choose?

"I'm sorry for anything I may have done to hurt you" and "I'm sorry for [specific thing] because it was wrong, and I love you" are the two approaches I've learned to use with Jesse after an argument. Even when I might not feel like I'm entirely at fault, these words are a vital part of how I address conflict. And honestly, it's not always easy. Sometimes I feel like I'm choking on my words. (Pride, is that you? Yes. It absolutely is.) And yet I do it anyway because our marriage is worth my humility. It's a commitment that goes beyond temporary feelings and momentary frustrations.

Just yesterday I sent a text that said, "Hey, I'm sorry. You were already having a bad day and I could have made it better. But I chose selfishness, and I made things worse. Just because this issue impacts me, it doesn't give me the right to tear you down because of it. I'm sorry. Will you forgive me?"

Preventing disconnection means choosing to unite even when you have the opportunity to divide.

You and your spouse get to be a team. You get to be one under God's covenant. You have the opportunity to grow together, being sanctified and shaped into Christ's image each day. This journey involves frequent apologizing and forgiving.

When I see older couples who have been married for decades, especially the ones who still show love and affection in public, I can't help but wonder, *How many times did they have to forgive each other to get here?* The happiest couples aren't those who never make mistakes or have perfect partners. There's no such thing. Instead, they are the ones who take responsibility for their mistakes, apologize sincerely, and forgive when their partner does the same.

You may have heard it said that "if you win the fight, the Enemy wins. If your spouse wins the fight, the Enemy wins. If God wins, you both win."

If your goal is to win while your spouse loses, you're both going to feel empty and disappointed. Marital conflicts should never lead to scoring personal wins, because the goal isn't to fight one another but to defeat or overcome the external pressures that can threaten your relationship. When one partner focuses only on winning an argument, it might lead to a quick victory, but it can damage trust and intimacy in the long run. On the flip side, if one partner constantly backs down to avoid conflict, it can create an imbalance and leave issues unresolved.

When conflicts are approached with a focus on God and with an eternal perspective, both partners benefit.

The strength of a marriage is measured not by how often a couple argues but by how they find their way back to one another afterward. The real difference between couples who stay connected and those who quietly drift apart isn't how little they fight but how willing they are to repair after the hurt.

Repair can seem simple, but it carries incredible weight. It's the moment one person softens their tone, reaches for a hand, or offers a small smile that breaks the tension. It's still offering to make them a coffee, even when you're fighting. Or a bit of humor to lighten the air after the apology, or the courage to say, "I didn't mean to hurt you."

The key to apologizing well is taking accountability for your actions. I've learned to start conversations with "I feel . . ." or "I'm sorry that I . . ." instead of focusing solely on Jesse's mistakes. However, if you're dealing with someone who struggles to acknowledge their faults or apologizes only to repeat the behavior, it might require more time and possibly outside help.

Remember, don't build a wedge, build a bridge. Every day, piece by piece.

8. Psst . . . How Not to Apologize

I shared a post on social media a few years ago about how not to apologize, and to my surprise, it went viral. Many of the comments revealed that while people understood the importance of apologizing, they hadn't realized there were unhelpful ways to go about it.

Following are a few examples of apologies that might be counterproductive.

Justifying Yourself:

"I'm sorry, but . . ."

- *Why it isn't helpful:* This type of apology begins with an acknowledgment but immediately shifts to excuses or justifications. The "but" negates the sincerity of the apology and directs attention away from the hurtful action.
- *What to do instead:* Offer a direct apology without any qualifiers. For example, say, "I'm sorry for what I did." Ditch the qualifiers and excuses. This approach shows genuine remorse and addresses the issue directly.

Deflection:

"I guess I'm just a horrible person/ dad/mom/wife/husband."

- *Why it isn't helpful:* Deflection through self-criticism sidesteps the real issue and focuses on self-pity rather than addressing the impact of your actions. It shifts the conversation away from the problem and can make the apology seem insincere or self-serving.
- *What to do instead:* Focus on owning up to your actions and their impact on the other person. A more effective response would be, "I recognize that I hurt you, and I am committed to understanding how I can do better." This helps your partner feel acknowledged while also demonstrating a willingness to improve.

Blaming Your Partner:

"I did do that, but I did it because you did this."

- *Why it isn't helpful:* This approach shifts the focus from taking responsibility for your actions to blaming the other person. While they may have done something wrong, it fails to address your part of the issue and can lead to further conflict and resentment.
- *What to do instead:* Own your actions and their effects on the other person without linking your apology to past grievances. For example, "I'm sorry for how I reacted. I will work on managing my responses better in the future."

- *Why it isn't helpful:* If you're not actively listening to your partner's concerns, your apology may come across as insincere. When you're dismissive of details or emotions, your spouse is likely to feel unheard and unloved. Helpful apologies require that you truly hear and understand the impact of your actions on the other person.

- *What to do instead:* Practice active listening by paying attention to the other person's feelings and perspectives. Avoid distractions and show that you understand their concerns by reflecting back what you've heard. For example, you might say, "I understand that saying [specific comment] hurt you, and I'm sorry for that. I'll make an effort to be more mindful of how my words affect you in the future."

9. Praise and Protect Your Spouse in Public

One crucial lesson I've learned in recent years is this: We should be a force to be reckoned with when it comes to protecting our spouses—their peace, their reputation, their joy, their mental health, and most important, their relationships with God.

Oof. This one can hit hard. We've all had those moments when we're tempted to discredit or criticize our spouses in front of close friends or acquaintances. Often we do this not out of a malicious heart but rather from a need to seek validation or justify our feelings and actions. We're looking for support in our own hurt and find ourselves seeking affirmation for our negative feelings toward our spouses.

But let me say this: Few things will make our spouses feel

smaller than when we belittle them in front of other people or behind their backs. Gossiping about your spouse just keeps the drama going. It stokes an unnecessary and damaging fire and is bound to drive a wedge in your marriage. Proverbs 26:20–21 tells us that just like a fire dies out without fuel, arguments fizzle out when gossip stops. Adding fuel to the fire with gossip only keeps it burning. But once you stop, the fire eventually dies down.

Keep this in mind: Sharing your marital problems with others, especially from a one-sided perspective and in a negative light, not only affects how others view your spouse but also complicates your own perspective. Friends and family may not have the full picture and could hold on to the negative impression you've painted, even after you've made amends with your spouse.

This inevitably makes resolving issues more difficult and likely keeps old conflicts alive. Your friends haven't walked through the process of healing like you and your spouse have, so they will likely bring up past problems as if they're current issues. Or you may find yourself having to defend your spouse against the negative image you've created, even after the problems have been resolved.

Ephesians 5:33 identifies love and respect as crucial aspects of oneness. We do not respect or love one another when we try to elevate ourselves in the view of others while shaming or even jokingly putting down our spouses. If you are struggling in your marriage, the goal should be to go together to speak with someone who has proven themselves to be wise, godly, and unbiased toward your relationship.

Focus on building up your spouse, not tearing them down.

10. Live Without Secrets

When we live without secrets, we build a marriage without deceit. Trust is an antidote to unfaithfulness.

Secrets build on secrets. The longer we get used to telling mistruths—even small white lies—the easier it becomes to live in those lies and weave a web of deceit.

Recent research reveals that one in five people are keeping a major secret from their spouses, with many of these secrets being held for years.[2] To build the trust necessary to prevent unfaithfulness, we must start by communicating openly and confronting difficult truths.

Ask yourself, *Am I trapped by a secret that needs to be shared? Is this secrecy fostering deception and disconnection? Am I justifying my actions out of fear of abandonment? Am I gravitating toward people who only affirm my sinful desires instead of challenging me to grow in faith and integrity?*

If you're hiding, know that you are still seen. If you're broken, you are not unloved. Jesus sacrificed himself for your sins and rose again to offer you freedom and redemption from the secrecy that binds you. Confessing your secrets may be painful and come with consequences, but he promises never to leave you broken. He is a God not of condemnation but of grace and forgiveness.

11. *Always* and *Never*

We learned early on as a couple that using absolutes like *never* and *always* in our conversations is unproductive and also very harmful. We believe in this so strongly that we've even taught our boys that such terms rarely reflect ongoing issues accurately.

Think about those disagreements in which you find yourself saying, "You always treat me this way," or, "You never do what you say you're going to do." The problem with these statements is that they generalize and box your partner into a fixed role, ignoring any growth they may have experienced. It's more constructive to address specific behaviors and acknowledge progress than to resort to absolutes.

When you catch yourself using absolutes, step back and reframe your language. For example, say, "I'm sorry, the term *always* isn't fair in this instance," or, "Let me correct myself—it's not *never*, but it does feel common." This helps to create a more constructive dialogue and acknowledges the complexities and growth in your partner's behavior.

12. Bandaids Don't Fix Bullet Holes

This is a gentle but necessary reminder that bandaids don't fix bullet holes.

Forgiveness and grace are indeed essential in marriage, but they don't replace the need for kindness and gentleness. An apology alone, especially after angry words or a harsh attack on someone's character, isn't always enough to heal the hurt. Often it takes more than just saying "I'm sorry" to mend the wound.

I once knew someone who would lash out at night, unleashing their frustrations and hurtful words on those around them. The next morning, they would send a quick text and offer a half-hearted apology, expecting it to resolve the damage done. They believed that forgiveness should be immediate because of our Christian faith, but the reality is that healing requires more than just an apology. It needs open conversation, remorse, and a commitment to change.

Are we called to forgive as Christians? Absolutely—"seventy times seven," as stated in Matthew 18:22. But that doesn't mean someone we have hurt with our words will forget what was said or that the relationship will be the same as it was before.

I teach my boys that once toothpaste has been squeezed out of the tube, it can't be put back in. The same goes for our words and actions. They leave a lasting impact on our spouses, children, friendships, and family relationships.

Jesse often reminds us, "God gave us two ears and one mouth

for a reason." Our words have power. While our intentions may be pure, people in our lives will feel the weight of our actions, not of our intentions.

Let me say it again for emphasis: People in your life will feel the weight of your actions, even if your intentions are good.

As the saying often attributed to Ralph Waldo Emerson wisely states, "What you do speaks so loudly that I cannot hear what you say."

When speaking to your spouse and children, are you cautious and thoughtful? Are you slow to speak and quick to listen? Do your words, even in moments of frustration and anger, bring life and healing like Jesus' words did, or do they bring destruction?

The call to be humble, to love our spouses above ourselves, and to be slow to speak and slow to anger is not easy. But the more intentional we are about choosing to repair, to notice tension quickly and reach for each other instead of retreating or attacking, the happier we will be.

CHAPTER 16

NOTHING CHANGES IF NOTHING CHANGES

Our greatest weakness lies in giving up. The most certain way to succeed is always to try just one more time.

—Thomas Edison

One thing I've learned in my life is that perspective is earned. Every struggle and every moment of heartbreak helps us to grow, learn, and gain perspective. The ups and downs we go through in marriage aren't all for naught.

On the week I was set to finish this chapter, I came home from church with Jesse, Sutton, and Saxon, excited for the day ahead. But as we walked through the door, we noticed that our little doggy, Milo, wasn't himself. We'd loved Milo for nine years. We rescued him two months before Sutton was born. He'd been around for the births of both boys, all of the birthdays and small achievements, and so much of our marriage.

We, and even our friends and extended family, connected through our love for Milo; it was a universal experience to adore him and shower him with affection. He was a household name in our little community, so to speak. And he surely didn't give you much choice to pet him, either. Pets were a must for our attention-loving, sweet little guy.

We lost him quickly and unexpectedly to cardiac arrest.

Just a couple of days later, we received the news that my sweet Gram had passed away—the matriarch of our family. She was the one who helped care for me during my parents' divorce and the glue that kept our family connected through years of change. She lived through the difficulties of World War II in England and came to the United States from London at age twenty-three, where she built her own business from scratch. Our tight-knit family was blessed to gather around her bed during her final hours, sharing stories and memories of the profound impact she'd had on our lives.

Needless to say, Jesse and I cried a lot that week.

I share this because, in my grief, I found myself asking God, *Lord, why did this happen? Why the shock and gravity of loss? Why so many tears and so much aimlessness for our family, especially when my mind is meant to be here, in this book, to serve you and minister to my audience? I don't understand it.*

I know it wasn't God's doing, but the feelings of confusion and pain were hard to shake.

What I felt in my heart after my prayer was this: Perspective is earned through experience. It doesn't simply show up overnight. Perspective and empathy come from facing difficulties and give us the ability to connect with people in a way we never have before. Loss teaches us to cherish what we have, and to cherish it dearly.

Tell them to cherish it, Lindsey.

So here it is. You guys, please, please, please cherish your people. Be responsible with their hearts; they have only one. Our relationships, in the end, are truly all that matter.

From the very beginning of this book, my desire has been to connect with you, to relate to your experience, and to remind you that you're not alone in the inevitable ups and downs of marriage. As I navigated this wave of grief in my life, I discovered that while loss is profoundly painful, it also opens our eyes to the value of life and of our relationships. Loss is a bittersweet reminder of just how fragile life can be and how fleeting it is.

You may recall having felt a similar urge to cherish your life more after experiencing a loss or attending a funeral.

We change when we lose someone, don't we?

We often commit to becoming better versions of ourselves—reaching out to loved ones or old friends and loving harder than we ever have before. We become more attuned to the struggles of others, more willing to offer support, and more appreciative of love in every form.

Yet it's all too easy to let this commitment fall by the wayside as time passes, giving space to the playlist of failures and should-haves to echo in our minds when it's too late to make things right.

It is guaranteed that one day your favorite people will no longer be on this earth. There is no promise that your husband or wife will be with you by the time you get into bed tomorrow.

How would you love your spouse and children differently today if you knew you wouldn't ever see them again? Would you choose kindness over criticism?

Would you take the time to share your gratitude for everything they do?

Would you look them in the eyes or hold them tightly for a few extra minutes?

We have to value God, this life, our experiences, and our marriages enough to ask ourselves, *Are these arguments really worth it when eternity is at hand?* If you lost your wife, would you regret not helping her out more or not telling her what a great wife and mother she was? Would you wish you had shown your husband just how much you loved, respected, and desired him? Would you both wished you had kept God at the center of your home, even when the world was pulling and tugging at your hearts?

Every disagreement, every moment of frustration can feel monumental in the heat of the moment, but in the grand scheme of things, is it worth the toll it takes on your relationship?

I want you to take a moment to remember why you fell in love in the first place. It's far too easy to get caught up in what your spouse is lacking and overlook the amazing qualities that drew you together.

Think back to the spontaneous adventures, late-night talks, laughter, and shared dreams. Let those memories inspire you to create new experiences together and take the first steps toward growth.

How Are Your Roots?

Psalm 119:105 beautifully reminds us of the trust we are called to place in God: "Your word is a lamp for my feet, a light on my path" (NIV). God illuminates each step we take, and I love that the terminology refers to a lamp. He doesn't refer to a floodlight that brightens the entire landscape with light but refers to a lamp that merely sheds light on the ground right in front of us. And while we can't see the entire journey of our marriages ahead of us—what they will feel like or look like in six months or a year—we get a snippet of the next step. God guides us one step at a time. It's an invitation to trust him, even when the way feels unclear.

It's a slow but refining process.

Healing and compromise won't happen overnight. They begin when you're ready and willing to build a solid foundation and take that first step of trust—holding tight when things get tough.

Colossians 2:6–7 says, "As you therefore have received Christ Jesus the Lord, so walk in Him, rooted and built up in Him and established in the faith, as you have been taught, abounding in it with thanksgiving."

Do you see the word *rooted*? A tree's root system provides the stability the tree needs to withstand tumultuous circumstances. When trees are well rooted, they don't easily fall during storms. The deeper their roots, the more stable they are.

How are your roots?

You may have faced many seasons of testing and trials in your relationship, and the reality is that you likely won't see how strong or weak your roots are until they have been put to the test.

But it takes time for your roots to grow, and if you've had too much happen too quickly—too much damage, too much exposure, too much temptation—your root system may not yet be strong enough to endure the weight of responsibility in a marriage.

Quick fixes and surface-level connections don't provide the stability needed for lasting love. Just as trees need to consistently soak in water and sunlight, we need to soak in our time with Scripture, prayer, and community to thrive in our marriages. This is where transformation takes place.

What does God want for and from your marriage? Do you take time to silence the noise of the world and even quiet your own opinions?

Friends, it's very difficult to hear God's voice when you've already made up your mind about what you want him to say.

When we root ourselves in God's Word and gospel truth, we begin to understand his character and his promises. We become more like him and learn to trust him more fully, which gives us the strength to face our challenges with a stronger identity as a couple.

And when those roots run deep, you're better equipped to withstand the storms that come your way.

The War Against Your Marriage

I believe that the new definition of generational wealth is growing up in a home where people apologize and repair conflict, knowing and believing that love doesn't leave when things get hard. It doesn't abandon. It doesn't quit. It stays. It fights.

Because it will get hard. We can't allow ourselves to be surprised by that anymore.

Make no mistake: This world, and the gates of hell, are against marriage. Your marriage.

The world tells us to prioritize ourselves and our own happiness, encouraging us to leave relationships that don't fulfill us. Very few things in our society encourage fighting for a lasting relationship.

People feel more comfortable hearing others gossip about their spouses than celebrating the good in them.

Millions turn to lust and porn, but discussing sex within marriage remains taboo.

Our generation advocates for human rights and social justice yet devalues covenants such as traditional marriage.

Many in our world are convinced that they're more clever and informed than ever, and yet:

- We're more anxious than any culture at any time in the history of the world.
- We're more tormented by discontentment and insecurity than ever before.
- We're more wayward in our purpose.

- We don't know what unconditional love is.
- We're more isolated and lonely than any generation before us.

We can have everything this world offers, but if we don't have Jesus, we're aimless. Our fight is not against flesh and blood; we're in a spiritual war. As individuals and as couples, we have to keep God at the center of every decision, word, and action.

Your marriage is not disposable, despite what the world may suggest. It's a battleground for love, growth, and transformation. Your family is worth fighting for, and understanding this helps you see the stakes involved.

Can you imagine how incredible it would be if we released our marriages to God and became the generation that makes the most drastic, positive dent in the devastating statistics on divorces and affairs in history?

It begins with you.

How Did We Make It Here?

While writing this book, I found myself in a room with a couple who were navigating some really tough decisions as they planned for their divorce. They discussed budgets, custody arrangements, and holiday splits. It was a heavy conversation, filled with weighty choices that would change their entire lives. One moment stood out to me: During a brief lull in the conversation, I heard the husband whispering with a tone of disbelief, "How did we get here?"

About twenty minutes later, the wife asked herself the same question, her voice trembling with tears: "How did we get here?"

She answered her own question: "We played with fire until it burned our entire house down."

These moments spent dividing everything a couple has built together are a reality for nearly half of all Americans.

It takes only a spark—a little leeway, a bit of fire play—to ignite destruction in your marriage. The first secret, the little lie told, the act of disrespect or quiet resentment left to fester is all it takes to light a blaze in your relationship. And if it goes unchecked, it won't just smolder. It will consume.

In the future, you can ask either, "How did we get here?" as you sign the divorce papers or "How did we make it here?" while reminiscing in rocking chairs on the countless times you chose to forgive, love, and fight for each other, even when it felt impossible.

Both fear and faith demand that you believe in something you cannot see. You get to choose which one leads your life.

This is where the beauty of choice comes in. Tomorrow you can wake up and repeat the same old patterns, living with tension and anxiety, tiptoeing around one another and the difficult subjects. Or you can choose a different path.

Because nothing changes if nothing changes.

I repeat this simple truth often on my podcast because I believe it carries so much weight in every area of our lives. If you keep living the way you always have, you'll continue getting the same results. Change requires effort. When you decide to try and put forth even 1 percent more effort every day, you start building something better. It's scary, sure, but isn't staying the same even scarier? You get one life. You get to take action. You get to build a life that you're proud of.

If you want your spouse to be something to you, start by embodying that very thing. Want fun? Be fun. Want romance? Be romantic. If you long to feel served and valued, serve your spouse. If you desire friendship, be a friend to them.

Whatever situation you feel stuck in will not improve until anger, resentment, and judgment are set aside. Compassion and understanding must take precedence.

Take time to ask yourself these questions about your spouse:

- What was missing in their past that may have caused this issue?
- What hurt is motivating their behavior?
- What brokenness needs to be touched with love?
- What is lacking that needs to be learned?

If You Could Say Anything

As I was writing this last chapter, I thought to myself, *Linds, if you could write anything to this generation of couples who are working to keep their marriages afloat after five to thirty years, those who are distracted or bored or desiring something new, what would you say to them?* Here it is:

1. Jesus changes everything. Let go of your control, each other's mistakes, and obsession over patterns and habits, and burn those issues to the ground. Just get your eyes back on Jesus and in his Word.

The boredom you feel, the lull in your relationship, the desire for freedom or something new—everyone who has ever been married has felt it. Your marriage is going to be monotonous. It is going to be humdrum and stagnant. It's also going to be novel and exciting and fun. A good marriage grows through everything when Christ remains at the center.

2. Get outside of yourself. It's easy to feel miserable in our marriages when we focus solely on our own needs and priorities and the things that aren't right. We have got to stop being so curved in on ourselves. You're likely not broken beyond repair, but it requires humility to look inward and recognize where you may be falling short, rather than just pointing fingers at your spouse's faults.

It's likely that, to some degree, you're self-sabotaging. Be honest with yourself. What aren't you letting go? What conversation is on repeat in your home? For what do you need to forgive yourself? Which unhealthy patterns are you allowing yourselves to cycle through over and over?

Friends, we can't be above asking for forgiveness. We can't be above acknowledging that we are wildly imperfect in our marriages. We can't be above forgiving our partners when God has already forgiven us for so much.

It's helpful to approach forgiveness with the understanding that your vision might be impaired. Ask yourself, *How might I be misperceiving something I believe to be true that may not actually be true?*

Matthew 7:3–5 reminds us that we don't just have a dust speck in our eyes, we have a plank. In other words, we should assume that our own vision is distorted before pointing out what we believe is wrong in someone else. Jesus isn't saying your spouse doesn't have flaws; he's asking you to begin with humility. Before confronting your partner's weaknesses, are you willing to examine your own blind spots? Are you willing to consider that your issues might actually be contributing more to the tension than you realize?

What if, in humility, we created space for our partners to be different—different from us, different from our expectations? What if we took the time to spot hypocrisy within ourselves? To identify areas where we struggle to extend grace simply because someone doesn't align with our way of thinking? Our marriages would change.

3. Your thoughts create your experience. How you think about your partner can affect how you view your entire relationship.

When you have repetitive thoughts and assign truth to them, they eventually evolve into beliefs. These beliefs become a cognitive filter that influences how you perceive events. This filter supports what you believe to be true while overlooking things that don't match those beliefs. The thoughts that result dictate how you communicate with and react toward your partner.

You must learn to take your thoughts captive to change how you view, respond to, and respect your spouse.

Have you ever heard the story of the man who carried his wife to the door every day? He was completely done with their marriage, ready to file for divorce. But when he told his wife, she said, "Fine, I'll give you a divorce, but first, for the next hundred days, you have to carry me to the door every day and kiss me goodbye. Only then will I sign the papers."

He agreed, mostly to get it over with. Every day, he picked her up, cradled her in his arms, and carried her to the door. At first it felt awkward and forced, a chore that reminded him just how disconnected they had become.

For her, it was a desperate attempt to reconnect. She asked him to do this because she knew something he didn't—that even a small act could soften their hardened hearts. She hoped that being close, even briefly, might crack open the door they had slammed shut on one another.

And slowly, it worked. Day by day, the act of carrying her and kissing her goodbye changed him. It was no longer just a task to check off his daily list but a moment of connection. He remembered why he fell in love with her in the first place. He noticed little things he'd stopped paying attention to, like the way her smile could warm up a room and how her green eyes sparkled when they reflected the sun.

She softened too. The daily closeness in this small gesture reminded them both not only what they had lost but also what they could still have. These moments weren't magic, but they were enough to rekindle something they thought was gone forever.

By the end of the hundred days, the man didn't want a divorce. He didn't want to lose her. What had started as a reluctant obligation had turned into a rediscovery of each other.

This story illustrates how acts of service and intimacy can change everything. When you feel disconnected, it's tempting to give up or wait for something to fix itself. But healing starts with showing up and choosing to move toward your spouse, even when you don't feel like it.

Life is hard enough as it is without carrying all of the issues and struggles from the past five, ten, or twenty-five years into the next twenty years of marriage. God wants you to be free—free from the heartache, the details that hurt you, and the habits that bind you.

I recently told Jesse, "After thirteen years of marriage, I would marry you even harder now than I did back then." The honeymoon phase has been over for a long time, but our experiences and time together have deepened my love and appreciation for him, which has built a love that's stronger than ever before.

We haven't gotten here without heartache or pain. But we're doing the dang thing together. And I pray that you choose the same for yourselves.

Burning your house down may happen accidentally or unintentionally, but reconnecting with your spouse will not. So for the road, here's one final activity to do with your spouse.

FIFTEEN CONNECTING QUESTIONS TO ASK EACH OTHER EVERY MONTH

1. In what two instances this month did you feel that I served you well?
2. In what ways, if any, do I make you feel disrespected or unloved? What, if anything, have I done in the past month that made you feel really loved?

3. In this season of your life, what are the best and most practical ways I can serve you?
4. In my own life right now, do you see that I am seeking Jesus, or am I focusing on the wrong things?
5. What is one practical step I need to take to make our marriage better?
6. What is one fun thing you always want to do that I don't give you the opportunity to do?
7. Have I made you feel sexy and attractive this month? If so, how?
8. If you could change one thing to make our marriage better, what would it be?
9. What are some practical things that we can do as a couple to love the people around us better?
10. What have I done recently that made you feel good in front of other people?
11. What have I done recently that made you feel disrespected in front of other people?
12. What is something I've done sexually that you've really enjoyed, or what is something you wish we would do more?
13. What was your favorite date night with me this month, and why?
14. What are three things you love about me right now?
15. What is one thing you wish I understood better about you?

Are you ready to put down the match and pick up a bucket of water?

This culture is louder than ever, seducing you with cheap alternatives to true intimacy with flashing screens, filtered bodies, and a million false definitions of success. It tells you that the grass is greener somewhere else; that if it's hard, it's wrong; that if your spouse doesn't meet your every need, you're justified in leaving. But that voice is not truth. That's deception. That's the slow drift that ends in divorce court and legacy loss.

Let me remind you of something no algorithm will: Your marriage is holy ground.

It doesn't have to end in ashes. That slow burn of disconnection, resentment, silence, or avoidance doesn't have to consume everything good. You are not powerless.

Through Christ, you have the strength to choose a different ending.

And maybe that's the entire message of this book: That redemption is always possible. Not just for the perfect marriages or the easy seasons, but for the mess, the ruins, for those of you who are barely holding on.

The world will keep telling you to walk away. To self-protect. To settle. To numb the pain. To move on. But Jesus calls you to stay. To be rooted. To press in. To love in a way that reflects his love for us. To honor your covenant even when it stretches you to the edge of yourself.

This isn't a passive endurance of two strangers coexisting under the same roof. It's an active, fiery, soul-deep intentionality.

And it starts with you. Not them. Not someday. Today.

You don't need to rebuild your entire house overnight. Just start with one brick. One apology. One confession. One step toward honesty. One small refusal to let the Enemy have the final word. That's how you begin again.

So here's the question you'll have to answer with your life:

Will you burn it all down, or will you become someone who rebuilds it, one day at a time, in love, in truth, and in fireproof grace?

Marriage is holy. And hard. And it's so incredibly worth it. You weren't given your marriage to simply survive it. You were given this sacred bond to display the gospel to each other and to the world.

If you need someone to tell you what matters most in a world that's forgotten, let it be this: Faithfulness still matters. Integrity still matters. Marriage still matters. It matters for your family, for the generations to come, and for the glory of the one who brought you together.

You already know what to do.

Now go and live like it.

ACKNOWLEDGMENTS

*T*hank you.

Jesse: I love you so much. Thank you for being the most patient and kind man I've ever known. I never could have reached this beautiful place in my life and career without your humor, consistency, lemon-water deliveries, and unconditional love and support. Your presence, both as a dad and a husband, has made life sweeter than I ever thought possible. Thank you for always showing up, for being safe, steady, and sure, and for doing the work with me when marriage inevitably gets tough. We are imperfect, but I am so deeply proud of how far we've come. You are my person and my best friend.

Sutton and Saxon: You are my world, and you inspire me to be better every single day. Thank you for believing in me every step of the way. From your confetti-and-cake celebration to asking about the book process five times a day, you've made this journey so much fun. Thank you for being so proud of me, for sharing with everyone that Mom has a published book, and for asking at every bookstore, "Which shelf is *Don't Burn Your Own House Down* on?" Your unconditional love, contagious joy, and passion for life are some of the greatest gifts God has ever given me. I do it all for you two! I love you both to pieces. You are my joy.

Meg: Thank you for being my protector, cheerleader, supporter, and friend, and for exemplifying what it means to love your family well. You are an encouragement through both your life and your words. Thank you for always believing I'll follow through and for being so sure I'll do it well. I'm so grateful to have you as my big sister. I love you to pieces, and you inspire me every day!

Dad: Thank you for always encouraging me to seek adventure, travel the world, meet new people, and prioritize education and research. You showed me the value of giving generously—not just my money but my knowledge, kindness, and time. You taught me never to shy away from asking tough questions or seeking out solutions, even when it's uncomfortable; those conversations have helped shape this book. I love you!

Mom: Thank you for reminding me time and again to pursue what I love and to do it well. I'll never be able to voice how grateful I am that you encouraged me to fill my bookshelves from such a young age while continuously fueling my dreams. You've been my greatest support from day one, always reminding me of my potential and never letting me settle for anything less than what you knew I was capable of. You're a living example of what it means to be a woman who loves her family and serves God with all her heart. You are so special to me!

My incredible friends and family: I wish I could name each of you because you've helped turn my dream into a reality. Your support has meant the world to me. Thank you for indulging my endless questions and for allowing me to dive into the depths of your marriages. Thank you for reading the chapters, answering every phone call during my moments of fear or anxiety, and celebrating each step of this journey like it was your own. Your stories, experiences, and lives are a gift, and I'm grateful to share them in the hope of helping others. I love each of you so very much.

My agent, Chris: You have made the process of writing

my very first book so immensely enjoyable. Your belief in me and consistent investment from day one has been a tremendous encouragement. You brought a sense of stability and calm to my chaos and anxiety. Thank you for fighting for me, for placing your trust in me, and for giving me the confidence to make this book a reality. Working with you has been a privilege. Thank you for giving me a chance! I am forever indebted to you.

My editor, Keren: From the very first draft to the final pages, your insights and thoughtful feedback have shaped this work into something I am so deeply proud of. Thank you for helping me stay true to my voice and writing style, for reminding me—again and again—that the words God placed on my heart were enough, and that I didn't need to be like anyone else or bend to the world's expectations. Thank you so much for helping me bring this project to life.

My copyeditor, Brian: Thank you for your endless patience and steady guidance throughout this process. Your sharp eye, skill, and genuine kindness have meant so much to me. I'm especially grateful for how you handled my last-minute changes with such grace and for understanding how much the little details mattered to me. Your flexibility, encouragement, and care have made this entire experience a joy. I'm so thankful for all you've poured into these pages.

My loyal audience: Thank you for sticking with me, whether you've just joined or have been around for the past ten years. I am incredibly grateful for each of you. From the very beginning of this journey, writing a book has been my ultimate dream.

Your questions, late-night messages, emails, and insights have all played a significant role in shaping the heart of this book. You've been my sounding board, my motivators, and my community. This book is as much yours as it is mine. I pray that it makes even a small difference in your lives, as you've made an immeasurable difference in mine.

NOTES

Chapter 1: Marriage Temperature Check

1. Lars Tornstam, "Loneliness in Marriage," *Journal of Social and Personal Relationships* 9, no. 2 (May 1992): 197–217, https://doi.org/10.1177/0265407592092003.
2. A. Barbour, "Research Report: Dyadic Loneliness in Marriage," *Journal of Group Psychotherapy, Psychodrama and Sociometry* 46, no. 2 (1993): 70–72.
3. Sara Muftic and Kathy Nickerson, "The Truth About Affairs and Cheating: Your Top Twenty Questions Answered with Research and Statistics," Dr. Kathy, the Relationship Psychologist, accessed October 15, 2025, https://drkathynickerson.com/blogs/relationship/the-truth-about-affairs-and-cheating-your-top-20-questions-answered-with-research-and-statistics.
4. Jordan Peterson, "Lecture: Biblical Series III; God and the Hierarchy of Authority," May 29, 2017, YouTube, 2:38:12, www.youtube.com/watch?v=R_GPAl_q2QQ.
5. Cammie Dennis, excerpt from chapter 3, "Everything I've Learned About Love, So Far," in *There's Coffee in the Pot* (self-published, 2024), 150. Used with permission.

Chapter 2: How I Almost Burned My Own House Down

1. Gary Chapman, *The Five Love Languages: The Secret to Love That Lasts* (Chicago: Northfield Publishing, 2015), 31.
2. Craig Groeschel, "When Your Mind Is out of Control,"

Life.Church, July 14, 2024, YouTube, 32:48, www.youtube.com
/watch?v=8dgSQzQ-oPs.

3. Francis Chan and Lisa Chan, *You and Me Forever: Marriage in Light of Eternity* (Claire Love Publishing, 2014), 96.

4. Anna Miller, "Can This Marriage Be Saved?" *Monitor on Psychology* 44, no. 4 (April 1 2013): www.apa.org/monitor/2013/04/marriage.

5. Esther Perel, *The State of Affairs: Rethinking Infidelity* (New York: HarperCollins, 2017), 17.

6. Lindsey Maestas, "Secrets from a Divorce Lawyer: Why Divorce Isn't the Answer," *Living Easy Podcast*, episode 96, June 13, 2022, https://podcasts.apple.com/us/podcast/96-secrets-from-a-divorce-lawyer-why-divorce-isnt/id1481805272?i=1000566220386.

Chapter 3: Make the Dang Coffee

1. Zita Oravecz et al., "Psychological Well-Being and Personality Traits Are Associated with Experiencing Love in Everyday Life," *Personality and Individual Differences* 153 (January 2020), https://doi.org/10.1016/j.paid.2019.109620.

Chapter 4: Defrosting Your Marriage

1. Darren Whitehead, "What's Beneath the Surface?" COTC Franklin, August 13, 2023, YouTube, 1:02:14, www.youtube.com/watch?v=4lFM6t0X_ZQ.

2. Craig Fowler and Megan R. Dillow, "Attachment Dimensions and the Four Horsemen of the Apocalypse," *Communication Research Reports* 28, no. 1 (2011): 16–26, https://doi.org:10.1080/08824096.2010.518910.

3. Ellie Lisitsa, "The Four Horsemen: Contempt," Gottman Institute, May 13, 2013, www.gottman.com/blog/the-four-horsemen-contempt/.

4. Susan L. Brown, "Marriage and Child Well-Being: Research and Policy Perspectives," *The Future of Children* 20, no. 2 (2010): 1–19.

5. "Differentiation of Self," The Bowen Center for the Study of the Family; My People Patterns, "Differentiation of Self," April 7, 2023.

6. Lysa TerKeurst, *Good Boundaries and Goodbyes: Loving Others Without Losing the Best of Who You Are* (Nashville: Thomas Nelson, 2022), 42.

Chapter 6: Forgive Each Other (Even for the Little Things)

1. John Piper, "How Can Couples Heal After Adultery?" *Ask Pastor John*, episode 1440, February 28, 2020, www.desiringgod .org/interviews/how-can-couples-heal-after-adultery.

2. Rick Warren, *The Purpose Driven Life: What on Earth Am I Here For?* (Grand Rapids: Zondervan, 2012), 143.

Chapter 7: More Scrolling, More Problems

1. "The Dopamine Cliff: Understanding the Crash in ADHD," Focus Bear, May 28, 2024, www.focusbear.io/blog-post/the -dopamine-cliff-understanding-the-crash-in-adhd?utm _source=chatgpt.com.

2. Anna Lembke, *Dopamine Nation: Finding Balance in the Age of Indulgence* (New York: Dutton, 2021).

3. Brandon T. McDaniel and Sarah M. Coyne, "Technoference: The Interference of Technology in Couple Relationships and Implications for Women's Personal and Relational Well-Being," *Psychology of Popular Media Culture* 5, no. 1 (2016): 85–98, https://scholarsarchive.byu.edu/facpub/4023.

4. Malcolm Gladwell, *The Tipping Point: How Little Things Can Make a Big Difference* (New York: Back Bay Books, 2002).

Chapter 8: Marriage Doesn't Suffocate

1. H. Brevy Cannon, "Across Races, Couples That Pray Together Are Happier, Study Finds," UVA Today, August 11, 2010, https://news.virginia.edu/content/across-races-couples-pray -together-are-happier-study-finds.

Chapter 9: Your Mind and Body Glow-Up

1. James Clear, *Atomic Habits: An Easy and Proven Way to Build Good Habits and Break Bad Ones* (New York: Avery, 2018).
2. C. S. Lewis, *The Weight of Glory* (San Francisco: HarperOne, 2001), 26.
3. Natalie Brooks, *The Power of Habit: Transform Your Life with Positive Routines* (Cheryl Eyes, 2024), 1.
4. E. M. Gromada and J. Wong, "Couples' Sleep Patterns and Relationship Satisfaction: A Review of the Literature," *Journal of Marriage and Family* 84, no. 3 (2022): 712–27.
5. Kyrsten Sackett-Fox et al., "Better Together: The Impact of Exercising with a Romantic Partner," *Journal of Social and Personal Relationships* 38, no. 11 (2021), https://doi.org/10.1177/02654075211012086.

Chapter 10: Becoming Best Friends Again

1. C. S. Lewis, "Equality," *The Spectator* 171 (August 27, 1943): 192, https://archive.spectator.co.uk/article/27th-august-1943/8/equality.
2. Kyrsten Sackett-Fox et al., "Better Together: The Impact of Exercising with a Romantic Partner, *Journal of Social and Personal Relationships* 38, no. 11: 3078–96, https://doi.org/10.1177/02654075211012086.
3. Elaine Hatfield et al., "Emotional Contagion," *Current Directions in Psychological Science* 2, no. 3 (1994): 96–100, https://doi.org/10.1111/1467-8721.ep10770953.
4. Giacomo Rizzolatti and Laila Craighero, "The Mirror-Neuron System," *Annual Review of Neuroscience* 27 (2004): 169–92, https://doi.org/10.1146/annurev.neuro.27.070203.144230.

Chapter 11: Are We Actually in This Together?

1. John Gottman, "Turn Towards Instead of Away," The Gottman Institute, accessed June 7, 2025, www.gottman.com/blog/turn-toward-instead-of-away/.
2. The Associated Press, "Can a Six-Second Kiss Each Day Lead

to a More Intimate Relationship?" AP News, last modified July 31, 2024, https://apnews.com/article/six-second-kiss-intimacy -wellness-f16d21abf7206a3de92cce99453c46dc.

3. Linda Bloom and Charlie Bloom, "Kissing Adds Years to Your Life," *Psychology Today*, July 16, 2019, www.psychologytoday.com /us/blog/stronger-at-the-broken-places/201907/kissing-adds -years-to-your-life.

4. Sherri Gordon, "What Are the Five Love Languages?" Verywell Mind, updated February 5, 2024, www.verywellmind.com/can-the -five-love-languages-help-your-relationship-4783538.

Chapter 12: Responsibility Tug-of-War

1. Lauren Berlant, *On the Inconvenience of Other People* (Durham, NC: Duke University Press, 2022).

2. C. S. Lewis, *The Screwtape Letters* (New York: HarperOne, 2009), 16.

Chapter 13: Money Is a Spiritual Issue—and a Divorce Issue

1. Oxford Reference (n.d.), "Hedonic Treadmill," accessed November 16, 2020, www.oxfordreference.com/view/10.1093/oi /authority.20110803095928134.

2. Matt Chandler, "Hearts of Generosity," sermon, The Village Church, Flower Mound, TX, November 11, 2019, YouTube, 46:54, www.youtube.com/watch?v=IDryrQo8MZU.

3. Maria Cohut, "Financial Hardship Is a Top Risk Factor for Suicide Attempts," *Medical News Today*, September 8, 2020, www .medicalnewstoday.com/articles/financial-hardship-is-a-top-risk -factor-for-suicide-attempts.

Chapter 15: Don't Give Your Spouse Your Leftovers

1. James H. Fowler and Nicholas A. Christakis, "Dynamics of Happiness: The Social Contagion of Joy," *American Journal of Sociology* 113, no. 5 (2008): 722–65.

2. Taryn Hillin, "Survey Says One in Five People Are Keeping a Major Secret from Their Spouse," *HuffPost*, August 1, 2014, www.huffpost.com/entry/secrets-survey_n_5642818.